W9-CHK-791

Implementing Standards-Based Mathematics Instruction

Implementing Standards-Based Mathematics Instruction

A Casebook for Professional Development

SECOND EDITION

Mary Kay Stein
Margaret Schwan Smith
Marjorie A. Henningsen
Edward A. Silver

Foreword by James Hiebert

NATIONAL COUNCIL OF
TEACHERS OF MATHEMATICS
1906 Association Drive, Reston, VA 20191
www.nctm.org

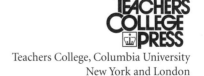

Teachers College, Columbia University
New York and London

Published simultaneously by Teachers College Press, 1234 Amsterdam Avenue, New York, NY 10027 and National Council of Teachers of Mathematics, 1906 Association Drive, Reston, VA 20191-1502.

Copyright © 2009 by Teachers College, Columbia University

All rights reserved. No part of this publication may be reproduced or transmitted in any form or by any means, electronic or mechanical, including photocopy, or any information storage and retrieval system, without permission from the publisher.

Library of Congress Cataloging-in-Publication Data

Implementing standards-based mathematics instruction : a casebook for professional development / Mary Kay Stein . . . [et al.]. — 2nd ed. / new foreword by James Hiebert.
      p. cm.
  Includes bibliographical references and index.
  ISBN 978-0-8077-4957-9 (pbk. : alk. paper)
    1. Mathematics—Study and teaching (Middle school)—Case studies. I. Stein, Mary Kay.
  QA135.6.I467 2009
  510.71'2–dc22   2008055108

ISBN 978-0-8077-4957-9 (paper)
NCTM Stock Number: 13498

Printed on acid-free paper

Manufactured in the United States of America

16   15   14   13   12   11   10   09   8   7   6   5   4   3   2   1

To all the teachers with whom we have worked over the past decade who have embraced the ideas presented in the "purple book," as the first edition of this work is commonly known. You have provided us with important insights into the challenges and rewards associated with engaging students in cognitively demanding mathematical activity. By striving to improve instruction in your classrooms, despite the complexities and pressures of real school settings, you have increased your students' opportunities to succeed in mathematics class and beyond. We appreciate and applaud your efforts.

Contents

Foreword *by James Hiebert*   ix

Acknowledgments   xiii

Introduction   xv

PART I: THE MATHEMATICAL TASKS FRAMEWORK

1. **Analyzing Mathematics Instructional Tasks**   1
   Defining Levels of Cognitive Demand of Mathematical Tasks   2
   Matching Tasks with Goals for Student Learning   4
   Differentiating Levels of Cognitive Demand   5
   Gaining Experience in Analyzing Cognitive Demands   8
   Moving Beyond Task Selection and Creation   12

2. **Using Cognitively Complex Tasks in the Classroom**   14
   The Evolution of Tasks During a Lesson   14
   Patterns of Task Setup and Implementation   17

3. **Learning from Cases**   23
   Theoretical Considerations   23
   Moving on to Considerations of One's Own Practice   25
   Advantages to Guided Reflection   27

PART II: THE CASES

4. **Introduction to the Cases**   31
   The Cases and Supporting Materials   31
   How to Orchestrate Teacher Learning from the Cases   33

5. **Linking Fractions, Decimals, and Percents Using an Area Model**   37
   The Case of Ron Castleman   37
   Discussion Questions   46
   Teaching Notes   47
   Possible Solution Strategies   51

6. **Multiplying Fractions with Pattern Blocks**   **56**
    The Case of Fran Gorman and Kevin Cooper   56
    Discussion Questions   67
    Teaching Notes   68

7. **Giving Meaning to Measures of Central Tendency**   **72**
    The Case of Trina Naruda and Ursula Hernandez   73
    Discussion Questions   82
    Teaching Notes   82

8. **Using Algebra Tiles to Multiply Monomials and Binomials**   **88**
    The Case of Monique Butler   88
    Discussion Questions   96
    Teaching Notes   96

9. **Organizing Data**   **101**
    The Case of Nicole Clark   101
    Discussion Questions   107
    Teaching Notes   108

10. **Solving Problems**   **112**
    The Case of Jerome Robinson   112
    Discussion Questions   118
    Teaching Notes   118
    Possible Solution Strategies   121

PART III: USING THE CASES

11. **Assisting the Learning of Teachers**   **131**
    Transformative Professional Development   132
    Key Professional Activities Related To Mathematical Tasks   137
    Conclusion   149

12. **Assisting the Learning and Professional Practice of Principals** **151**
    Conducting Observations and Arranging for Tailored
        Professional Development   153
    Providing Schoolwide Resources for Ongoing
        Teacher Development   160
    Conclusion   163

References   **165**

Index   **171**

About the Authors   **181**

Foreword

Perhaps the major challenge facing those who wish to improve the mathematics learning of U.S. students is taking seriously the fact that teaching must change. Teaching is increasingly recognized as the key lever for improving learning, but changing teaching means something quite different from what the popular press would lead us to believe. It *does not* mean raising the certification requirements for teachers, creating alternative routes to licensure, or even recruiting more qualified candidates. Although recruiting talented teachers is always welcome, changing *teaching* is not about changing *teachers*—it is a different kind of task and requires different kinds of actions. Changing teaching requires, first and foremost, treating teaching as an object of study, a complex skill that can be studied and improved.

Treating teaching as an object of study is not common in the United States. Teaching usually is seen as the prerogative of individual teachers. Behind classroom doors, each teacher must figure out what works best for him or her. Naturally gifted teachers, says this folklore, blossom into effective teachers, and the profession just needs to find more of them. But this view means the profession can never improve beyond what a minority of teachers can figure out on their own. Even more damaging, this view denies two basic truths about teaching. The first is that teachers do not invent the methods they use—they inherit them from having watched their teachers teach when they were students. This means those naturally gifted teachers often use the same methods as everyone else. The second truth is that all teachers, gifted and not-so-gifted, can improve their practice. They can do so by studying carefully what they do and learning how they can do it better. By engaging all teachers in studying teaching, the profession as a whole can improve, and the learning opportunities of students in all classrooms can improve.

The uncommon value of this book is found in the way it treats teaching as an object of study. It engages all teachers in studying and improving teaching. It focuses directly on the details of teaching and on the methods used to interact with students about the content. It is these details that make all the difference. How teachers pose problems to students; how they work on problems with students; and how they engage students in analyzing and discussing and solving problems—these are the details of teaching that determine students' opportunities to learn. These are the details of teaching that matter. And these are the details explored throughout this book.

Why are the details of working on math problems the details of teaching that matter? Because students spend most of their time in math class working on problems, and, consequently, that's what sets the boundaries on what students will learn. One of the first things that the research team working on the TIMSS 1999 Video Study noticed was that eighth-graders all over the world— in countries as different as Australia, the Czech Republic, Hong Kong, Japan, the Netherlands, Switzerland, and the United States—spend an average of 80% of their time in math class working on math problems (see also Hiebert et al., 2003).

Here is where the details matter. What differed across countries was *how* the students worked on the math problems. In some countries, students did most of the mathematical work; in other countries, teachers did most of the work for the students. In some countries, students were asked to wrestle with problems they didn't already know how to solve; in other countries, students first watched the teacher demonstrate a solution procedure and then practiced the same procedure on similar problems. Imagine being a student in these different classrooms. The experiences would be completely different. The subject of mathematics would look completely different. The opportunities to learn would be completely different. This is how much teaching matters. The way in which the same topics are taught can change completely what students learn.

The framework the authors of this book provide for analyzing how problems are worked on during class beautifully captures the major differences we saw among the countries in the TIMSS Video Study. The framework directs attention to those exact details of teaching that shape the learning opportunities for students: what mathematical thinking is required by the problem, how this thinking is affected by how the problem is posed, and how this thinking is supported or undermined by the way in which teacher and students interact about the problem during class. To repeat, for emphasis, the critical questions are: What mathematical learning opportunities does the problem afford, and how are these opportunities sustained or diminished as the problem is posed and worked on during class?

If the learning goals for U.S. students include understanding concepts, using procedures flexibly, or even remembering procedures from year to year, then the results from the TIMSS Video Study along with numerous previous descriptions of math classrooms show that students need different opportunities from the ones provided in most U.S. classrooms on most days. Math problems need to be worked on in different ways. Teaching needs to change in just the ways highlighted in this book.

But how can teaching change? How can teachers who are currently teaching in one way learn to teach in a different way? The answer is simple to say but really hard to do—by studying teaching and improving one's practice a little each day, each week, each month; by *learning* how to teach differently. The contribution of this book is that it directs teachers' attention to exactly those aspects of teaching that teachers must learn to do differently. It focuses teachers' study of teaching on how to work on math problems with students. It brings these details of teaching to awareness and reveals that these are conscious, deliberate choices teachers can make, and that it is these choices that matter most for students' learning.

But the authors do more than focus teachers' attention on the key details of teaching. The authors respect both the complexity of teaching *and* the capabilities of teachers. They treat teaching as an object of study *and* they treat teachers as professionals who can study and improve their own practice. Of course, teachers are the only ones who can improve teaching; no one else can do this for them. But too often, educators suggest either that improving teaching is easy or that improving teaching is beyond the "pay-grade" of teachers. The authors of this book trust teachers to engage in the difficult work of changing their own teaching and, in turn, transforming the standard practice of the profession.

The authors succeed by applying their principles for helping students learn mathematics more deeply to the materials in this book in order to help teachers learn about teaching more deeply. How can students' learning be facilitated? By being clear about the learning goals for students, by planning instructional activities aligned with these goals, and by implementing these activities in ways that do not diminish the cognitive and mathematical demands of the activities. How can teachers' learning be facilitated? By being clear about the learning goals for teachers, by planning activities that are aligned with these goals, and by engaging teachers in work that does not diminish the intellectual demands of teaching. The authors apply these principles with equal effectiveness in both contexts.

Teaching is a complex, intellectually demanding skill. It will improve only through the hard and unrelenting work of teachers who study their practice and improve it over time. The authors of this book provide a guide that directs teachers to study the details of practice that matter for students. It is a book that offers the best kind of help—pointing teachers to the aspects of teaching that matter, refusing to diminish the intellectual challenge of this work, and investing in teachers to lead the profession toward a higher level of standard practice.

—James Hiebert

Acknowledgments

In the decade since the first edition of the "purple book" was published, we have been amazed and heartened by the attraction and traction that the ideas we put forth in that volume have had. Professionals across the United States and even in other countries have found these materials to be useful with diverse audiences for many different purposes, and they have expanded our own view of how and with whom these materials might be successful. We have been invited to make presentations about the ideas in this book at local, state, national, and international conferences, and we continue to learn from our interactions with teachers, teacher educators, researchers, and administrators in those settings.

Our work with two groups of teachers in particular inspired us to write this second edition: the teachers in western Pennsylvania who participated in the NSF-funded ESP project and the teachers in Michigan who participated in the BIFOCAL project. The work of these teachers over several years provided us with important insights on how to support teacher learning with and through these materials, and it served as the foundation for Chapter 11 in this second edition. Similarly, our work with administrators in urban districts across the country has heightened our awareness of how principals can become better instructional leaders from engaging with these materials, and this has informed Chapter 12.

We are indebted to Victoria Bill whose insights continue to inform our practice of working with teachers, coaches, and administrators. Her perspective on the importance of providing teachers with practical tools that they can use to do their "real" work has shaped our thinking and our materials and has pushed us to do better. Along with her colleagues at the Institute for Learning at the University of Pittsburgh, she has been a champion of the purple book and has brought the mathematical tasks framework to hundreds of teachers in urban school districts across the country. We also acknowledge the insights provided by Valerie Mills, Judith Flowers, Diane Briars, Susan Friel, and a host of other professionals who have used our materials and enriched our thinking about their utility.

Introduction

Imagine walking into a seventh-grade classroom that has just begun a unit on measuring two- and three-dimensional figures. Following an efficient check of the previous night's homework, the lesson begins with a definition of terms and a review of formulas for finding the area and perimeter of rectangles. Then the teacher demonstrates how to compute the perimeter and area of two rectangles on the blackboard—one with a length of 15 inches and a width of 7 inches, the other having four sides, each labeled 50 yards in length. Afterward, the teacher assigns 20 similar problems from the students' textbooks. As students work individually at their desks, applying the formulas to the labeled diagrams, the teacher walks around the room. Most of her assistance falls into one of two categories: (1) help with two-digit multiplication and (2) reminders of which formula to use for area versus perimeter. As the period draws to a close, the teacher tells the students to finish working on the 20 problems for homework and to do the word problem that appears at the bottom of the page (see Figure I.1).

Research has documented the prevalence of lessons such as the one just described (Fey, 1981; Stodolsky, 1988; Hiebert et al., 2003). Both the sequence of classroom activities (homework check followed by teacher lecture and demonstration followed, in turn, by student practice) and the level of student engagement and thinking required by the instructional task (application of a learned procedure to a set of similar problems) can be regularly observed in middle school classrooms throughout the United States (Stigler & Hiebert, 1997).

Now imagine walking into a different middle school classroom. These seventh-grade students are also working on a unit that involves measuring two- and three-dimensional figures, but the kind of thinking required of these students is quite different. As the students walk into the room, the teacher directs their attention to the task displayed on the blackboard (see Fencing Task shown in Figure I.2) and asks them to begin to work immediately in their small groups. She tells the students that they will have the entire period to work on this task and reminds them that, as usual, they may quietly get whatever paper, tools, or manipulatives they need to complete the task.

FIGURE I.1. A word problem from a unit on two- and three-dimensional measurement.

Martha's Carpeting Task

Martha was recarpeting her bedroom, which was 15 feet long and 10 feet wide. How many square feet of carpeting will she need to purchase?

Unlike their counterparts in the first scenario, these students must do more than apply a formula in order to be successful. They must figure out a way to generate and systematically test different pen configurations in order to identify which rectangular shape creates the maximum area for the rabbits they are raising using 24 (and later 16) feet of fencing. They also need to engage in the process of mathematical generalization by figuring out how to maximize the area for any amount of fencing. By asking them to organize their work so someone else could understand it, the task also demands that students learn to explain their thinking and reasoning.

During the class period, the teacher walks around to the various groups asking questions and, in some cases, providing hints about how to proceed, but never showing students exactly how to go about solving the problem. As the period draws to a close, none of the groups has completed the task but several have begun systematically laying out different pen configurations for the same amount of fencing. Several others are well on their way to discovering that a square would enclose the greatest amount of area for any given amount of fencing. All students are deeply engaged with the task and are actively talking to their partners about how to justify, organize, and communicate their thinking.

The Fencing Task is very different from the types of tasks most middle-school students typically encounter in mathematics classrooms. Students are rarely confronted with such tasks and—unlike the students portrayed in the above scenario—will probably not respond with the kind of thinking and reasoning that is intended. In some cases, students might press the teacher to provide them with a formula that could be used to solve the problem or with a clear pathway to the solution. In other cases, students might focus on extraneous aspects of the problem such as the size of the rabbits, the amount of space they will need, and the cost of fencing. In yet other cases, students might get sidetracked from the mathematics altogether, producing elaborate drawings of rabbits and pens.

FIGURE I.2. A mathematical task that might be associated with unpredictable student responses.

The Fencing Task

Ms. Brown's class will raise rabbits for their spring science fair. They have 24 feet of fencing with which to build a rectangular rabbit pen to keep the rabbits.

  a. If Ms. Brown's students want their rabbits to have as much room as possible, how long would each of the sides of the pen be?

  b. How long would each of the sides of the pen be if they had only 16 feet of fencing?

  c. How would you go about determining the pen with the most room for any amount of fencing? Organize your work so that someone else who reads it will understand it.

The Fencing Task is typical of the kinds of problems that the National Council of Teachers of Mathematics (NCTM) has recommended that teachers incorporate into their instructional repertoires (NCTM, 1989, 1991, 1995, 2000). In fact, versions of the Fencing Task can be found in most standards-based curricula that are consistent with NCTM recommendations for mathematics teaching and learning. As increasing numbers of teachers embrace the NCTM reforms and begin to use these curricula, we can expect more and more cognitively challenging tasks such as the Fencing Task to appear in our nation's classrooms. Many teachers and students, however, will be encountering such tasks for the first time.

Our work in the QUASAR[1] Project (Silver, Smith, & Nelson, 1995; Silver & Stein, 1996) and working with teachers in a variety of projects since then (most notably, the ESP and BIFOCAL Projects[2]) has taught us a lot about the difficulties and the triumphs associated with using challenging tasks in the classroom. In QUASAR's 5-year effort to improve the way mathematics was taught and learned in six urban middle schools, we sought to understand the nature of classroom instruction and the relationship between classroom instruction and student learning. One strand of this research focused on the instructional tasks[3] used in project classrooms. Since instructional tasks form the basis of students' opportunities to learn mathematics, the types of tasks used and the nature of student engagement with the tasks seemed a promising site for investigation.

Two things were central to this research. First, as illustrated by our opening scenarios, all tasks are not created equal—different tasks require different levels and kinds of student thinking. We refer to the kinds of thinking needed to solve tasks as their *cognitive demands.* Second, the cognitive demands of tasks can change during a lesson.[4] A task that starts out challenging, such as the Fencing Task, might not induce the high-level thinking and reasoning that was intended as the students actually go about working on it.

The Mathematical Tasks Framework, shown in Figure I.3, was developed to guide the analysis of classroom lessons in the QUASAR Project. It provides a fluid representation of how tasks unfold during classroom instruction. In the framework, tasks are seen as passing through three phases: First, as they appear in curricular or instructional materials or as created by teachers; next, as they are set up or announced by the teacher in the classroom; and finally, as they are carried out or worked on by students. All of these, but especially the third phase (i.e., implementation), are viewed as important influences on what students actually learn (illustrated by the triangle in Figure I.3).

This framework was used to analyze hundreds of project lessons between 1990 and 1995. This research has yielded two major findings: (1) mathematical tasks with high-level cognitive demands were the most difficult to implement well, frequently being transformed into less-demanding tasks during instruction; and (2) student learning gains were greatest in classrooms in which instructional tasks consistently encouraged high-level student thinking and reasoning and least in classrooms in which instructional tasks were consistently procedural in nature.

As we began to share these findings with teachers and teacher educators, we found that they resonated with the way in which we had characterized mathematical instructional tasks (i.e., by their cognitive demands) and with our way of representing how tasks unfold during a lesson (i.e., task phases as depicted in the Mathematical Tasks Framework). After teachers learned about

FIGURE I.3. A representation of how mathematical tasks unfold during classroom instruction (Stein & Smith, 1998).

The Mathematical Tasks Framework

(Reprinted with permission from *Mathematics Teaching in the Middle School,* copyright © 1998 by the National Council of Teachers of Mathematics. All rights reserved.)

the framework, they began to use it as a lens for reflecting on their own instruction and as a shared language for discussing instruction with their colleagues. Teachers' identification with the framework led us to consider how we could take this research (both the framework and findings) and use it to create tools that would be helpful to teachers and teacher educators who are trying to improve their practice. This effort to take research into practice has culminated in this book.

Since the first edition was published in 2000, we have been using the Mathematical Tasks Framework and the materials contained in this book as the focus of our professional work with preservice and practicing teachers. We, along with our students and colleagues, have used these materials with teachers who are preparing to teach mathematics at the elementary, middle school, and secondary school levels, and also with teachers who are already certified to teach. In teacher preparation programs, they have been used in methods courses and also in courses whose intent is to teach mathematics content. We have used them with teachers in professional development projects in urban and suburban school settings; with teachers in large and small school districts; with veteran and novice teachers; and with teachers whose base curriculum is quite innovative as well as with those who are using more conventional mathematics textbooks. In addition, these materials have been used in a university-based principal preparation program and in professional development sessions with principals from urban school districts across the country.

FOCUS OF THE BOOK

The centerpiece of this book is a set of instructional cases. As with all cases, ours are situated in place, time, and subject matter, evoking the daily worlds of teachers and students and their classrooms (Shulman, 1996). Our hope is to take readers beyond the generic notions of "effective teaching behaviors" and lists of "teacher shoulds" and into a familiar world where intention, uncertainties, chance, and judgment prevail.

Cases do not become teaching tools, however, until one asks: "What is this a case of?" According to Shulman (1986), this question represents the key move made when teaching with cases.

> A case, properly understood, is not simply the report of an event or incident. To call something a case is to make a theoretical claim—to argue that it is a "case of something," or to argue that it is an instance of a larger class. (p. 11)

In this book, the question "What is this a case of?" is taken very seriously: Each case is "a case of" a research-based pattern of teaching and learning, viewed through the lens of the Mathematical Tasks Framework. Together, the cases represent the most prevalent ways in which cognitively challenging mathematical tasks play out during classroom lessons.

This purposeful connection to a broader set of ideas serves as an important complement to the "here-and-now" details of the cases themselves. The teaching and learning patterns and ideas associated with the Mathematical Tasks Framework bring conceptual and pedagogical power to discussions of and reflections on the cases, adding coherence, memorability, and generalizability to what is learned.

OVERVIEW OF THE BOOK

The book is organized in three main parts. In the first part, readers will learn about the concepts, frameworks, and research findings that undergird the cases. In Chapter 1 we describe and provide examples of how mathematical instructional tasks vary with respect to the kind of thinking (i.e., cognitive demand) they require of students. These ideas have particular relevance for teachers as they are selecting or designing tasks (the first phase of the Mathematical Tasks Framework) or for principals or other leaders as they examine curricula for possible adoption. In Chapter 2 we provide descriptions of ways in which our research has suggested that the cognitive demands of tasks typically evolve and change during classroom instruction (the second and third phases of the framework). In Chapter 3 we outline our theory of how teachers move from reading and discussing cases of mathematics instruction to the improvement of their own practice.

Part II is comprised of actual materials for use in classes, seminars, or other instructional settings. Chapter 4 offers an introduction to the materials and their use. Each of the remaining chapters in this part of the book consists of a narrative case, which the reader is invited to analyze using the Mathematical Tasks Framework. All of the cases are written in the first person, revealing teachers' goals for their lessons and their thought processes at crucial decision points faced during the lesson. Thus, the reader is drawn into the teachers' thinking and feelings, thereby promoting a firsthand view of the challenges and rewards of teaching in this way.

A word about how the cases were created: The cases are based on real teachers and events, drawing on detailed documentation (videotapes and write-ups) of classroom lessons and interviews with teachers about the documented lessons. At times, cases collapse several lessons from a single teacher or enhance certain aspects of a lesson in order to bring out the research-based pattern of teaching and learning. It should be noted, however, that the instructional tasks themselves have remained unaltered. Moreover, every attempt has been made to stay true to the predispositions and general teaching habits of the teacher who inspired the case.

Part III is new to the second edition. It contains two chapters, both of which discuss the ways in which the materials in this book can be used to support the learning of teachers and administrators, drawing on our work over the past decade. Chapter 11 illustrates the various ways in which teacher educators or professional developers might use these materials to aid in the professional growth of teachers, including how to directly improve teachers' instruction practices. Chapter 12 discusses ways in which principals (or those who work with principals or principals-in-training) might use these materials to become better instructional leaders of teachers who are attempting to teach with cognitively demanding tasks.

FOR WHOM IS THIS BOOK WRITTEN?

This book is written primarily for teachers and teacher educators who have made a commitment to provide students with increased opportunities to experience mathematics as meaningful, challenging, and worthwhile. However, with the addition of Chapter 12, which is directed specifically toward principals, the book gains more immediate relevance to administrators and other leaders who are interested in learning how to foster reform efforts at the school or district levels.

Although individuals could benefit from reading this book alone, we believe that the real power of the ideas and strategies contained herein is derived from group discussion. Working alongside their peers, especially with the guidance of an experienced facilitator, individuals can gain richer insights into what makes a task challenging, how classroom events influence the unfolding of tasks, and ways in which one can productively reflect on one's own practice.

When using this book in group settings, individuals generally assume one of two roles: participants (usually teachers or principals who are attempting to improve their practice) or facilitators (professional educators who are supporting teachers' and principals' improvement efforts). Although most of this book is written for both facilitators and participants, at times we specifically address the facilitator, providing suggestions for how to use the materials.

It is our hope that the Mathematical Tasks Framework and the cases of instructional practice presented in this book will help teachers realize that they are not alone when they experience frustrations incorporating high-level tasks into their instructional practice. By reading this book and discussing it with like-minded educators, we hope teachers will begin to recognize when their instruction is and is not living up to its potential and what they can do to get the most out of cognitively challenging tasks. Similarly, principals will have a new gauge by which to judge instructional practice in their buildings and a fresh set of ideas about how to support teachers who want to make a difference.

NOTES

1. QUASAR (Quantitative Understanding: Amplifying Student Achievement and Reasoning) was a national project aimed at improving mathematics instruction for students attending middle schools in economically disadvantaged communities in ways that emphasized thinking, reasoning, problem solving, and the communication of mathematical ideas. The project was funded by the Ford Foundation, directed by Edward A. Silver, and headquartered at the Learning Research and Development Center at the University of Pittsburgh. The authors of this book were researchers on the QUASAR Project.

2. ESP (Enhancing Secondary Mathematics Teacher Preparation) was a project funded by the National Science Foundation (NSF) and directed by Margaret Schwan Smith; BIFOCAL (Beyond Implementation: Focus on Challenge and Learning) was a project funded by NSF and by the Michigan State University Mathematics Education Endowment Fund and directed by Edward A. Silver. Both projects provided support to teachers as they endeavored to enact more rigorous instruction in their own classrooms and take on leadership or mentoring responsibilities within their schools or districts.

3. An *instructional task* was defined as a segment of classroom activity devoted to the development of a mathematical idea.

4. Although we recognize the importance of considering the development of mathematical ideas and concepts over time, our research focused on the development of students' thinking during one classroom episode.

PART I

THE MATHEMATICAL TASKS FRAMEWORK

CHAPTER 1

Analyzing Mathematics Instructional Tasks

Mathematical tasks can be examined from a variety of perspectives, including the number and kinds of representations evoked, the variety of ways in which they can be solved, and their requirements for student communication. In this book, we examine mathematical instructional tasks in terms of their cognitive demands. By cognitive demands we mean the kind and level of thinking required of students in order to successfully engage with and solve the task.

In this chapter, we describe a method for analyzing the cognitive demands of tasks as they appear in curricular or instructional materials (the first phase of the Mathematical Tasks Framework shown in Figure I.3 in the Introduction). Unlike the remainder of the framework, which describes task evolution *during* a classroom lesson, the initial phase of the framework focuses on tasks *before* the lesson begins, that is, the task as it appears in print form or as it is created by the teacher.

Why are the cognitive demands of tasks so important? Opportunities for student learning are not created simply by putting students into groups, by placing manipulatives in front of them, or by handing them a calculator. Rather, it is the level and kind of thinking in which students engage that determines what they will learn (NCTM, 1991). Tasks that require students to perform a memorized procedure in a routine manner lead to one type of opportunity for student thinking; tasks that demand engagement with concepts and that stimulate students to make purposeful connections to meaning or relevant mathematical ideas lead to a different set of opportunities for student thinking. Day-in and day-out, the cumulative effect of students' experiences with instructional tasks is students' implicit development of ideas about the nature of mathematics—about whether mathematics is something they personally can make sense of, and how long and how hard they should have to work to do so.

Since the tasks with which students become engaged in the classroom form the basis of their opportunities for learning mathematics, it is important to be clear about one's goals for student learning. Once learning goals for students have been clearly articulated, tasks can be selected or created to match these goals. Being aware of the cognitive demands of tasks is a central consideration in this matching. For example, if a teacher wants students to learn how to justify or explain their solution processes, she should select a task that is deep and rich enough to afford such opportunities. If, on the other hand, speed and fluency are the primary learning objectives, other types of tasks will be needed. In this chapter, readers will learn how to differentiate among the various levels of cognitive demand of tasks, thereby laying a foundation for more careful matching between the tasks teachers select for the classroom and their goals for student learning.

DEFINING LEVELS OF COGNITIVE DEMAND
OF MATHEMATICAL TASKS

The example shown in Figure 1.1 illustrates four ways in which students can be asked to think about the relationships among different representations of fractional quantities. Each of these ways places a different level of cognitive demand on students. As shown on the left side of the figure, tasks with lower-level demands would consist of memorizing the equivalent forms of specific fractional quantities (e.g., $\frac{1}{2} = .5 = 50\%$) or performing conversions of fractions to percents or decimals using standard conversion algorithms in the absence of additional context or meaning (e.g., convert the fraction $\frac{3}{8}$ to a decimal by dividing the numerator by the denominator to get .375; change .375 to a percent by moving the decimal point two places to the right to get 37.5%). These lower-level tasks are classified as *memorization* and *procedures without connections to understanding, meaning, or concepts* (hereafter referred to simply as *procedures without connections*), respectively. When tasks such as these are used, students typically work 10 to 30 similar problems within one sitting.

Another way in which students can be asked to think about the relationships among fractions, decimals, and percents—one that presents higher-level cognitive demands—might also use procedures, but do so in a way that builds connections to underlying concepts and meaning. For example, as shown in Figure 1.1, students might be asked to use a 10×10 grid to illustrate how the fraction $\frac{3}{5}$ represents the same quantity as the decimal .6 or 60%. Students would also be asked to record their results on a chart containing the decimal, fraction, percent, and pictorial representations, thereby allowing them to make connections among the various representations and to attach meaning to their work by referring to the pictorial representation of the quantity every step of the way. This task is classified as *procedures with connections to understanding, meaning, or concepts* (hereafter referred to simply as *procedures with connections*).

FIGURE 1.1. Lower-level vs. higher-level approaches to the task of determining the relationships among different representations of fractional quantities (Stein & Smith, 1998).

Lower-Level Demands

Memorization

What are the decimal and percent equivalents for the fractions ½ and ¼ ?

Expected Student Response:

½ = .5 = 50%

¼ = .25 = 25%

Procedures Without Connections

Convert the fraction ⅜ to a decimal and a percent.

Expected Student Response:

Fraction	Decimal	Percent
⅜		

$$\begin{array}{r} .375 \\ 8\,\overline{)3.000} \\ \underline{24} \\ 60 \\ \underline{56} \\ 40 \\ \underline{40} \end{array}$$

.375 = 37.5%

Higher-Level Demands

Procedures With Connections

Using a 10 × 10 grid, identify the decimal and percent equivalents of ⅗.

Expected Student Response:

Fraction	Decimal	Percent
60/100 = ⅗	60/100 = .60	.60 = 60%

Doing Mathematics

Shade 6 small squares in a 4 × 10 rectangle. Using the rectangle, explain how to determine each of the following: a) the percent of area that is shaded, b) the decimal part of area that is shaded, and c) the fractional part of area that is shaded.

One Possible Student Response:

a) One column will he 10% since there are 10 columns. So four squares is 10%. Then 2 squares is half a column and half of 10%, which is 5%. So the 6 shaded blocks equal 10% plus 5%, or 15%.

b) One column will be .10 since there are 10 columns. The second column has only 2 squares shaded so that would he one half of .10, which is .05. So the 6 shaded blocks equal .1 plus .05, which equals .15.

c) Six shaded squares out of 40 squares is 6/40, which reduces to 3/20.

(Reprinted with permission from *Mathematics Teaching in the Middle School*, copyright © 1998 by the National Council of Teachers of Mathematics. All rights reserved.)

Another high-level task (classified as *doing mathematics*[1]) would entail asking students to explore the relationships among the various ways of representing fractional quantities. Students would not—at least initially—be provided with the conventional conversion procedures. They might once again use grids, but this time grids of varying sizes (not just 10 × 10) would be used. As shown in Figure 1.1, students could be asked to shade six squares of a 4 × 10 rectangle and to represent the shaded area as a percent, a decimal, and a fraction. When students use the visual diagram to solve this problem, they are challenged to apply their understandings of the fraction, decimal, and percent concepts in novel ways. For example, once a student has shaded the six squares, he or she must determine how the six squares relate to the total number of squares in the rectangle. In Figure 1.1, we see an example of a student's response to this task that illustrates the kind of mathematical reasoning used to come up with an answer that makes sense and that can be justified. In contrast to the tasks with lower-level demands discussed earlier, in *procedures-with-connections* or *doing-mathematics* tasks, students typically perform far fewer problems (sometimes as few as two or three) in one sitting.

MATCHING TASKS WITH GOALS FOR STUDENT LEARNING

As illustrated by the above discussion, not all mathematical tasks provide the same opportunities for student learning. Some tasks have the potential to engage students in complex forms of thinking and reasoning while others focus on memorization or the use of rules or procedures. In our work with teachers in the QUASAR Project, we discovered the importance of matching tasks with goals for student learning. Take, for example, the case of Mr. Johnson (Silver & Smith, 1996). Mr. Johnson wanted his students to learn to work collaboratively, to discuss alternative approaches to solving tasks, and to justify their solutions. However, the tasks he tended to use (e.g., expressing ratios such as $15/25$ in lowest terms) provided little, if any, opportunity for collaboration, exploration of multiple solution strategies, or meaningful justification. Not surprisingly, class discussions were not very rich or enlightening. The discourse focused on correct answers and describing procedures, doing little to further students' ability to think or reason about important ideas associated with ratio and proportion.

Mr. Johnson's experience (and that of many teachers with whom we have worked) makes clear the need to start with a cognitively challenging task that has the potential to engage students in complex forms of thinking if the goal is to increase students' ability to think, reason, and solve problems. Although starting with such a task does not guarantee student engagement at a high level, it appears to be a necessary condition since low-level tasks rarely result in high-level engagement (Stein, Grover, & Henningsen, 1996).

This is not to suggest that all tasks used by a teacher should engage students in cognitively demanding activity, since there may be some occasions on which a teacher might have other goals for a particular lesson, goals that would be better served by a different kind of task. For example, if the goal is to increase students' fluency in retrieving basic facts, definitions, and rules, then tasks that focus on *memorization* may be appropriate. If the goal is to increase students' speed and accuracy in solving routine problems, then tasks that focus on *procedures without connections* may be appropriate. Use of these types of tasks may improve student performance on tests that consist of low-level items and may lead to greater efficiency of time and effort in solving routine aspects of problems that are embedded in more complex tasks. However, focusing exclusively on tasks of these types can lead to a limited understanding of what mathematics is and how one does it. In addition, an overreliance on these types of tasks could lead to the inability to apply rules and procedures more generally, that is, to similar but not identical situations, or to recognize whether a particular rule or procedure is appropriate across a variety of situations (NCTM, 1989; 2000). Hence, students also need opportunities on a regular basis to engage with tasks that lead to deeper, more generative understandings regarding the nature of mathematical processes, concepts, and relationships.

DIFFERENTIATING LEVELS OF COGNITIVE DEMAND

The Task Analysis Guide (shown in Figure 1.2) consists of a listing of the characteristics[2] of tasks at each of the levels of cognitive demand described earlier in the chapter: *memorization, procedures without connections, procedures with connections,* and *doing mathematics.* When applied to a mathematical task (in print form), this guide can serve as a judgment template (a kind of scoring rubric) that permits a "rating" of the task based on the kind of thinking it demands of students.

For example, the guide would be helpful in deciding that the Fencing Task (shown in Figure I.2 in the Introduction) was an example of *doing mathematics* since the characteristics of this level most clearly describe the kind of thinking required to successfully complete the task. Specifically, no pathway is suggested by the task (i.e., there is no overarching procedure or rule that can simply be applied for solving the entire problem and the sequence of necessary steps is unspecified) and it requires students to explore pens of different dimensions and ultimately to make a generalization regarding the pen that will have maximum area for a fixed amount of fencing.

FIGURE 1.2. The characteristics of mathematical tasks at each of the four levels of cognitive demand (Stein & Smith, 1998).

THE TASK ANALYSIS GUIDE

Memorization Tasks

- Involve either reproducing previously learned facts, rules, formulae, or definitions OR committing facts, rules, formulae, or definitions to memory.
- Cannot be solved using procedures because a procedure does not exist or because the time frame in which the task is being completed is too short to use a procedure.
- Are not ambiguous—such tasks involve exact reproduction of previously seen material and what is to be reproduced is clearly and directly stated.
- Have no connection to the concepts or meaning that underlie the facts, rules, formulae, or definitions being learned or reproduced.

Procedures without Connections Tasks

- Are algorithmic. Use of the procedure is either specifically called for or its use is evident based on prior instruction, experience, or placement of the task.
- Require limited cognitive demand for successful completion. There is little ambiguity about what needs to be done and how to do it.
- Have no connection to the concepts or meaning that underlie the procedure being used.
- Are focused on producing correct answers rather than developing mathematical understanding.
- Require no explanations, or explanations that focus solely on describing the procedure that was used.

Procedures with Connections Tasks

- Focus students' attention on the use of procedures for the purpose of developing deeper levels of understanding of mathematical concepts and ideas.
- Suggest pathways to follow (explicitly or implicitly) that are broad general procedures that have close connections to underlying conceptual ideas as opposed to narrow algorithms that are opaque with respect to underlying concepts.
- Usually are represented in multiple ways (e.g., visual diagrams, manipulatives, symbols, problem situations). Making connections among multiple representations helps to develop meaning.
- Require some degree of cognitive effort. Although general procedures may be followed, they cannot be followed mindlessly. Students need to engage with the conceptual ideas that underlie the procedures in order to successfully complete the task and develop understanding.

Doing Mathematics Tasks

- Require complex and nonalgorithmic thinking (i.e., there is not a predictable, well-rehearsed approach or pathway explicitly suggested by the task, task instructions, or a worked-out example).
- Require students to explore and understand the nature of mathematical concepts, processes, or relationships.
- Demand self-monitoring or self-regulation of one's own cognitive processes.
- Require students to access relevant knowledge and experiences and make appropriate use of them in working through the task.
- Require students to analyze the task and actively examine task constraints that may limit possible solution strategies and solutions.
- Require considerable cognitive effort and may involve some level of anxiety for the student due to the unpredictable nature of the solution process required.

(Reprinted with permission from *Mathematics Teaching in the Middle School*, copyright © 1998 by the National Council of Teachers of Mathematics. All rights reserved.)

When determining the level of cognitive demand provided by a mathematical task, it is important not to become distracted by superficial features of the task and to keep in mind the students for whom the task is intended. Both of these considerations are discussed below.

Going Beyond Superficial Features

Determining the level of cognitive demand of a task can be tricky at times, since superficial features of tasks can be misleading. Low-level tasks, for example, can appear to be high-level when they have characteristics of reform-oriented instructional tasks (NCTM, 1991; Stein et al., 1996), such as requiring the use of manipulatives; using "real-world" contexts; involving multiple steps, actions, or judgments; and/or making use of diagrams. For example, some individuals have considered Martha's Carpeting Task (shown in Figure I.1 in the Introduction) a high-level task because it is a word problem and it is set in a real-world context. Similarly, some have considered commonly used fraction tasks—which ask students to find the sum of two proper fractions with unlike denominators and then to show the answer using fraction strips—high-level because they use manipulatives. But we would classify these tasks as low-level because typically well-rehearsed procedures (for Martha's Carpeting, the formula for determining area, and for the fraction task, the rule for adding fractions with unlike denominators) are strongly implied by the problems. In both cases, the tasks would be considered to be *procedures-without-connections* tasks since there is little ambiguity about what has to be done or how to do it, there is no connection to concepts or meaning required, and the focus is on producing the correct answer.

It is also possible for tasks to be designated low-level when in fact they should be considered high-level. For example, the Lemonade Task—in which students have to determine which of two recipes for lemonade is more "lemony": Recipe A, which has 2 cups of lemon concentrate and 3 cups of water, or Recipe B, which has 3 cups of lemon concentrate and 5 cups of water—has been considered by some an example of a *procedures-without-connections* task because it "looks like" a standard textbook problem that could be solved by applying a rule or because it lacks "reform features" (such as requiring an explanation or justification). However, we have described this task as *doing mathematics* since no pathway for solving the problem is suggested (either explicitly or implicitly). Specifically, the task requires students to compare two situations and to determine which recipe has the higher proportion of concentrate. To do so, students must make sense of the problem situation and maintain a close connection to the meaning of ratio and to the question being asked. So even though tasks might "look" high- or low-level, it is important to move beyond their surface features to consider the kind of thinking they require.

Considering the Students

Another consideration when deciding the level of challenge provided by a task is the students (their age, grade level, prior knowledge and experiences) and the norms and expectations for work in their classroom. Consider, for example, a task in which students are asked to add five two-digit numbers and explain the process they used. For a fifth- or sixth-grade student who has access to a calculator and/or the addition algorithm, and for whom "explain the process" means "tell how you did it," the task could be considered routine. If, on the other hand, the task is given to a second grader who has just started work with two-digit numbers, who has base-10 blocks available, and/or for whom "explain the process" means you have to explain your thinking, the task may indeed be high-level. Therefore, when teachers select or design instructional tasks, all of these factors must be considered in order to determine the extent to which the task is likely to provide an appropriate level of challenge for their students.

GAINING EXPERIENCE
IN ANALYZING COGNITIVE DEMANDS

One way we have found to help teachers learn to differentiate levels of cognitive demand is through the use of a task-sorting activity. The long-term goal of this activity is to raise teachers' awareness of how mathematical tasks differ with respect to their levels of cognitive demand, thereby allowing them to better match tasks to goals for student learning. A task-sorting activity can also enhance teachers' ability to thoughtfully analyze the cases (which appear in Part II of this book), and ultimately, to become more analytic and reflective about the role of tasks in instruction.

The eight tasks shown in Figure 1.3 represent a subset of tasks we have used for this purpose (an expanded set of middle school tasks can be found at *http://www.tcpress.com* and additional task sets can be found in Smith, Stein, Arbaugh, Brown, & Mossgrove, 2004). These tasks cover all four categories of cognitive demand and they vary with respect to a range of superficial features across these categories. For example, both Tasks A and D require an explanation or description, yet Task A is considered high-level *(doing mathematics)* and Task D is considered low-level *(procedures without connections)*. Alternatively, both Tasks A and C are considered *doing mathematics*, yet they differ with respect to the use of manipulatives, a "real-world" context, and the use of a diagram.

FIGURE 1.3. Sample tasks that have been used in a sorting activity.

TASK A
Manipulatives/Tools: Counters

For homework Mark's teacher asked him to look at the pattern below and draw the figure that should come next.

Mark does not know how to find the next figure.
A. Draw the next figure for Mark.
B. Write a description for Mark telling him how you knew which figure comes next.

QUASAR Project - QUASAR Cognitive Assessment Instrument - Release Task

TASK B
Manipulatives/Tools: None

Part A: After the first two games of the season, the best player on the girl's basketball team had made 12 out of 20 free throws. The best player on the boy's basketball team had made 14 out of 25 free throws. Which player had made the greater percent of free throws?

Part B: The "better" player had to sit out the third game due to an injury. How many baskets out of an additional 10 free throw "tries" would the other player need to make in order to take the lead in terms of greatest percentage of free throws?

Adapted from *Investigating Mathematics*. Glencoe Macmillan/McGraw-Hill. New York, New York, 1994.

TASK C
Manipulatives/Tools: Calculator

Your school's science club has decided to do a special project on nature photography. They decided to take a little over 300 outdoor photos in a variety of natural settings and in all different types of weather. Eventually they want to organize some of the best photos into a display and enter the state nature photography contest. The club was thinking of buying a 35mm camera, but someone in the club suggested that it might be better to buy disposable cameras instead. The regular camera with autofocus and automatic light meter would cost about $40.00 and film would cost $3.98 for 24 exposures and $5.95 for 36 exposures. The disposable cameras could be purchased in packs of three for $20.00 with two of the three taking 24 pictures and the third one taking 27 pictures. Single disposables could be purchased for $8.95. The club officers have to decide which would be the best option and they have to justify their decisions to the club advisor. Do you think they should purchase the regular camera or the disposable cameras? Write a justification that clearly explains your reasoning.

TASK D
Manipulatives/Tools: None

The cost of a sweater at J. C. Penney's was $45.00. At the "Day and Night" sale it was marked 30% off of the original price. What was the price of the sweater during the sale? Explain the process you used to find the sale price.

TASK E
Manipulatives/Tools: Pattern Blocks

½ of ⅓ means one of two equal parts of one-third

one-third   ½ of ⅓ or ½ × ⅓ = ⅙

Find ⅓ of ¼. Use pattern blocks. Draw your answer.

one-fourth   ⅓ of ¼ or ⅓ × ¼ = ☐

Find ¼ of ⅓. Use pattern blocks. Draw your answer.

one-third   ¼ of ⅓ or ¼ × ⅓ = ☐

TASK F
Manipulatives/Tools: Square Pattern Tiles

Using the side of a square pattern tile as a measure, find the perimeter (i.e., distance around) of each train in the pattern block figure shown below.

Train 1   Train 2   Train 3

TASK G
Manipulatives/Tools: Grid Paper

The pairs of numbers in a-d below represent the heights of stacks of cubes to be leveled off. On grid paper. sketch the front views of columns of cubes with these heights before and after they are leveled off. Write a statement under the sketches that explains how your method of leveling off is related to finding the average of the two numbers.

9   5   7   7
a) 14 and 8   b) 16 and 7   c) 7 and 12   d) 13 and 15

By taking 2 blocks off the first stack and giving them to the second stack, I've made the two stacks the same. So the total # of cubes is now distributed into 2 columns of equal height. And that is what average means.

Taken from *Visual Mathematics* (Bennett & Foreman, 1989).

TASK H
Manipulatives/Tools: None

Give the fraction and percent for each decimal.

.20 = _____ = _____
.25 = _____ = _____
.33 = _____ = _____
.50 = _____ = _____
.66 = _____ = _____
.75 = _____ = _____

(Reprinted with permission from *Mathematics Teaching in the Middle School,* copyright © 1998 by the National Council of Teachers of Mathematics. All rights reserved.)

Whether our tasks are chosen as the basis for a sorting activity, new tasks are created for this purpose, or some combination of tasks is used, it is important to vary tasks with respect to a range of features across categories of cognitive demand. Figure 1.4 provides a complete listing of the cognitive demands and features represented in the eight tasks shown in Figure 1.3. The analysis of tasks that vary in these ways will require going beyond superficial features to focus on the kind of thinking in which students must engage in order to complete the tasks.

Developing a Shared Meaning

The benefits of a task-sorting activity, as described in the previous section, accrue not simply from completing the sort, but rather from a combination of small- and large-group discussions that provide the opportunity for conversation that moves back and forth between specific tasks and the characteristics of each category as illustrated in the Task Analysis Guide (Figure 1.2) and negotiating definitions for the categories. We have found that participants do not always agree with each other—or with us—on how tasks should be categorized, but that both agreement and disagreement can be productive.

For example, we have found that there is often complete (or near) consensus that Task E should be classified as *procedures with connections*. The discussion about the task often brings out the fact that the task focuses on *what it means* to take a fraction of a fraction (as opposed to using an algorithm such as "multiply the numerators and multiply the denominators") and that it cannot be completed without cognitive effort (i.e., students have to think about what their actions mean as they work through the problem). For other tasks, such as Task A, there is often little agreement. Some consider Task A an example of *procedures without connections,* some as *procedures with connections,* and others as *doing mathematics.* The ensuing discussion often highlights the fact that there is no procedure or pathway stated or implied for Task A, yet the Task Analysis Guide has included the use of a procedure as a hallmark of tasks that were classified as *procedures without connections* and *procedures with connections.* A more focused look at the characteristics of *doing mathematics* can bring out the fact that tasks in this category require students to explore and understand the nature of relationships—a necessary step in extending and describing the pattern in Task A. The discussion generally concludes with teachers deciding it is a *doing-mathematics* task. By using the Task Analysis Guide as a template against which to judge this and other "little consensus" tasks, the group has a principled basis for the decisions it makes.

FIGURE 1.4. Cognitive demands and features of the eight sample tasks shown in Figure 1.3.

Task	Level of Cognitive Demand	Explanation of Categorization	Features
A	Doing mathematics	There is no pathway suggested by the task. The focus is on looking for the underlying mathematical structure.	• Requires an explanation • Uses manipulatives • Involves multiple steps • Uses a diagram • Is symbolic/abstract • Is "textbook-like"
B	Procedures with connections	The task focuses attention on the procedure for finding percents, but in a meaningful context.	• Has "real-world" context • Involves multiple steps • Is "textbook-like"
C	Doing mathematics	There is no predictable pathway suggested by the task and it requires complex thinking.	• Requires an explanation • Has "real-world" context • Involves multiple steps • Uses a calculator • Is "textbook-like"
D	Procedures without connections	The task requires the use of a well-established procedure for finding the sales price. There is no connection to meaning.	• Requires an explanation • Has "real-world" context • Involves multiple steps • Is "textbook-like"
E	Procedures with connections	The task provides a procedure for taking a fraction of a fraction but connects the procedure to meaning.	• Uses manipulatives • Involves multiple steps • Uses a diagram • Is symbolic/abstract
F	Procedures without connections	The task provides a procedure for finding the perimeter but requires no connection to meaning.	• Uses manipulatives • Uses a diagram • Is symbolic/abstract
G	Procedures with connections	The task provides a procedure for finding the average that focuses on the underlying meaning of average.	• Requires an explanation • Involves multiple steps • Uses a diagram • Is symbolic/abstract
H	Memorization	The task requires the recall of previously learned information. No understanding is required.	• Is "textbook-like"

It is easy to get sidetracked with discussions about how a specific group of students would solve a particular task or to become overly concerned about achieving complete consensus on every task. (This has happened to us more than once!) The goal is not to achieve complete agreement but rather to provide teachers with a shared language for discussing tasks and their characteristics and to raise the level of discussion among teachers toward a deeper analysis of the relationship between the tasks they select or create and the level of cognitive engagement that will be required of students. It is important to remind participants to consider the purpose of the task-sorting activity more generally—to begin to consider how and why tasks differ and how these differences can impact opportunities for student learning.

Continuing to Differentiate Cognitive Demands

A task-sorting activity provides one way in which teachers can begin to differentiate cognitive demands of tasks. Two additional approaches, more closely connected to teachers' practice, can also be helpful in this regard.

One approach is to ask teachers to collect the tasks used during classroom instruction over a defined period of time (e.g., 3 weeks). Then the teachers can use the Task Analysis Guide to identify the cognitive demands of the tasks they collected and evaluate whether the collection provided sufficient opportunity for development of thinking, reasoning, and problem solving as well as basic skills.

Another suggestion is to have teachers use the Task Analysis Guide to evaluate the tasks in a unit or chapter of their textbook or instructional materials. This could lead to a discussion of the balance of instructional tasks provided by the materials and/or to having teachers rewrite the tasks that were identified as low-level so as to raise the level of cognitive demand of the task (i.e., change low-level tasks into high-level tasks).

MOVING BEYOND TASK SELECTION AND CREATION

This chapter has focused on analyzing the cognitive demands of tasks as they appear in curricular materials or as they are created by teachers. In the remainder of this book, we will focus on the ways in which tasks that are set up at a high-level play out *during* classroom instruction. There are at least two reasons for restricting our focus to high-level tasks from this point forward. First, the widespread dissemination of the Standards documents (NCTM, 1989, 1991, 1995, 2000) has made teachers and staff developers keenly aware of the need to challenge student thinking and the publication of several innovative curricula such as *Connected Mathematics* (Lappan, Fitzgerald, Friel, Fey, & Phillips, 1998) and *Mathematics in Context* (The Mathematics in Context Development Team, 1998) has provided teachers with access to a storehouse of challenging mathematical tasks. Hence, high-level tasks are being used with increased frequency in our nation's classrooms. Second, in contrast to low-level tasks, which are almost always faithfully implemented, the enactment of high-level tasks is less predictable and often leads to unintended and unanticipated outcomes (Stein et al., 1996).

In the next chapter, we will focus on understanding the complexities encountered when tasks leave the printed page and become entangled with the thoughts and actions of the teachers and students who give them life during classroom lessons. This is a critical part of the story for teachers who are committed to ensuring that students are not only *exposed to,* but also *benefit* from, high-level tasks.

NOTES

1. The category *doing mathematics* includes many different types of tasks that have the shared characteristic of having no pathway for solving the task explicitly or implicitly suggested and therefore requiring nonalgorithmic thinking. This category includes tasks that are nonroutine in nature, are intended to explore a mathematical concept in depth, embody the complexities of real-life situations, or represent mathematical abstractions.

2. These characteristics are derived from the work of Doyle on academic tasks (1988) and Resnick on high-level thinking skills (1987), and from the examination and categorization of hundreds of tasks in QUASAR classrooms (Stein et al., 1996; Stein, Lane, & Silver, 1997).

CHAPTER 2

Using Cognitively Complex Tasks in the Classroom

A major aim of the QUASAR Project was to provide students with increased opportunities for thinking, reasoning, problem solving, and mathematical communication. Student learning could not be expected to deepen or become more conceptually rich, it was argued, unless students were regularly, actively, and productively engaged with cognitively challenging mathematics.

Classroom observations conducted by project researchers suggested that most QUASAR teachers were successful in *identifying and setting up* challenging instructional tasks. Nearly three-fourths of the observed and coded instructional tasks placed high-level cognitive demands on students (Stein et al, 1996). These same observations, however, showed that simply selecting and beginning a lesson with a high-level task did not guarantee that students would actually think and reason in cognitively complex ways. In fact, only about 40% of the tasks that started out at a high-level remained that way as the students actually engaged with them (Stein et al., 1996). A variety of factors were found to conspire to reduce the level of cognitive demand of a task once it was unleashed into the classroom environment. The difficulty of maintaining the cognitive demands of a task during implementation was also a key finding of the TIMSS video analysis (Stigler & Hiebert, 2004). In that analysis, none of the tasks that were set up at a high level was implemented as intended.

THE EVOLUTION OF TASKS DURING A LESSON

The fact that tasks take on lives of their own after being introduced into classroom settings has been noted by a variety of classroom researchers (Doyle, 1988; Doyle & Carter, 1984; Stein et al., 1996). In fact, if one wishes to examine *task use in the classroom,* a reconceptualization of the term *task* is in order. As mathematical tasks are enacted in classroom settings, they become intertwined with the goals, intentions, actions, and interactions of teachers and students. Therefore, we have found the need to conceptualize mathematical instructional tasks as not only the problems written in a textbook or a teacher's lesson plan (the focus of Chapter 1), but also the *classroom activity* that surrounds the way in which those problems are set up and actually carried out by teachers and students. Defined in this way, mathematical instructional tasks become situated squarely in the interactions of teaching and learning. When tasks are conceptualized as classroom-based activity, it is not unusual for their cognitive demands to change as they unfold during a lesson. The Mathematical Tasks Framework that was introduced earlier is a visual representation that summarizes the unfolding of tasks in response to the dynamics of teaching and learning in the classroom (see Figure I.3).

The first phase—tasks as they appear in curricular or instructional materials—was discussed in detail in Chapter 1. In this chapter, our focus is on the setup and implementation phases. The *setup phase* includes the teacher's communication to students regarding what they are expected to do, how they are expected to do it, and with what resources. The teacher's setup of a task can be as brief as directing students' attention to a task that appears on the blackboard and telling them to start working on it. Or it can be as long and involved as discussing how students should work on the problem in small groups, working through a sample problem, and discussing the forms of solutions that will be acceptable.

It is not unusual for a teacher to alter the cognitive demands of the task as she is setting it up for her class. In other words, she may, either purposefully or unwittingly, change the task from how it appeared in the curricular or instructional print materials from which she originally took her idea. For example, consider the Fencing Task, which appeared in the Introduction (Figure I.2). A teacher who thinks that her students are not ready for such an open-ended problem might prepare a worksheet to guide them systematically through a set of solution steps. This worksheet might include the formulas for area and perimeter and a partially completed table that would "lead" students to the discovery that as the pen dimensions approached a square, the area approached its maximum value. The use of this worksheet would take away the challenge introduced by the unstructured nature of the task and hence change its cognitive demands.

The *implementation phase*[1] (also referred to as the *enactment phase*) starts as soon as the students begin to work on the task and continues until the teacher and students turn their attention to a new mathematical task. During the implementation phase, both students and the teacher are viewed as important contributors to how the task is carried out. Although the students' levels of cognitive engagement ultimately determine what is learned, the ways and extent to which the teacher supports students' thinking and reasoning is a crucial ingredient in the ultimate fate of high-level tasks (Henningsen & Stein, 1997; Stein et al., 1996). For example, teachers can promote sense-making and deeper levels of understanding by consistently asking students to explain how they are thinking about the task. Or, conversely, they can cut off opportunities for sense-making by hurrying students through the tasks, thereby not allowing the time to grapple with perplexing ideas. (See Figure 2.1 for the variety of ways in which students' thinking can be supported or hindered.)

FIGURE 2.1. Factors associated with maintenance and decline of high-level demands (Stein & Smith, 1998).

Factors Associated with the Decline of High-Level Cognitive Demands	**Factors Associated with the Maintenance of High-Level Cognitive Demands**
1. Problematic aspects of the task become routinized (e.g., students press the teacher to reduce the complexity of the task by specifying explicit procedures or steps or perform; the teacher "takes over" the thinking and reasoning and tells students how to do the problem).	1. Scaffolding of student thinking and reasoning.
	2. Students are provided with means of monitoring their own progress.
2. The teacher shifts the emphasis from meaning, concepts, or understanding to the correctness or completeness of the answer.	3. Teacher or capable students model high-level performance.
	4. Sustained press for justifications, explanations, and/or meaning through teacher questioning, comments, and/or feedback.
3. Not enough time is provided to wrestle with the demanding aspects of the task or too much time is allowed and students drift into off-task behavior.	5. Tasks build on students' prior knowledge.
4. Classroom management problems prevent sustained engagement in high-level cognitive activities.	6. Teacher draws frequent conceptual connections.
5. Inappropriateness of task for a given group of students (e.g., students do not engage in high-level cognitive activities due to lack of interest, motivation, or prior knowledge needed to perform; task expectations not clear enough to put students in the right cognitive space).	7. Sufficient time to explore (not too little, not too much).
6. Students are not held accountable for high-level products or processes (e.g., although asked to explain their thinking, unclear or incorrect student explanations are accepted; students are giving the impression that their work will not "count" toward a grade).	

(Reprinted with permission from *Mathematics Teaching in the Middle School*, copyright © 1998 by the National Council of Teachers of Mathematics. All rights reserved.)

During the implementation phase, the cognitive demands of high-level tasks can easily transform, usually into less-demanding forms of student thinking. The ways in which cognitively challenging tasks typically transform during the implementation phase is discussed in depth in the next section of this chapter.

The ultimate reason for focusing on instructional tasks is to influence student learning (see final triangle in Figure I.3). Research has demonstrated that the cognitive demands of mathematical instructional tasks are related to the level and kind of student learning. Within the QUASAR Project, students who performed best on the QUASAR Cognitive Assessment Instrument[2] were in classrooms in which tasks were more likely to be set up *and* implemented at high levels of cognitive demand (Stein & Lane, 1996; Stein et al., 1997). For these students, having the opportunity to work on challenging tasks in a supportive classroom environment translated into substantial learning gains on an instrument specifically designed to measure student thinking, reasoning, problem solving, and communication. Similarly, recent research conducted by Boaler and Staples (2008) suggests that the success of students at Railside (one of the high schools participating in their study) was due in large part to the high cognitive demand of the curriculum and the teachers' ability to maintain the level of demand during enactment through questioning. Together, these findings suggests the importance of being mindful, both at the outset *and* during the various task phases, of the kinds of cognitive activity with which students *should be* and *actually are* engaged in the classroom.

PATTERNS OF TASK SETUP AND IMPLEMENTATION

In a 3-year study of classroom instruction at four QUASAR middle schools (Henningsen & Stein, 1997; Stein et al., 1996), a handful of patterns emerged that captured characteristic ways in which high-level tasks unfolded during instruction. These patterns and the classroom-based factors associated with them are described below.

Maintenance of High-Level Cognitive Demands

Some tasks that were set up to place high levels of cognitive demand on student thinking were indeed implemented in such a way that students thought and reasoned in complex and meaningful ways. Take, for example, what happened in Ms. Fox's class when students were introduced to the Fencing Task (Figure I.2). Students started out by describing an assortment of pen configurations that could be built with 24 feet of fencing. As they kept coming up with new configurations, they realized they needed to keep track of the shapes they had already tried. This led them to construct a table that identified the dimensions of each configuration along with its area. Eventually, by looking for patterns across many configurations, students arrived at a conjecture regarding the shape that produced the largest area, and then tested that conjecture with a different amount of fencing (i.e., a different perimeter). During this time, Ms. Fox circulated among the groups, asking questions such as "How do you know you have all of the possible pen configurations?", "Which has the most room?", and "Do you see a pattern?". These questions led students to see the need to organize their data, make conjectures, and test them out.

Indeed, throughout our data, when tasks were enacted in this way there were usually a large number of support factors present in the classroom environment. As shown in Figure 2.1, these included the selection of tasks that built on students' prior knowledge, appropriate teacher scaffolding of student thinking (i.e., assisting student thinking by asking thought-provoking questions that preserve task complexity), sustained pressure for explanation and meaning, and the modeling of high-level thinking and reasoning by the teacher or more capable peers.

Other tasks that were set up to place high levels of cognitive demand on students' thinking, however, exhibited declines in terms of how students actually went about working on them. When the cognitive demands of tasks declined during the implementation phase, a different set of factors tended to be operating in the classroom environment (see Figure 2.1). These factors involved a variety of teacher-, student-, and task-related conditions, actions, and norms. Tasks that declined during the implementation phase generally transformed into one of the forms of student cognitive activity described below.

Decline into Procedures Without Connection to Meaning

Instead of engaging deeply and meaningfully with the mathematics, students ended up utilizing a more procedural, often mechanical and shallow, approach to the task. In this type of decline, one of the most prevalent factors operating in the environment was teachers' "taking over" and doing the challenging aspects of the tasks for the students.

For example, shortly after Ms. Jones gave her seventh-grade students the Fencing Task (Figure I.2), she was dismayed to see that they were not making much progress—some students were already off-task and many others were complaining that the task was too difficult. Not knowing where to begin, the students began to urge her to give them some help. Wanting them to feel successful and stay engaged, Ms. Jones pointed out to the students that the problem involved finding the area of all the rectangles that had a perimeter of 24. She told her students that they needed to make a chart of all possibilities, starting with a 1 × 11, and then find the area for each using the formula area = length × width. Although Ms. Jones's actions were well intended (and understandable), when she provided students with a procedure for solving the problem, students' opportunities for mathematical thinking were diminished.

High-level tasks (such as the Fencing Task) tend to be less structured, more difficult, and longer than the kinds of tasks to which students are typically exposed. Students often perceive these types of tasks as ambiguous and/ or risky because it is not apparent what they should do, how they should do it, and how their work will be evaluated (Doyle, 1988; Romagnano, 1994). In order to deal with the discomfort that surrounds this uncertainty, students often urge teachers to make these types of tasks more explicit by breaking them down into smaller steps, specifying exact procedures to be followed, or actually doing parts of the task for them. When the teacher gives in to such requests, the challenging, sense-making aspects of the task are reduced or eliminated, and the opportunity to develop thinking and reasoning skills and meaningful mathematical understandings is lost.

Decline into Unsystematic Exploration

Unsystematic exploration differs from the other categories previously discussed since it is not used to describe tasks as they appear in curricular materials or as they are set up by the teacher and it was not represented in the QUASAR researchers' original coding scheme. Rather, this category emerged from the analysis as a way to describe some *doing-mathematics* tasks that were not proceduralized but still not adequately implemented. In this type of decline, students approached the task seriously and attempted to perform mathematical processes such as conjecturing, looking for patterns, discussing and justifying, and so forth. However, they failed to progress toward understanding the important mathematical ideas embodied in the tasks. Take, for example, Mr. Chambers's experience with the Fencing Task. Although his seventh-grade students worked conscientiously during the entire period, they focused on aspects of the problem (e.g., How big were the rabbits? How much space did the rabbits need? How much would the fencing cost?) that were not central to answering the questions posed. Although students' thinking required decision making and involved some mathematics, it did not move the students toward the generalization that the largest area for a fixed perimeter would be a square—the point of the task.

In cases such as that of Mr. Chambers, teachers appeared to desire to maintain the complexity of the task; they usually didn't take over and/or oversimplify tasks. But they also did not provide the kind and the extent of support that teachers provided when high levels of cognitive activity were maintained. For example, the sensitive, thought-provoking questions that Ms. Fox interjected at crucial points of students' explorations were absent. Another factor that seemed to be associated with this pattern was too much time for students to work on the task; without needed supports they floundered, failing to make progress toward mathematical understanding.

Decline into Nonmathematical Activity

In these cases, students often displayed a variety of off-task behaviors such as playing absentmindedly with their manipulatives or talking with their partners about subjects far afield from mathematics. This often happened when the task was not matched appropriately to students' prior learning experiences and/or expectations were not specific enough to guide students into an appropriate mathematical space. Another factor that played a significant role in this type of decline (to a much greater extent than in other kinds of decline) was classroom-management problems. When students were free to roam the room and talk with friends during group-work time, or to disrupt the class with requests for materials, then all students' abilities to engage with complex tasks were sacrificed.

Tasks can also decline into no mathematical activity when the teacher does not keep the focus on mathematics. In these situations, students are engaged in activity, but the activity tends to be nonmathematical in nature. For example, when Ms. Jackson used the Fencing Task in her class, she asked each student group to produce a poster on a large sheet of newsprint, showing their work in an organized way. The students' attention turned immediately to the creation of posters as works of art rather than as the result of mathematical activity, producing elaborate drawings of rabbits and pens and titling their work in calligraphy. In this situation, the teacher failed to keep an eye on the mathematics, settling instead for more affective outcomes such as students' working well together.

These four patterns—all of which began with a task classified as *doing mathematics*—represent a subset of the most prevalent patterns of task setup and implementation identified in our research. All of the prevalent patterns are identified in Figure 2.2.[3] As shown in the figure, each pattern has been found to be associated with a set of classroom-based factors that appear to influence the path of task evolution. It is interesting to note that when the level of cognitive demand is maintained, the same five factors are generally present. When tasks decline, however, the set of factors varies depending on the nature of the decline.

FIGURE 2.2. Common patterns of task setup and implementation and most-frequently associated factors. For each pattern, the factors are ordered from most- to least-frequently observed.

PATTERNS		High-Level Demands	Factors Most Often Associated with Specific Patterns of Maintenance and Decline
Task Setup	Task Implementation		
Doing mathematics →	Doing mathematics	Maintained	• Task builds on students' prior knowledge • Scaffolding • Appropriate amount of time • High-level performance modeled • Sustained pressure for explanation and meaning
Doing mathematics →	Procedures without meaningful connections	Declined	• Challenges become nonproblems • Focus shifts to correct answer • Too much or too little time
Doing mathematics →	Unsystematic exploration	Declined	• Inappropriateness of task for students • Too much or too little time • Challenges become nonproblems
Doing mathematics →	No mathematical activity	Declined	• Inappropriateness of task for students • Classroom management problems • Too much or too little time
Procedures with connections →	Procedures with connections	Maintained	• Task builds on students' prior knowledge • High-level performance modeled • Appropriate amount of time • Sustained press for explanation and meaning • Scaffolding
Procedures with connections →	Procedures without connections	Declined	• Challenges become nonproblems • Focus shifts to correct answer • Inappropriateness of the task for students

In Part II of this book, we present cases of classroom instruction that exemplify each of these six patterns (shown in Figure 2.2) and the factors associated with them. It is our hope that these cases will help teachers identify when and why various patterns occur in a more self-conscious and consistent manner than they might normally do on their own. This will, in turn, help teachers become more alert to the potential for slippage between intention and action in their teaching. The self-monitoring and reflection required to analyze instruction in this way represents an important first step toward providing students with the enhanced learning opportunities they need in order to develop into powerful mathematical thinkers.

Before introducing the cases, we conclude Part I of the book with a chapter that provides an overview of our theory of how teachers learn from cases.

NOTES

1. In our framework, task implementation refers to the enactment of a task in the classroom by teachers and students. In our more current writings, including this book, we frequently use the term *enactment* as a synonym for the term *implementation*. Enactment appears to avoid the sometimes negative connotations associated with implementation (i.e., implementation as mindless performance of mandated practices), and the misinterpretation that teachers can be thought about only as implementors rather than as constructors. By contrast, enactment connotes the view that instructional tasks are co-constructed through the thoughts and actions of the teacher and her students during the course of instruction. We have continued to label this phase "tasks as *implemented* by students" in the framework, however, in order to preserve continuity with past publications.

2. For additional information on the QUASAR Cognitive Assessment Instrument, see Lane (1993), Lane and Silver (1995), and Silver and Lane (1993).

3. The two patterns not discussed in the preceding paragraphs involve tasks that were set up as *procedures with connections* (see the final two patterns in the figure).

CHAPTER 3

Learning from Cases

Although the professions of business, law, and medicine have used cases for de-
cades to teach the main ideas, skills, and underlying principles of their practice,
the use of cases in teacher education is relatively recent. After Lee Shulman's
1986 American Educational Research Association (AERA) presidential address
in which he called for the development of a *case knowledge of teaching*, a variety
of practitioners and researchers began writing, using, and studying cases as tools
for educating teachers. The use of the case method can now be observed in a variety of teacher-education and staff-development programs across the country.

THEORETICAL CONSIDERATIONS

Professional users of the case method are often asked what teachers learn
from cases and how they learn it. Their answers vary, often in relationship to
the kind of case being used. For example, *dilemma-driven* cases close with a
pedagogical problem to be solved (see, for example, cases edited by Barnett,
Goldenstein, & Jackson, 1994). Exposure to these kinds of cases aims to help
teachers (1) realize that teaching is an inherently dilemma-ridden enterprise
and (2) learn how to think about the trade-offs involved in selecting one
course of action over another.

The cases in this book are of a different kind. We think of them as *paradigm* cases (Shulman, 1992), that is, cases that embody certain principles or
ideas related to the teaching and learning of mathematics. Exposure to our
cases aims to assist teachers to develop (1) an understanding of mathematical
tasks and how their cognitive demands evolve during a lesson and (2) the skill
of critical reflection on their own practice guided by reference to a framework
based on these ideas.

Our ultimate goal is to influence instructional practice through teacher
reflection. Teachers often report that, without guidance, it is difficult to get a
handle on how to think about their own instruction. For example, when teachers first view a video of their own practice, they often lack a coherent focus
and thus experience reflection as a frustrating attempt to decipher and bring

meaning to the myriad actions and interactions that constitute classroom activity. Our intention is to help teachers learn one particular way in which to critically examine classroom activity: by viewing it through the lens of the Mathematical Tasks Framework.[1]

The role of cases is to situate the abstract ideas of the Mathematical Tasks Framework in episodes of classroom practice. Like teachers' understanding of their own practice, the ideas embedded in our cases come bundled with context-specific details; they are intertwined with decisions made by specific teachers on particular days, about specific topics and particular students. Teachers recognize and resonate with the "here-and-now" events depicted in the cases and readily make comparisons with their practice. In fact, we've witnessed teachers spontaneously comparing specific events in their own lessons with events in our cases. For example, midway through the semester of her elementary mathematics methods course, Rosa and her classmates were involved in a discussion of the case of Fran Gorman and Kevin Cooper (see Chapter 6). Several weeks later, in a written analysis of a mathematics lesson she had taught—one of the course assignments—Rosa reflected on her use of manipulatives in her teaching and concluded that she was "just like Fran." She went on to make connections between what had occurred in her classroom and what had happened in Fran's.

Although Rosa's identification of similarities between her practice and Fran's practice was helpful in the analysis of this one particular lesson, it will not necessarily lead to broad-based improvement of her practice. In order to "grab hold" of classroom events, to learn from examples, and to transfer what has been learned in one event to learning in similar events, teachers must learn to recognize events as instances of something larger and more generalizable. Only then can knowledge accumulate; only then will lessons learned in one setting suggest appropriate avenues of action in another.

This is where each case's connection to a larger set of ideas comes into play. With each case's grounding in the concepts of cognitive demand and patterns of task enactment, this connection has been "hard-wired" into our cases. As described earlier, each of our cases is a "case of" a cognitively challenging task playing out in the classroom in a particular pattern of task enactment centered around the idea of cognitive demands.

Once teachers begin to view our cases as cases of various patterns of task enactment, they can begin to reflect on their own practice through the lens of the cognitive demands of tasks and the Mathematical Tasks Framework. Teachers must learn this connection over time; it cannot be assumed. The cases are an important learning tool in this regard because they serve as a mediating device between teachers' reflection on their own practice and their ability to interpret their own practice as instances of more general patterns of task enactment.

How do cases play this mediating function? When facilitators assist teachers to view the cases through the lens of the Mathematical Tasks Framework, teachers (1) become sensitive to important cues in teaching episodes (e.g., Was the teacher tuned into students' needs? Was teacher assistance to struggling students just right, too much, or too little?) and (2) learn how to interpret those cues as influences on students' opportunities to engage productively with tasks. This is done in the relaxed, nonthreatening environment of the case discussion. However, because teachers naturally compare their own classroom lessons with the cases, they will also be gaining insights into ways of attending to and interpreting events in their own day-to-day instruction.

MOVING ON TO CONSIDERATIONS OF ONE'S OWN PRACTICE

In this section, we review a variety of ways in which the Mathematical Tasks Framework, enhanced by teachers' work with cases, can be connected to teachers' own practice. We begin with suggestions for how a discussion group can complement their conversations surrounding the cases in this book with artifacts drawn from their own classrooms. We then move on to a discussion of how two teachers can use the Mathematical Tasks Framework as a tool for observing and discussing each others' lessons. Finally, we end with a scenario in which a teacher reflects on her own instruction using a videotape.

Reflecting in a Case-Based Discussion Group

We envision this book being used by a group of practitioners who meet regularly to discuss the cases either formally (e.g., during a course or professional development session) or informally (e.g., study group). There are several activities in which such a group could engage that would help to bridge the space between the events depicted in the cases and teachers' own practice. For example, teachers could be encouraged to discuss specific events in their own classes in which they thought that tasks did or did not live up to their potential. In fact, it has been our experience that teachers often spontaneously apply the Mathematical Tasks Framework to recollections of their own practice, thereby beginning the process of analyzing their practice in terms of the cognitive demands it places on students and sometimes allowing them to gain insight into how they might have done things differently (see Stein & Smith, 1998).

Another option would be for teachers to bring in videotapes of mathematics lessons for the group to view. Together, they could reflect on the lesson, identifying the levels of cognitive demand that the task placed on students during the setup and implementation phases. In the process, teachers would begin to notice certain cues on the videotape to which they have attended during their case discussions, such as the extent to which the teacher tunes into students' needs, the manner in which the teacher provides assistance, and whether the teacher assists students to do the work rather than doing it for them. By serving as an object of shared discussion, videotapes are an especially good way of solidifying a common language for discussing classroom instruction and for beginning the process of connecting ideas learned in case discussions to teachers' day-to-day practice. (Additional suggestions regarding how these materials could be used to support teacher learning can be found in Chapter 11.)

Reflecting with a Partner

Teacher colleagues who have participated in case discussions can also take turns observing each other during actual classroom instruction. Because they have developed a shared language for talking about instructional events, the teachers will find it easy to decide on a common focus and to communicate meaningfully with one another. As the instructional task is being set up, for example, the observer will want to focus on the messages being conveyed, both implicitly and explicitly, to the students. What are they being asked to do? How are they being asked to do it? With what resources? The answers to these questions will reveal the cognitive processes required to successfully complete the task.

As students work on the task, the observer will want to watch carefully in order to discern how deeply students are grappling with significant mathematical ideas. Based on many discussions of task-implementation phases in the cases, the observer will be drawn toward certain cues: Are students dealing with mathematical meaning as they work? Is their talk grounded in mathematical reasoning and evidence? Or are they staying at the level of memorized procedures and symbols that are disconnected from underlying ideas?

Following the class, the teacher and observer will be able to use the ideas and language of the Mathematical Tasks Framework to discuss the lesson. For example, they may find it useful to begin by coming to agreement on what constituted the task-setup and the task-implementation phases. Then they can turn their attention to the cognitive demands of the task at each of these phases. Our experience suggests that the observer should first provide her judgments regarding the cognitive demands at each phase; then the teacher can comment on the observer's judgments, noting both agreements and disagreements. In this way, the observer is forced to offer critical judgments and is less likely to be tempted to "gloss over" differences of opinion—differences that are important for growth.

If the observer and teacher agree that one or more tasks were set up at a high level of cognitive demand, they will also want to identify the factors that either supported or inhibited student engagement at a high level. The list of factors shown in Figure 2.1 can be helpful in this discussion, but should move beyond the general descriptors provided in the figure to more closely identify the factor(s) in the observed lesson. This is the part of the framework that teachers, by and large, find the most fascinating, probably because it reflects most directly on things they are doing well or that they can improve.

Reflecting Individually

Rather than asking others to observe them, some teachers videotape themselves. This enables them to reflect on their own instruction in a convenient, unhurried, and private manner. Reflection using videotape is carried out in the same manner as described above, identifying what occurs at both the setup and implementation phases.

Videotapes of instruction can be used in partner or group settings as well as privately by a single teacher. Using videotape offers several advantages over discussions based on memory or notes. First, memories and notes cannot capture as much detail as videotape. Second, videotape allows teachers to watch and review a segment, trying to discern exactly what was going on as students worked on a particular task.

ADVANTAGES TO GUIDED REFLECTION

As discussed in the previous section, the Mathematical Tasks Framework provides a lens through which to view the cases as well as to reflect on one's own practice. It is the latter that is critical for improving practice and ultimately for ensuring that students have the opportunity to successfully engage in cognitively challenging tasks. According to the *Principles and Standards for School Mathematics* (NCTM, 2000, p. 19), "to improve mathematics instruction, teachers must be able to analyze what they and their students are doing and consider how those actions are affecting students' learning."

Whenever the framework has been used for individual or partner reflections, teachers and teacher educators have cited several advantages to its use.

First, the framework helps to draw teachers' attention to what students are actually doing and thinking about during classroom lessons. Sometimes teachers have a tendency to focus too much on themselves. (For example, "Did I explain that concept adequately?" "Did I provide clear enough directions?") While self-scrutiny is important, teachers can also learn about their effectiveness by scrutinizing what their students are doing.

Second, the framework provides explicit standards against which to judge practice. Reflection performed in the absence of some criteria of what constitutes exemplary practice may not lead to improved instruction (Richardson, 1990). In this regard, one teacher educator who has used this framework in ongoing professional development work with teachers remarked that it has helped to provide a "critical edge" to her postobservation discussions with teachers.

Finally, as indicated earlier in this chapter, the framework provides a way of connecting the specifics of an individual teacher's practice to a larger set of ideas about teaching and learning. Shulman (1992) has noted the power of a knowledge base that integrates the specifics of classroom practice with larger theories about instruction and learning. Encouraging teachers to raise their interpretations of classroom actions to this more general level can allow them to see specific classroom events as "cases of" something larger, more coherent, more meaningful, and, perhaps, more memorable.

NOTES

1. Obviously, mathematical tasks and the cognitive demands they place on students comprise but one piece of a much larger pedagogical/mathematical puzzle. We claim only to provide a framework for analyzing practice, not *the* framework. After learning to use the Mathematical Tasks Framework as a guide for reflection, teachers will, it is hoped, be able to move on to the use of additional frameworks (e.g., discourse) as needed.

PART II
THE CASES

CHAPTER 4

Introduction to the Cases

In Part I, we presented the conceptual ideas and research findings that underlie our approach to case design and interpretation, and our method of guided reflection. In Part II, we turn our attention to the "how to" of case analysis and discussion. In this introductory chapter, the cases and their supporting materials are described. We then move on to suggestions for how to orchestrate teacher learning from the cases.

THE CASES AND SUPPORTING MATERIALS

The cases span a range of mathematical topic areas, including those that have been mainstays of the mathematics curriculum in the middle grades (e.g., fractions, decimals, and percents) and others that are relative newcomers or less frequently taught curricular topics (e.g., algebra, data organization and analysis). The cases also have embedded within them a range of issues in addition to the featured concepts of task implementation and cognitive demand. For example, "The Case of Fran Gorman and Kevin Cooper" raises issues related to the ways in which teachers confer with their colleagues in team-planning situations. As such, the cases can be seen as a storehouse of discussion catalysts for a variety of mathematical, pedagogical, and reform issues. Table 4.1 summarizes the issues that are embedded in each of the six cases that appear in the book.

There are two types of cases: single and dual. Each of the single cases (Monique Butler, Nicole Clark, and Jerome Robinson) exemplifies one of the patterns of task decline discussed in Chapter 2. The dual cases (Ron Castleman, Fran Gorman and Kevin Cooper, Trina Naruda and Ursula Hernandez) provide two different enactments of the same task—one that retains the task's high cognitive demands and one in which those demands are reduced. By providing an example of a "good" enactment, these dual cases give readers a picture of what can happen when things go well, including the classroom-based factors that support students' high-level thinking and reasoning. For this reason, we have placed the dual cases first and recommend retaining this sequence, especially for readers who may not yet have an image of teaching with high-level tasks.

TABLE 4.1. The issues embedded in each of the six cases that appear in Chapters 5 through 10.

Chapter	The Case of . . .	Math Content	Other Issues
5	Ron Castleman	Fractions, decimals, percents	Role of procedures in reform mathematics; teacher self-reflection
6	Fran Gorman Kevin Cooper	Multiplication of fractions	Team planning; use of manipulatives
7	Trina Naruda Ursula Hernandez	Mean, median, mode, and range	Teacher collaboration; special education inclusion; bilingual education
8	Monique Butler	Multiplication of monomials and binomials	Impact of standardized testing on instruction; group work
9	Nicole Clark	Data organization and analysis	Students' self-esteem; English Language Learners
10	Jerome Robinson	Problem solving	Content coverage; role of problem solving

Each case is accompanied by a set of materials that will help participants prepare for a case discussion. These ancillary materials are described below.

The Tasks

At the beginning of each case chapter, we present a version of the mathematical task featured in the case.[1] These tasks have been selected because, in our judgment, they have potential to elicit high-level thinking and reasoning on the part of middle-school students. In some cases, the tasks may also be cognitively challenging to teachers.

Discussion Questions

Each case ends with a set of questions that can be used for group discussion and/or individual reflection. The questions focus readers' attention on important aspects of the case: the teacher's goals, student learning, and the conditions that supported or inhibited student learning.

Teaching Notes

The teaching notes begin with general comments regarding what can be learned from reading and discussing the case. The notes then move into a detailed analysis of the cognitive levels of the task at the setup and implementation phases, followed by a discussion of the classroom-based factors that are associated with the way in which the task played out. This analysis explicates what the case is a "case of," that is, the ideas the case authors want teachers to learn from the case.

The teaching notes also include an additional layer of interpretation that focuses on other issues raised by the case. In the case of Ron Castleman (Chapter 5), for example, the relationship between procedural and conceptual knowledge is raised as an important topic for consideration. The notes identify the issue and suggest points the facilitator may wish to raise in the discussion. Finally, in some cases, the teaching notes also include various solutions and/or solution strategies to the task featured in the case.

HOW TO ORCHESTRATE
TEACHER LEARNING FROM THE CASES

In order to gain the most from the set of cases,[2] we recommend using them in conjunction with Chapters 1 and 2, which outline the Mathematical Tasks Framework and ways of identifying the cognitive demands of tasks. Through periodic reference to the Mathematical Tasks Framework, teachers will learn how to travel back and forth between the details of practice and the broader generalizations that provide wider applicability and deeper insight. Moreover, when the same group of teachers uses this framework over time, they develop a common language with which to talk about their instruction.

Some teacher educators have, however, used the cases in other ways. For example, instructors of methods courses for pre-service teachers sometimes pick and choose particular cases to be used as "cases of" other topics of interest for their particular course, such as classroom discourse or the use of manipulative materials to teach rational number operations. Similarly, professional developers have used some or all of the cases to exemplify certain aspects of the *Professional Standards for Teaching Mathematics* (NCTM, 1991). For example, most, if not all, of the cases can be used to highlight the teacher's and the students' roles in classroom discourse. Several cases also point to considerations regarding tools for enhancing discourse, including the use of manipulative materials as models and the ways in which pictures, diagrams, tables, and graphs can be used—both productively and nonproductively—in the course of teaching mathematical concepts.

Whether or not the cases are used in conjunction with the Mathematical Tasks Framework, it is important for facilitators to keep in mind their learning objectives and how each case discussion can help them to realize those objectives. Although free-flowing discussions can sometimes lead to important revelations, starting with well-defined objectives will result in a more coherent and productive learning experience for participants. We now turn to suggestions for preparing for, leading, and following up on case discussions.

Preparing for the Discussion

Effective case discussions require preparation on the part of both the facilitator and the participants. We suggest that participants work through the task featured in the case before reading the case, and that they have the opportunity to discuss as a group various ways of solving the task. This is especially crucial for those tasks whose complexity becomes increasingly apparent as one is exposed to their multiple solution paths and/or solutions or for participants who may have limited experience themselves in engaging in challenging mathematical tasks. By working through the tasks as learners, teachers will be able to secure each task's underlying principles and ideas firmly in their own knowledge base, before moving on to the added complexity of analyzing the pedagogical factors that influence students' opportunities to learn the core mathematics embodied in the tasks.

We also suggest that teachers spend time individually with the case before jumping into a group discussion. Because reading the case and reflecting on it can take some time, it is a good idea, if possible, to have the teachers read the case before meeting as a group, rather than taking group time to do this. Facilitators may want to guide teachers' individual reflections on a case by asking them to respond to the following three questions:

- What are the main mathematical ideas in the case?
- What evidence is there that the students learned these ideas?
- What did the teacher do to facilitate or inhibit students' learning of these ideas?

We have found that these questions help orient teachers to key issues and set the stage for productive discussion.

Facilitators should also prepare by reading the case and reviewing the teaching notes. From the facilitator's point of view, it is critical to think about the case as it relates to one's learning objectives. For example, if the facilitator wants teachers to develop an understanding of how Fran proceduralized the multiplication of fractions task (see Chapter 6), she needs to flag those portions of the case that provide evidence of when and how Fran did this.

Facilitating the Case Discussion

We usually begin the case discussion with small groups of three to five individuals and then move on to a discussion involving the entire group. One or more of the discussion questions provided at the end of the case can serve as a focus for these discussions. For the dual cases, these discussions might alternatively focus on the similarities and differences between the two parts of the case (e.g., How are Fran and Kevin the same and how are they different?); this serves to highlight the fact that the same task (and some of the same student responses to the task) can be handled differently, with different outcomes.

During the large-group discussion of the case, it is important for the facilitator to strike a balance between allowing the discussion to drift aimlessly and overcontrolling the direction of the discussion. Asking questions that encourage focused discussion and listening closely to participants so as to recognize new, yet related, ideas are both key to successful facilitation.

Facilitators also want to consider ahead of time how they plan to end the discussion. Sometimes it may be advantageous to send participants away without closure so that they can actively think about issues in a self-directed way before the next session. Other times it is better to provide a brief summary of the discussion and to place it in a larger (or more general) context, be it an interpretation related to the Mathematical Tasks Framework or one related to another "big idea" in mathematics teaching and learning. As participants connect the particulars of each case to a framework or a set of more general ideas, the knowledge derived from experience with cases is made more coherent.

After the Case Discussion

On occasion, we have asked teachers to return to their initial set of re-flections (the set of questions that they completed independently before meeting as a group) and to answer them again. This provides a measure of how their thinking has changed as a result of the case discussion. Other possible follow-up activities might include having participants consider what the teacher (portrayed in the case) might do the following day in class in order to engage students at a high level, what the teacher could have done during the class that might have led to a different learning outcome, or how the participants might discuss the lesson with the teacher if they were colleagues who had observed the class.

Connecting to Teachers' Practice

Following the analysis of each case, teachers can be invited to engage in one or more activities in which the mathematical and pedagogical ideas discussed in the case are connected to their own teaching practice. This process, which is critical to transforming participants' own practice will be discussed in more detail in Chapter 11. In addition, numerous suggestions regarding the use of cases to transform mathematics teaching and learning can be found in a three-volume set published by Smith, Silver, and Stein in 2005 (Smith, Silver, & Stein with Boston, Henningsen, & Hillen, 2005; Smith, Silver, & Stein with Henningsen, Boston, & Hughes, 2005; Smith, Silver, & Stein with Boston & Henningsen, 2005).

NOTES

1. The task presented is not always exactly identical to the one that is set up by the teacher in the case. We have adapted some tasks so that they make more sense for adult learners in seminar-type situations. The point is to provide a context for exploring the mathematical ideas at the heart of the case rather than to replicate the teacher's classroom setup.

2. This section of Chapter 4 contains information that is particularly important for facilitators of case discussions. Teachers may want to skip this section and move on to the first case, which appears in Chapter 5.

CHAPTER 5

Linking Fractions, Decimals, and Percents Using an Area Model

FIGURE 5.1. Opening activity to be completed prior to reading the case of Ron Castleman.

Shade 6 of the small squares in the rectangle shown below.

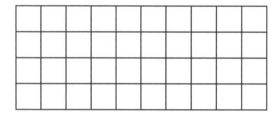

Using the diagram, explain how to determine each of the following:
- (a) the percent of area that is shaded
- (b) the decimal part of area that is shaded
- (c) the fractional part of area that is shaded

THE CASE OF RON CASTLEMAN

Ron Castleman is an experienced teacher who demands much from his students. Before entering teaching, he was an engineer for a major corporation. Although he was considered successful at his work, he found himself unfulfilled in important ways and so, at mid-career, he returned to school to obtain a master's degree in teaching. Majoring in secondary mathematics was a natural choice, given his background and love of the discipline. Interestingly, his natural ability at mathematics turned into a stumbling block rather than an asset once he began teaching middle school. Ron prided himself on not being the kind of teacher who present- ed meaningless algorithms. However, he found that his ways of thinking about concepts and procedures made very little contact with seventh grad- ers' ways of thinking about them. He often became frustrated when his students didn't "get it" and blamed the students for not paying attention or not trying hard enough.

It took Ron a long time to figure out why he was having such a difficult time connecting with his students. After several years of teaching, however, he learned not only to talk to his students but also to listen to them. This enabled him to begin to comprehend how they were understanding (or mis- understanding) mathematics. Over the years, one of the strategies that he found most useful for encouraging students to talk about mathematics was the use of diagrams. Ron believed that diagrams, although not a panacea by any means, provided a tool for reasoning. With them, he had seen math- ematics come alive for his students.

For the past several years, Ron has been teaching from a curriculum that makes extensive use of visual diagrams. He thinks that he and his stu- dents are beginning to communicate with each other in meaningful ways about important mathematical concepts, but he sometimes worries that procedures—those wonderfully quick and efficient ways of getting from point A to point B—may be getting lost in the process. His main struggle during the past year has been finding a balance between encouraging the development of conceptual understanding and the facile use of efficient procedures.

Ron Castleman Talks About His Classes

My seventh-grade students and I had been working with fractions and decimals for several weeks. We began by learning the traditional conversion algorithms (e.g., $\frac{3}{5}$ = 3 divided by 5 = .6), but then moved on to investiga- tions of the meaning of fraction and decimal concepts. We did this by using manipulatives and visual diagrams to focus on portions of a unit whole and place value. For example, we used decimal squares divided into tenths and hundredths (see Figure 5.2) to illustrate how the areas covered by $\frac{3}{5}$, $\frac{6}{10}$, .6, $\frac{60}{100}$, and .60 are all the same.

Most recently, we began working with percents. The lion's share of the time was spent emphasizing the meaning of percent by using various manipu- latives and visual diagrams.

FIGURE 5.2. Decimal squares that illustrate that the areas covered by ⅗, ⁶⁄₁₀, .6, ⁶⁰⁄₁₀₀, and .60 are equivalent.

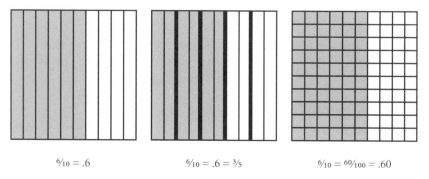

$⁶⁄₁₀ = .6$ $⁶⁄₁₀ = .6 = ⅗$ $⁶⁄₁₀ = ⁶⁰⁄₁₀₀ = .60$

Both of my seventh-grade classes were nearing the end of the unit and I was anxious that they begin to pull together all of their work on rational numbers. On this particular day, I decided to have the students work with all three representations—fractions, decimals, and percents—at the same time. My goal was for the students to figure out the percent, decimal, and fraction representations of shaded portions of a series of rectangles. In particular, I wanted the students to use the visual diagrams to determine their numerical answers rather than relying on the traditional algorithms that we had learned at the beginning of the unit. I hoped this would help them develop conceptual understandings of each of these forms of representing fractional quantities and the relationships among them.

I planned on doing the same lesson with both my second-period and my sixth-period classes. This would give me my lunch period to reflect on the earlier class and make adjustments based on what worked and what didn't work. The two classes are amazingly similar in their makeup and in how they react to lessons, so I often find that this strategy works well. (Sometimes I try out the lesson on the sixth-period class first so that the second-period students are not always the guinea pigs!)

Second-Period Mathematics Class

Setup. At the beginning of the lesson, I passed out a set of three problems and asked the students to focus on the first one (shown in Figure 5.1 at the beginning of this chapter).

I expected the students to be challenged by this problem because it would be the first time that they would be working on a grid that was not 10 × 10.

This would add a layer of complexity because subregions constituting tenths or hundredths, for example, would not be automatically evident, but rather would have to be reasoned out based on students' understandings of fractional relationships.

As we discussed the problem, I indicated that I wanted them to actually use the diagram to figure out the answers to each part and that there was more than one way to do so. In my verbal instructions to the students, I clearly stated that I wanted them to be prepared to give explanations and/or to illustrate diagrammatically why their responses made sense. I told the students to work on the first problem for about 10 minutes with their partners. Then we would go over it as a class, with students demonstrating how they went about using the diagram to solve the problem.

Implementation. As students started to work in their pairs, I circulated around the room observing their approach to the problem. All students easily shaded the 6 squares. My first observation of student difficulty was their lack of success in figuring what percent the 6 squares were of the total diagram. Some had gleefully written 6%, failing to notice that the total number of squares was not 100, but 40. Most, however, did notice that the diagram was not the usual 10 × 10 grid, and that 6% would not be the correct answer. We had not learned an algorithm for determining the answer to "6 is x% of 40" and students appeared stumped as to how to proceed. I let them struggle for a short time, but became increasingly uncomfortable with their lack of progress. Several students, feeling frustrated by their inability to quickly determine the answer, began to press me for an algorithm to use to figure the correct percent. I hesitated. I did not want to provide the students with a method for finding the percent (e.g., $6/40 = x/100$); I wanted them to use the diagram, but I wasn't sure how to get them to do so. Many students appeared to have run into a brick wall and were becoming increasingly uneasy with the ambiguity.

After a quick assessment of the problem, I noticed that starting with part C (What fractional part of the area is shaded?) would perhaps be easier. As I visited pairs, I suggested that they begin by figuring the fraction first. My instincts were correct; most students successfully used the rectangle to figure that the 6 shaded squares would be represented by the fraction $6/40$, which could be reduced to $3/20$. What happened next, however, was surely not in my game plan, but I found myself incapable of stopping it. Students excitedly noticed that they could now do part B (What decimal part of the area is shaded?) by simply dividing 3 by 20 and coming up with the decimal answer of .15. And once they knew that the decimal representation was .15, they quickly turned to the "tried-and-true" method of moving the decimal point two places to the right to convert from decimals to percents. At this point, they believed that they had completed the problem and waited for me to visit their group to verify that their calculations were correct. I, however, was not convinced that they understood the reasoning behind the conversions they had performed, nor the relationship between the fraction/decimal/percent and the shaded area of the rectangle. They didn't seem to be using the diagram, not even to check the reasonableness of their answers.

It was now 15 minutes into the period and we needed to move along. After stopping by each table and marking their answers right or wrong, I said that it was time to share answers with the entire class and called on a pair of students, Jena and Ray, to display their methods and answers. I had noticed that these two students had made a calculation error and so I planned to make an appeal to return to the diagram to check the reasonableness of their answers. Jena and Ray had correctly figured ³⁄₂₀ as the answer to the part C, but had divided inaccurately and come up with an answer to part B of .015. Their answer to Part A was 1.5%. After they had displayed their calculations and answers, I said, "Look at the diagram. Does it look like only 1.5% of the rectangle is shaded?" Before they could answer, however, several students at their seats began pointing to the decimal placement error in the students' division problem. I felt that I couldn't ignore this either, so I did a quick review of the procedure for long division with decimals. Once the correct answer of .15 had been calculated, Jena and Ray quickly changed their percent answer to 15% and went back to their seats. I pointed out to the class that 15% surely seemed like a more reasonable estimate of the percentage of the shaded area than did the first answer of 1.5%.

Although we had already spent 20 minutes on this one problem and had displayed the correct answers to all three parts, I was reluctant to leave it because I still had the uneasy feeling that we had spent too much time worrying about correct answers and procedures and not enough time actually using the diagram to reason with. I decided to take a risk and call to the overhead Sharice and Krystal, the only two students in the class who had not resorted to algorithms to solve the problem. Although they had not come up with the right answer, they had at least tried to reason using the diagram. Sharice and Krystal started by shading 4 squares in the first column and 2 squares in the second column and then stating that 6% of the squares was shaded. (I knew their answer was incorrect, but was not sure what to do to get them to reconsider it. It didn't matter; while I was thinking of what to say, they moved on, eager to show their work for the next part of the problem.) For part B, they said that they did not have a specific answer, but that they had an idea. Krystal pointed to the rectangle and said, "There are 10 columns all together, which means that each column is worth ¹⁄₁₀. If one column was shaded, the answer would be .1 and if both columns were shaded the answer would be .2. So, the answer falls halfway in between." When I asked them how they could calculate or write ½ of $\frac{1}{10}$ as a decimal, they shrugged their shoulders. At this point, I turned to the class asking if anyone at their seats knew how to write $\frac{1}{2}$ of $\frac{1}{10}$ as a decimal. A couple of students volunteered incorrect answers. Feeling pressed for time, I reminded the class of previous work that we had done in which the word *of* was translated into a multiplication sign. As I wrote on the blackboard, I explained, "$\frac{1}{2} \times \frac{1}{10}$ equals $\frac{1}{20}$, which could be written by the equivalent fraction of $\frac{5}{100}$ or the decimal of .05." I went on to explain that the decimal representation for the 6 shaded squares would be .15 ($\frac{1}{10} + \frac{5}{100}$).

Checking my watch, I saw that we were now nearly 30 minutes into our 45-minute class period. I decided that we had spent enough time on this problem and that the students should begin work on the remaining two problems.

STOP

Discuss second-period class.

Reflection on Second Period

Over lunch, I thought about what had transpired during the second hour. I also had the chance to review students' papers on the three problems. Most had indeed completed all three problems. However, the overwhelming majority of students had jumped directly to the use of algorithms, with little if any evidence of actually having paid attention to the diagrams. Moreover, the procedures they had used were sometimes the wrong ones; often, they had been inaccurately executed. To my surprise, I found myself being less upset by sloppy execution than by the fact that many students had obviously failed to check the reasonableness of their answers.

In thinking over the lesson, I decided that my objectives were reasonable and that I had chosen and set up good tasks. And the students were certainly capable of doing what I had asked, if they would only slow down and take the time to really think about what they were doing. I decided to try again with my sixth-period class, but this time not to allow the clock to govern our pace. Also, I vowed not to allow the students' anxiousness about how to proceed get to me. If I could only find a way to support them without telling them how to do it....

Sixth-Period Mathematics Class

Setup. I set up the task in the exactly the same manner as I had with my second-period class, again stressing that they needed to use the diagram to figure out their answers. Once again, I promised to judge them by the quality of their explanations and visual reasoning processes in addition to whether they got the right answers.

Implementation. As students started to work in their pairs, I walked around the room observing their approach to the problem. As with the second-period class, my first observation of student difficulty was their lack of success in figuring what percent the 6 squares were of the total diagram. Once again, a few students had written 6%, failing to notice that the total number of squares was 40, not 100. Most, however, did notice that the diagram was not the usual 10 × 10 grid, and that 6% would not be the correct answer. This class had also not learned an algorithm for determining the answer to "6 is what % of 40" and, once again, the students appeared to be stumped regarding how to proceed. I held my breath and let them struggle.

It didn't take long for several students to begin to complain that it was too difficult because they had not been taught the rule for figuring the correct percentage when the number of squares was not 100. In response, I tried to redirect their attention to the diagram. I suggested that they might want to look carefully at the rectangle, noticing both the total number of squares and the ways in which the squares were organized into columns and rows. "How might you use this information to help you figure the percentage?" I would ask. This sustained them for awhile. They stopped bugging me for a formula and I could hear the quiet buzz of conversation as students began discussing possibilities with their partners, pointing to their diagrams as they spoke.

Almost 10 minutes had passed and I started to get nervous. Most students still had not correctly figured the percent of shaded squares. I noticed that students were engaged with the task, however, and several appeared to be holding quite animated discussions with their partners. Remembering my pledge to myself, I decided to let them go a few minutes longer.

As I visited pairs, I looked carefully at the various ways the students were attacking the problem. I observed that those students who were making the most progress had noticed that each column represented $\frac{1}{10}$ of the rectangle and that 6 squares could be seen as "filling up" 1½ columns. If a column was $\frac{1}{10}$ or 10%, then a "column and a half," they reasoned, would be 15%.

The students who were having the most difficulty were working with rectangles in which the shaded squares were not in columns, but rather were shaded horizontally in rows, in 2 × 3 rectangles, or in a scattered formation. This appeared to lead to difficulties in seeing the rectangle as divided into tenths. I tried to assist these students in finding other ways to figure the percentage by asking questions that would allow them to build on the particular configuration that they had shaded (see Figure 5.3).

FIGURE 5.3. Teacher questions that built on different shadings of six blocks (Stein & Smith, 1998).

Each row is what percent?

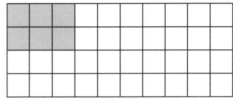

How many similar groups could you fit into the rectangle?

Each square is what percent of the total rectangle?

(Reprinted with permission from Mathematics Teaching in the Middle School, copyright 1998 by the National Council of Teachers of Mathematics. All rights reserved.)

In each instance, I would say, "Think about that. How might it help you figure out the percent?" Then I would leave them on their own to work on it a bit longer.

We were now about 20 minutes into the period and I noticed that most students had at least attempted all three parts of the problem. I decided that it was time to share strategies and rationales with the entire class. I called Jaleesa and Rachel to the overhead because they had approached Part A with a strategy that few others had used, one that I thought showed excellent thinking and reasoning. I asked them to explain their reasoning for Part A. Jaleesa wrote "6 × 2.5% = 15%" on the overhead transparency and then both girls began to return to their seats. I quickly intervened, asking them to return to the overhead projector and to provide a rationale for their method and their answer. Rachel explained that since there were 40 squares in the diagram and the whole diagram needed to represent 100%, each small square would have to equal 2½%. Since there were 6 shaded squares, they multiplied 2.5 times 6 to find out what percentage was shaded. I asked if other students had questions to ask of the girls about their solution method.

After Jaleesa and Rachel further clarified their method in response to questions from students at their seats, I thought that most of the students understood their approach. I took the opportunity created by this feeling of "we are all on the same page" to connect this pairs' reasoning strategies to an important mathematical idea. I noted that the girls began their explanation by stating that the rectangle equaled 100%. Michael asked, "How could something that wasn't subdivided into 100 equal 100%?" Derrick added, "Are you saying that 100% = 1? I thought that 100% = 100!" As students offered their views on these questions, we zeroed in on the important idea that 100% = 1 = 1.00. With respect to the current problem, we noted that 100% could be used to designate the whole rectangle, regardless of the number of parts into which the whole was subdivided.

Although we were now 30 minutes into the period, as a class, we had gone over only one strategy for one part of the problem. I decided to stick with the problem a bit longer and called a second pair of students to come to the overhead to display another way of figuring the percentage of shaded squares. Omar and Marcus had shaded 6 squares in the upper-left-hand corner of the rectangle and proceeded to figure the percent as shown in Figure 5.4. They explained their strategy and why it made sense while students at their seats listened and then asked a few questions.

FIGURE 5.4. The diagram displayed by Omar and Marcus.

$$90\% \div 6 = 15\%$$

Moving on to part B, I decided to call to the overhead Tim and Daniel. They had been working quite diligently, but had not yet reached an answer. Daniel began by pointing to the rectangle and saying, "There are 10 columns all together, which means that each column is worth ¹⁄₁₀. If one column was shaded the answer would be .1, and if two columns were shaded the answer would be .2. So, the answer falls halfway in between." When I asked them how they could figure out what ½ of ¹⁄₁₀ was, they were not sure. At this point, I provided them with 2 decimal squares (see Figure 5.2) and asked them if the squares could help them to figure out what ½ of ¹⁄₁₀ would be. Using the hundredths square, Tim reasoned that ¹⁄₁₀ was 1 column of 10 small squares (10 hundredths). One-half of ¹⁄₁₀, he noted, would be ½ of a column, or 5 small squares (5 hundredths). Returning to the original 40-square diagram, Daniel added that one column was ¹⁄₁₀ or 10 hundredths (even though it had 4 squares!) and that ½ of a column would still be half of that (that is, ½ of 10 hundredths) or 5 hundredths (even though it had 2 squares!). The boys concluded that their answer needed to be 10 hundredths (.10) plus 5 hundredths (.05) for a total of 15 hundredths (.15).

We had run out of time! Although more time was spent on this first problem than I had intended, I thought it had been necessary to set the students on the right track for the remaining problems. I told the students to complete the remaining two problems for homework and to write explanations about how they used the rectangle to figure out their answers.

STOP

Discuss Ron's reflections and the sixth-period class.

DISCUSSION QUESTIONS

Following the Second-Period Class

1. What are some mathematical issues Ron was concerned with during the lesson? Why are these important issues? What nonmathematical issues did Ron seem to be concerned about?
2. How would you describe the thinking Ron was asking students to engage in when he set up the task? Did Ron's goals change after the students began working on the task? Were Ron's goals accomplished?

Following the Sixth-Period Class

3. How would you describe the thinking Ron was asking students to engage in when he set up the task for his sixth-period class?

a. Did Ron seem to have the same initial goals for both classes?

b. Did the students in the sixth-period class engage with the task in the same way as those in the second-period class? What was learned in each class?

4. What classroom-based factors might have contributed to the different kinds of student engagement in the two classes?

a. What did Ron do differently in the two classes that might have supported (or not supported) students' engaging in the task as he intended? What, if anything, did he do that was the same?

b. What did the students do in each class that might have influenced their own learning and engagement with the task?

TEACHING NOTES

Ron Castleman is a teacher who knows his subject area well and who sincerely wants his students to know and understand mathematics in a deep way. He is also a teacher who learns from his experiences. He has changed his teaching practices to incorporate the use of visual diagrams and to include more student discussion. He also has established a "reflection routine" in which he uses his experiences in his second-period seventh-grade class to inform his approach in his sixth-period seventh-grade class.

This year, Ron has been struggling with how to balance the teaching of efficient procedures and the encouragement of students' development of conceptual understanding—a dilemma not unfamiliar to many teachers of mathematics. In this case, Ron encounters another, related dilemma. With the visually oriented curriculum, he has been able to introduce his students to increasingly complex and interesting problems. He is discovering, however, that the students sometimes prefer simpler, more straightforward tasks and can react anxiously to the uncertainty associated with not knowing immediately how to tackle a more complex, less structured task. Ron clearly wants his students to know *both* procedures and concepts, but he is having some difficulty getting them to discard the procedures and focus on meaning in the pair of lessons that are featured in this dual case. He is more successful in the second class (sixth period) than the first (second period). In order to understand this case, participants will have to recognize this and be able to identify the factors responsible for his greater success with the sixth-period class.

Cognitive Levels

The same task is used in both classes and is set up in essentially the same manner. In both classes, we consider the task—as set up—to be at the *doing-*

mathematics level. If the task is solved in the manner requested (i.e., by using the diagram and not using the traditional conversion procedures), it demands complex thinking and reasoning and a considerable amount of cognitive effort. The complexity of the task is largely derived from the fact that the grid is not a 10×10 square, and hence, students must construct novel ways of configuring the squares in order to determine the correct percentages and decimals (as opposed to relying on a grid that is conveniently laid out in tenths). When the visual diagram is used to solve the problem in this way, individuals are challenged to apply and use their understandings of fraction, decimal, and percent concepts in novel ways. When announcing the task to his students, Ron maintained these high levels of demand. He stressed that students should use the diagram to reason out their answers, noting that there was more than one way to do so. He also warned students that they should be prepared to give explanations and/or to illustrate diagrammatically why their responses made sense.

The ways in which students actually went about working on the task (the task-implementation phase) differed, however, in the two classes. We consider the implementation of the task during the second-period class to be at the level of *procedures without connections*. The vast majority of students performed algorithmic procedures that departed completely from the diagram. After starting with part C (finding the fraction), students found that they were able to use traditional conversion procedures that had previously been taught in order to find the answers to the other two parts (the decimal and percent representations). Moreover, the students did not even return to the diagram to check the reasonableness of their answers (e.g., two students got 1.5% for their answer and failed to recognize its absurdity).

During the sixth-period class, on the other hand, students did not start by finding the fraction, but rather did the problems in the suggested order; hence, they had to struggle with finding what percent of 40 the 6 shaded squares would be. Students were forced to use the diagram to reason out the answer, because they knew of no rules to find the answer. They used a variety of strategies to reason their way through the task, most of which required that they apply and use their understandings of percent, decimal, and fractions. We consider the implementation of the task during the sixth period to be at the level of *doing mathematics*.

Factors

Superficially, the implementation portions of the two lessons were conducted in similar ways: The students worked in pairs with careful teacher monitoring, the teacher made decisions based on what he noticed about student work, and the teacher called students to the front of the room to show their work. At a deeper level, however, Ron's actions in the two classes differed. Despite being faced with similar pressures as the two lessons unfolded, Ron handled the difficulties in very different ways in the two classes. These differences constitute the factors that enabled one lesson to stay at a high level while the other lesson declined into a procedural implementation. *These are the ideas toward which the case discussion should be steered.*

Maintaining problem complexity; assisting through scaffolding. During the second-period class, Ron inadvertently simplified the problem by suggesting that students start with finding the fraction; he did not repeat this mistake in the later class, however. When the sixth-period students pressed him for help, he instead urged them to look more closely at the visual organization of the diagram and to think about how that could be mapped onto mathematical ideas that could help them figure out the percentage, thus keeping the search for meaning and the connection to concepts foregrounded. He thus supported their thinking in a way that maintained the integrity of the task, rather than changing the task into a simpler procedure. At other points during the second-period class, Ron was also led into procedural spaces (e.g., he found himself demonstrating the long-division and multiplication-of-fractions algorithms). During the sixth-period class when Ron was faced with the same request for how to determine ½ of ¹⁄₁₀, Ron did not allow himself to be drawn into a procedural explanation, but rather supplied students with the decimal-squares representations, which allowed them, in turn, to reason the answer out on their own.

Another way in which Ron supported students' thinking while maintaining task complexity was the manner in which he built on whatever configuration of squares the students had shaded. Depending on which particular set of squares was shaded, Ron asked a different set of questions that could subtly steer the students toward the recognition of patterns that would be helpful in reasoning through the task.

Sustained press for justification, explanations, and meaning. During the morning class, Ron appeared to be more concerned with relieving students' anxieties than with having them struggle to construct meaning. There were subtle cues given to students that arriving at the correct answer was paramount (e.g., he stopped by each desk, marking their answers right or wrong) and that explanations were not really expected (students who were asked to justify their answer of .015 never had a chance to speak). In the afternoon class, however, Ron held students accountable for explanations and justifications throughout the implementation phase. For example, he did not allow the students who wrote "$6 \times 2.5 = 15\%$" to sit down until they had explained how they arrived at their answer and entertained questions from the class. Similarly, he demanded that the second pair of students reason their way through figuring ½ of ¹⁄₁₀ in a meaningful way.

Building on student knowledge and thinking. In both classes, Ron tried to build on students' prior knowledge, but he drew on different kinds of knowledge in the two classes. In the second-period class, Ron resorted to what they had learned about procedures, for example, how to perform long division or multiply fractions. In the sixth-period class, on the other hand, Ron tried to get students to use more conceptual forms of knowledge. For example, when the final pair of students had difficulty determining ½ of ¹⁄₁₀, he supplied them with the decimal-squares representations in an attempt to make accessible the hundredths place value and to illustrate (visually) the relationship between hundredths and tenths. Such translations between hundredths and tenths using the decimal-squares representations had previously been done in class and it was this knowledge that Ron chose to build on.

Teacher makes conceptual connections. Most of the connections that Ron made in the morning class were to procedures. In the afternoon class, the most directive segment was Ron's guiding the students toward the recognition that $100\% = 1 = 1.0$. Being able to identify the unit whole for percentages, fractions, and decimals is an important foundational concept for this kind of work and Ron took advantage of a "teachable moment" to point this out.

Modeling high-level thinking. In the second-period class, there was no opportunity for the students to see and hear what a "high-level solution process" to the problem would look like. In the sixth-period class, on the other hand, Ron was careful to select some students to present well-thought-out solutions to the entire class. Two of the whole-class presentations represented two viable methods of figuring the percentage; Ron made sure that the students explained their thinking processes as well as simply illustrating their answers. The final whole-class presentation was not completely worked out, but this provided an excellent opportunity for students to witness others "thinking out loud" about how to figure what ½ of ¹⁄₁₀ was.

Provision of enough time. Ron allowed himself to be pushed by the clock in the second-period class. Although students completed more problems, it is unclear that they understood as much as did the students in the sixth-period class. During the sixth-period class, Ron was aware of the passage of time but he did not allow it to close off productive student engagement. Students had enough time to work their way through the task in a meaningful way and to view how others had done so.

Additional Layers of Interpretation

An additional issue that this dual case raises for discussion is the manner in which students should be provided with opportunities to learn both deep-seated mathematical ideas and concepts *and* algorithmic procedures. This was a goal of Ron Castleman's, a goal with which he still appeared to be struggling. Indeed, the integration of procedural and conceptual knowledge or low-level and high-level skills is a concern and dilemma for many teachers of mathematics.

Ron taught the procedural algorithms first and then moved on to more conceptually based work. Participants may suggest that perhaps he should try the reverse order, beginning instead with the visually based work (indeed, this is the suggestion of the NCTM). By doing so, he will first be laying a conceptual foundation, without the interference of algorithms. After the students appear to have a good grasp of the meanings of percents, decimals, and fractions, they could be provided with the conventional conversion algorithms, with special attention to places where connections to underlying concepts could be made.

Another issue that could be discussed related to this case is the usefulness of teacher reflection for the improvement of instructional practice. Ron provides a good example of a teacher who reflects both on his own actions and on what students appear to be learning.

POSSIBLE SOLUTION STRATEGIES

Our discussion of possible solution strategies is presented in three sections based on three broad approaches to solving this problem. First, we discuss algorithmic solutions; we then move onto the discussion of solution strategies that are based on reasoning from the visual diagram. Finally, we end with a solution strategy that is based on extending the diagram.

Algorithms/Procedures

Algorithmic solutions are those based on learned procedures; students often implement these without understanding why or what they are doing.

Percent. Use a proportion to determine the percent.

$^6/_{40} = {}^N/_{100}$ *Since percent is based on 100.*
$40 \times N = 6 \times 100$ *Product of the means = the product of the extremes.*
$40 \times N = 600$
$N = {}^{600}/_{40}$
$N = 15$ *The 6 shaded blocks represent 15%.*

Decimal. Consider that 6 parts out of 40 are shaded and divide the numerator by the denominator following the appropriate procedures for decimal division. The 6 shaded blocks represent .15.

Fraction. The fraction is the number of parts shaded compared with the total number of parts in the whole. The 6 shaded blocks represent $^6/_{40}$ or $^3/_{20}$.

Reasoning from the Visual Diagram

Students may have shaded in the 6 squares in a variety of ways. Four different configurations of shading that we've often seen are illustrated in Figure 5.5. The way in which students might reason about each of these configurations to determine their percent and decimal answers is described below. We assume their understanding of fractions as part/whole relationships would make determining the fraction answer of $^6/_{40}$ or $^3/_{20}$ trivial; therefore, part C is not explained.

First configuration. Students may have begun by shading in 4 squares in the first column and 2 squares in the second column.
1. Percent. The entire rectangle represents 100%. Since there are 10 columns in the rectangle, the one column of 4 shaded squares will be $^1/_{10}$ of the rectangle, or 10%. The second column has only 2 squares shaded, or $^1/_2$ of the column. If the whole column is 10%, then half the column is 5%. Thus, the 6 shaded blocks that make up 1½ columns equal 10% plus 5% or 15%.
2. Decimal. The entire rectangle represents one whole. Since there are 10 columns in the rectangle, the one column of 4 shaded squares will be .1 of the rectangle or .10. The second column has only 2 squares shaded or half the column. Half of .1 or half of .10 is .05. (or the student might reason: ½ of $^1/_{10}$ is $^1/_{20}$ or $^5/_{100}$). Thus, the 6 shaded blocks that make up 1½ columns equal .1 plus .05, which equals .15.

FIGURE 5.5. Four configurations of shading associated with different solution strategies.

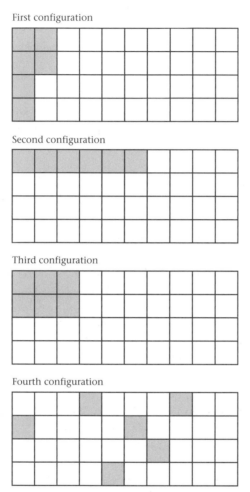

First configuration

Second configuration

Third configuration

Fourth configuration

Second configuration. Students may have begun by shading in 6 squares horizontally across the first row.

1. Percent. The entire rectangle represents 100%. Since there are 4 rows in the rectangle, one row is ¼ of the rectangle, or 25%. Since there are 10 blocks in a row, one block must represent 2.5%; 2 blocks would represent 5%; 4 blocks would represent 10%; and 6 blocks would represent 15%.

2. Decimal. The entire rectangle represents one whole. Since there are 4 rows in the rectangle, one row is ¼ of the rectangle, or .25. Since there are 10 blocks in a row, 6 blocks represent .6 of the row or .6 × .25 of the whole; .6 × .25 = .15.

Third configuration. Students may have begun by shading in 3 squares horizontally in each of the first two rows. We call this the "postage stamp" configuration.

1. Percent. The entire rectangle represents 100%. I can partition the rectangle into six groups of 2 × 3 sections, leaving one column on the end. The column on the end is ¹⁄₁₀ or 10% because there are 10 columns in the rectangle. That means the six 2 × 3 sections take up the remaining 90% of the rectangle. Ninety percent divided by 6 is 15%. So, one section of 6 blocks would represent 15%.

2. Decimal. The entire rectangle represents one whole. I can partition the rectangle into six groups of 2 × 3 sections, leaving one column on the end. The column on the end is ¹⁄₁₀ or .1 because there are 10 columns in the rectangle. That means the six 2 × 3 sections take up the remaining .9 of the rectangle, and .9 divided by 6 is .15. So, one section of 6 blocks would represent .15.

Fourth configuration. Students may have begun with a random shading of the 6 squares throughout the diagram.

1. Percent. The entire rectangle represents 100%. Since there are 40 blocks, 80% can be distributed across the 40 blocks by giving 2% to each block. That leaves 20%. Since 20 is half of 40, the 20% can be distributed across all the blocks by giving each block another .5%. Thus, each block would represent a total of 2.5% (2% +.5%). Two blocks would represent 5%, 4 blocks would represent 10%, and 6 blocks would represent 15% (or 6 times 2.5% =15%).

2. Decimal. The entire rectangle represents one whole. Each block is ¹⁄₄₀, but I don't know what the decimal equivalent of that is. If I think about putting the blocks together into pairs, then there would be 20 pairs and each pair of blocks would be ¹⁄₂₀ or .05 because there are 20 nickels in $1.00. So, the 6 blocks are 3 pairs or 3 nickels, which would be .15.

Reasoning by Extending the Diagram

In this solution strategy, students begin by extending the diagram to 10 × 10 (see Figure 5.6).

Percent. If there were 100 squares, then the number of shaded squares would equal the percent. There are 40 squares to begin with and 6 are shaded. If another 40 squares are added, then 6 more would be shaded. To get 100 squares you need to add 20 more. Since 20 squares is half the original 40 squares, then only half as many squares would be shaded. So 3 of the 20 squares would be shaded. Altogether then, 6 + 6 + 3 =15 of the 100 squares would be shaded. Fifteen out of 100 is 15%.

Decimal. If the whole is made up of 100 squares, then each shaded square represents .01. Since there are 15 squares shaded, this is equal to .15.

FIGURE 5.6. Extending the diagram in Ron Castleman's task to a 10 × 10.

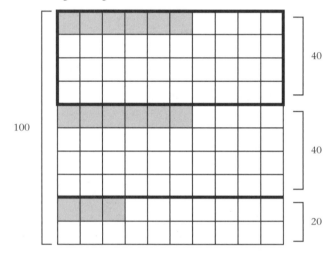

Multiplying Fractions with Pattern Blocks

THE CASE OF FRAN GORMAN AND KEVIN COOPER

Fran Gorman and Kevin Cooper, both teachers for more than 15 years, teach in a middle school that has recently been awarded a grant to improve its mathematics program so as to be more consistent with the National Council of Teachers of Mathematics's Principles and Standards for School Mathematics (2000). Having grown increasingly dissatisfied with their traditional, textbook-based approach to teaching mathematics, both Fran and Kevin enthusiastically supported their school's application to dramatically overhaul the way in which mathematics was taught. In particular, they were drawn to the Council's emphasis on teaching mathematics through the use of manipulatives. They were hopeful that a more concrete, "hands-on" approach would ground their students' learning in conceptual ideas more so than their current approaches did. When Fran and Kevin were honest with themselves, they had to admit that, currently, their students were learning little more than formulas, procedures, and definitions, usually without any idea of the mathematical ideas that underlay them.

As soon as their school was awarded the grant, Fran, Kevin, and their colleagues ordered classroom sets of pattern blocks, Cuisenaire rods, algebra tiles, fraction strips, and base-10 blocks and eagerly signed up for summer workshops that would teach them how to use them. In addition, along with their principal, they were able to work out a teaching schedule that allowed all of the seventh-grade teachers to share a common planning period each day. During these periods, teachers met together to share problems and successes and, more generally, to support each other during their initial year of change. Fran and Kevin, who each taught several sections of seventh-grade mathematics, were among the most regular participants in these meetings. With all of the classes heterogeneously grouped, Fran and Kevin found that they were able to make their way through the curriculum at roughly the same pace. They enjoyed planning units and lessons together, often meeting again afterward to reflect on how particular lessons went.

FIGURE 6.1. Opening activity to be completed prior to reading the case of Fran Gorman and Kevin Cooper.

1. Find ½ of ⅓. Use pattern blocks. Draw your answer.

Show ⅓   Show ½ of ⅓. ½ × ⅓ = ☐

2. Find ⅓ of ¼. Use pattern blocks. Draw your answer.

Show ¼   Show ⅓ of ¼. ⅓ × ¼ = ☐

3. Find ¼ of ⅓. Use pattern blocks. Draw your answer.

Show ⅓   Show ¼ of ⅓. ¼ × ⅓ = ☐

4. Find ⅔ of ¼. Use pattern blocks. Draw your answer.

Show ¼   Show ⅔ of ¼. ⅔ × ¼ = ☐

5. Find ¾ of ⅓. Use pattern blocks. Draw your answer.

Show ⅓   Show ¾ of ⅓. ¾ × ⅓ = ☐

6. Solve using pattern blocks.

    (a) ⅔ × ½ = ☐

    (b) ⅚ × ½ = ☐

(This task is adapted from *Fractions with Pattern Blocks*. It is reprinted with the permission of Creative Publications and may not be reproduced without written permission from the publisher.)

Fran Talks About Her Class

As I was at home recuperating from our family's hectic holiday schedule, I found myself thinking about how the new math project was going. Changing to a more meaning-oriented, hands-on approach to mathematics has not been easy. The newer problems demand that the students really think about what they are doing. If they don't, they can't solve the problems. Sometimes, when they get stuck, my students seem to be embarrassed because they realize that they really don't understand concepts well enough to use them—they are lost without their algorithms.

I've learned a lot, too: about new ways to think about old problems, and about how my students think. I've found that even my brightest students have some pretty astounding misconceptions! On the whole, however, I've been very pleased with the new approach and plan to stick to it as we enter our next and most challenging unit: multiplication and division of fractions.

If I were teaching the old way, this unit would be a cinch—the algorithms are easier than those for adding and subtracting fractions. But the mystery surrounding why we do what we do has always bothered me. I was determined that, this year, finally, my students would understand why they "invert and multiply!" However, I suspected that the students' weak underlying conceptions of what a fraction is, as well as their limited understandings of the importance of the unit whole, would lead to some confusion and a slow-going process. But slow-going isn't all that bad; by the time we are done with the fractions unit, my students will have learned to "stop and smell the roses!"

Luckily, I have Kevin to talk things over with. After several meetings, he and I came up with a plan. First, we would introduce the idea of multiplication as "x *of* y." We would start with whole numbers, for example, 5 cases *of* 24 bottles would equal 120 bottles; then we'd move to fractions (e.g., ½ *of* a ½ gallon of milk would equal ¼ gallon [or a quart]). This was the way in which multiplication was cast in the materials that Kevin and I decided that we liked the best (Zulie, 1988). As its title suggests, these materials utilize pattern blocks[1] to model the multiplication of fractions (see Figure 6.2 for an example).

At first, I thought that this approach would be too difficult because two hexagons were used to represent the unit whole. I was sure that this would really stump the students. But, after much discussion, Kevin and I decided that it was important for our students to grapple with the unit whole—something that most textbooks take for granted. With help, our students could handle it. Kevin and I also talked about wanting to get our students to understand that multiplication does not always increase the number that you end up with. Usually students have a hard time grasping this because, in everyday language, multiplying something always means getting more of it. Our hope was that

FIGURE 6.2. Example of using pattern blocks to model multiplication of fractions.

Find ½ of ½. Use pattern blocks. Draw your answer.

Show ½.   Show ½ of ½. ½ × ½ = ¼

the pattern blocks would help the students to be able to really see what they were doing when they took, for example, ⅓ of ½—and why the product, ⅙, *had* to be smaller than what they started out with.

My class had used pattern blocks quite a bit during the fall semester, so my students were very familiar with the shapes. In fact, many were so familiar with the pattern blocks that they often sketched the blocks rather than actually working with the blocks themselves.

Fran's Setup

This was the second day of the unit. During yesterday's lesson we had reviewed the meanings of fractions and of multiplication. Beginning with whole numbers, we discussed the "of" notion of multiplication; then we proceeded to fractions, at which time I introduced the use of pattern blocks as a way of modeling ½ of ½. After I modeled ½ of ½ using the pattern blocks, the students had time to work through two additional problems, under my guidance (⅓ of ½ and ¼ of ½).

To begin today's lesson, I asked Shawna, one of my best students, to come to the overhead projector to do the problem ⅙ of ½. She did not disappoint me. Without a single mistake, she used the pattern blocks to model the procedure and, without prompting, explained what she was doing and why she was doing it (see Figure 6.3).

For example, when she identified ⅙ of ½, she first showed and explained how six triangles would be contained in one hexagon, which was ½ of the entire unit. Then she pointed to one triangle, saying that it represented ⅙ of the ½ piece. She ended by going back to the two-hexagon unit, noting how the one triangle covered ¹⁄₁₂ of the entire unit. As she was presenting this, I smiled to myself. "Yes," I thought, "this is the way to go! The pattern blocks make it so clear why ⅙ of ½ would have to be ¹⁄₁₂."

FIGURE 6.3. Shawna's demonstration to the class.

Find ⅙ of ½. Use pattern blocks. Draw your answer.

Show ½.   Show ⅙ of ½. ⅙ × ½ = ⎡ ¹⁄₁₂ ⎤

There were no questions from the students, so I asked them to begin working on the remaining problems. The problems, which are shown in Figure 6.1, were distributed across two workbook pages; the first five supplied sketches of pattern blocks on which the students could overlay actual pattern block pieces (or on which they could simply sketch the pattern block pieces). The final two problems required that the students set up their own pattern block configurations (or sketches).

Although students had individual worksheets, they were told to work in pairs, making sure they asked their partner before me, if they ran into difficulty. "And please," I implored, "make sure to pay attention to what you are actually doing when you multiply these fractions. The pattern blocks will help you. You can either lay them on top of the worksheet or sketch them. But make sure that you use them so that you can see what is actually going on as you do these problems."

Fran's Implementation

I began walking around the room, stopping at nearly every desk to make sure that everyone was doing it correctly. The first student I came upon (Antonio) was having the exact difficulty that I had predicted. He was not seeing the unit whole as being comprised of *both* hexagons. Instead he had figured ½ of ⅓ using only one hexagon as the unit whole. He had marked off ⅓ of one hexagon and then noted that ½ of it was one triangle, which, in turn, was ⅙ of the hexagon (see Antonio's initial attempt in Figure 6.4). Although he got the right numerical answer this way, it did not cover the correct amount of area on his pattern blocks.

I leaned over his shoulder and gently explained to him that he had not followed the steps that had been modeled by Shawna at the beginning of the class and that he should start over. He looked disappointed, but dutifully removed his pattern blocks. To help him get started, I asked, "What fraction comes after

FIGURE 6.4. Antonio's work on the first problem.

Find ½ of ⅓. Use pattern blocks. Draw your answer.

Antonio's Initial Attempt:

Show ⅓.   Show ½ of ⅓. ½ × ⅓ = ⎡ ⅙ ⎤

Find ½ of ⅓. Use pattern blocks. Draw your answer.

Antonio's Second Attempt:

Show ⅓.   Show ½ of ⅓. ½ × ⅓ = ⎡ ⅙ ⎤

the word *of*?" After he correctly replied ⅓, I asked, "What is ⅓ of these *two* hexagons?" Antonio looked confused and did not answer. I asked, "What does the 3 in the denominator tell you?" This seemed to help, as he was then able to shade ⅓ of the two hexagons (see Antonio's second attempt in Figure 6.4).

At this point, Antonio appeared unsure of what to do next. Although I felt that his uncertainty was symptomatic of a deeper underlying confusion, I wanted to get him through this one problem. Then he could learn the procedure and (I hoped) repeat it for the other problems. I pointed to the term ½ and said, "The denominator tells us to divide the ⅓ piece into two parts; the numerator tells us that the answer is *one* of those two parts. Okay. Now start by drawing a line that divides the shaded part into two equal parts." To my surprise, he divided the ⅓ into four triangles (see Antonio's second attempt in Figure 6.4) instead of two parallelograms. But when I asked him how many triangles would be in ½ he said, "If you divided the ⅓ piece into two parts, you would have two triangles in each part." Maybe, I thought to myself, Antonio understands more than I thought. He seemed to be connecting the symbols with the diagrams pretty well.

"So," I asked, "how many of those [referring to the triangles in Figure 6.4] do we need for our answer?" He hesitated and I pointed to the numerator of 1 in ½. He grinned and pointed to one triangle! I became very frustrated at this point. I had the sense that he had lost where we were in the overall process.

Otherwise, how could he have answered one triangle when he had just said that two of them were needed for ½ of the ⅓ piece? With a deep sigh, I reminded him that ½ would need to include two triangles. He bobbed his head in agreement and then sat motionless staring at the pieces. "So what is your answer?" I asked. "One-sixth," he quickly replied. "Good," I said. "Go on to the next one." As I walked away, however, it occurred to me that he had answered much too quickly. Could he have simply multiplied the denominators together, thus circumventing the whole process? Or remembered the answer that he got using the wrong unit whole?

I had the feeling that I had spent too much time with Antonio, and sure enough, when I looked up there was a sea of hands asking for help. I asked a few of my stronger students to take care of students who were seated near them and I went on to the next closest student. Danielle (who was working on ⅓ of ¼) had not made the same initial mistake as Antonio, but she, too, was having her share of difficulties. I had a hard time understanding *what* she was doing, so I asked her to start over. This time, I was determined to keep up the momentum so that Danielle could stay with the process from beginning to end.

"What is the fraction after the word *of*?" I began. After she responded ¼ correctly, I asked her to show me ¼ of the two hexagons, reminding her that it would be one part out of four equal parts. After she had shaded ¼ of the two hexagons (see Figure 6.5), I quickly pointed to the term ⅓ and said, "The denominator tells us to divide the ¼ into three parts; the numerator tells us that the answer is one of those three parts. Okay. Now start by dividing the shaded area into three parts and label them." She did so without much trouble (see Figure 6.5). I then asked her to point to one of the thirds, which she did. "So," I said, "what is your answer?" When she replied ⅙, I groaned silently. Outwardly, I remained calm and reminded her that we were working with *two* hexagons. "How many triangles would it take to cover *both* hexagons?" I asked. After she responded correctly, I asked again. "So what is your answer?" She replied ¹⁄₁₂, quickly wrote it into the box, and moved onto the next problem. She appeared to be relieved to be finished with the problem. I, however, was not convinced that she understood it.

For the remaining 20 minutes, I continued to stop by every desk trying to get each student through the steps in an accurate and efficient manner. My hope was that this would enable students to repeat the procedure on their own for the remaining problems. As I began to reach students for a second time, I noticed that most seemed to be doing fairly well—as long as the numerators of the fractions were one. Barely anyone got problems four, five, and six, which had fractions with numerators greater than one, correct. "What does that mean?" I wondered to myself. "I guess that I will need to emphasize that step at the beginning of tomorrow's lesson."

FIGURE 6.5. Danielle's work on the second problem.

Find ⅓ of ¼. Use pattern blocks. Draw your answer.

Show ¼.   Show ⅓ of ¼. ⅓ × ¼ = $\boxed{1/12}$

Shared Meeting Time

The next period was the shared meeting time for seventh-grade mathematics teachers. As Fran left her room and turned to go down the stairway toward the conference room, she ran into Kevin. "How did it go?" he asked eagerly. He was scheduled to do the same lesson later in the day and, like Fran, was unsure whether the students would "get it" on their first try. "Okay, I think. We can talk about it in the meeting. Maybe the others will want to hear, too," Fran replied.

After getting settled, the four teachers took turns describing their most recent lesson. As each teacher spoke, the others were attentive and supportive, often providing praise for the teacher's initiative and creativity. Everyone had come prepared with handouts to share. Past experience told them that others probably would want to try the same activity in their class. When Fran's turn came, she handed out copies of the problem set she had just used (Figure 6.1) and explained how her students had worked through the problems with some assistance from her. She described how she had found it important to guide students through their first problem pretty intensively, but added that students then seemed to be able to repeat the procedure and continue on their own successfully. Fran considered sharing her concern about the last set of problems (the ones that her students had difficulty with), but decided she had talked long enough and that she could work through it on her own the next day. Maybe then she'd share what happened with the group. Her colleagues praised Fran's lesson, noting that it was one of the most creative uses of pattern blocks they had seen. They even discussed showcasing the lesson at the Spring Open House.

STOP

Discuss Fran's Lesson and the Shared Meeting Time

Kevin Talks About His Class

In general, I've been very pleased with my classes this year. I think that this new approach has really opened their eyes to mathematics—maybe for the first time. I've seen lots of "a-has!" I am, however, a little concerned about my afternoon classes today. I am not convinced that yesterday's introduction "sank in." I must say, too, that Fran's description of her class in today's meeting didn't relieve my concern much. I didn't say much at the time because I didn't want to appear critical. But I had expected to hear her say a lot more about what the kids were thinking about—what she was able to tell about how (or whether) they were understanding what they were doing. Isn't that the point of all of this anyway? At the meeting today, it seemed as though the whole point was how many different ways we can use pattern blocks!

Earlier in the week, Fran and I had some really good discussions. We talked a lot about how the students have to learn that when they are dealing with fractions (or percents for that matter), they had better know what the unit whole is. Fran really pushed hard on this point and was worried that her students would have a difficult time with the new materials because the unit whole was two hexagons. She didn't mention anything about this at the meeting today, so I guess that it turned out not to be such a big deal. Also, I was wondering if Fran's students had noticed that their answers were smaller values than what they started out with. Fran and I also discussed this earlier in the week. I know that I will want to focus on this if my students don't notice it on their own.

Kevin's Setup

Yesterday, I introduced the unit in the same way that Fran did. We reviewed the meanings of fractions and of multiplication. Beginning with whole numbers, we discussed the "of" notion of multiplication; then we proceeded to fractions, at which time I introduced the use of pattern blocks as a way of modeling $\frac{1}{2}$ of $\frac{1}{2}$. After I modeled $\frac{1}{2}$ of $\frac{1}{2}$ using the pattern blocks, the students had time to work through two additional problems, under my guidance ($\frac{1}{3}$ of $\frac{1}{2}$ and $\frac{1}{4}$ of $\frac{1}{2}$). To begin today's lesson, I asked Charlise to come to the overhead project to solve the problem $\frac{1}{6}$ of $\frac{1}{2}$. She used the pattern blocks to model the procedure and confidently explained what she was doing every step of the way—and why she was doing it.

When there were no questions from the students, I wasn't sure that they understood what Charlise had done. I hoped that their silence meant understanding, but my secret dread was that it indicated that they were so lost that they couldn't even think of a question to ask. I considered having another student model a second problem, but decided instead to let them begin working at their desks with a partner. I made a mental note to closely monitor their understanding as I visited each pair. Right before they began to work, I stressed that the sketches and pattern blocks would help them to understand what they were doing and why. "Make sure," I said, "to use the pattern blocks (or sketches) to keep track of where you are in the process and what it all means."

Kevin's Implementation

I began walking around the room. At first, I just watched and listened. Some students seemed to be getting it; many others, however, appeared to be having trouble. I reminded the class to talk with their partners as they were working.

After about 10 minutes, I decided that I should start to intervene and try to find out more about what the students were doing. The first student whose desk I came to (Charles) had figured ½ of ⅓ using only one hexagon as the unit whole. One-third of one hexagon had been shaded in and then cut in half and labeled ⅙. He had already written ⅙ in the box and gone on to the second problem. I pointed to the fraction ⅙ that he had written in the box and said gently, "You say your answer is ⅙. Why?" Charles calmly and confidently replied, "Because ½ of ⅓ is ⅙," pointing to the diagram as he spoke. "One-sixth of what?" I asked. "Of this," Charles replied, pointing to the first hexagon. There was no hint of tentativeness in his voice. I knew he needed to be challenged but wasn't quite sure how to do it. Not knowing what else to say, I asked, "Is that what the problem is asking? Think about it," and then walked away. I felt very uneasy. Had I provided enough information to set him on the right track?

Two students later, as I was looking over a correct response to the same problem, I got a brainstorm. "Jorge," I said, "come over here to Charles's desk." "Look, boys," I said. "You both have the same answer in the box: ⅙. But Jorge has two triangles shaded and Charles only has one. How can that be? Which one of you is right?" Then I left the two of them to hash it out.

I continued my rounds. The next student was completely mixed up. I could not understand what she was doing. When I asked her to explain how she had thought about the problem ⅓ of ¼, she admitted that she wasn't sure what she was doing. I noticed that her partner had correct answers (on the diagrams and in the boxes). I asked Tamara to explain to Maria what she had done—and hovered nearby to listen. What I heard took me by surprise. Tamara went directly to the symbolic sentence and showed Maria how to multiply numerator by numerator and denominator by denominator to get the answer of $\frac{1}{12}$. Then she went back to the diagram and showed Maria how to find $\frac{1}{12}$ of the two hexagons. This was not at all what I had in mind! I decided to halt the pairwork and bring the class together as a whole to talk through one more problem.

The two boys I had pulled together earlier (Charles and Jorge) eagerly volunteered to show how to do problem 1 ($\frac{1}{2}$ of $\frac{1}{3}$). I hadn't made it back to them, so I wasn't sure if they were on the right track. I did know, however, that they were at least using the diagram to reason with. I told them to go to the front of the room and demonstrate their work using the overhead pattern blocks.

Charles (with Jorge beside him for moral support) used the overhead versions of the pattern blocks to provide a wonderful explanation of how to find $\frac{1}{2}$ of $\frac{1}{3}$. At the end, I asked Charles to share with the class what he had done the first time through, when he had used only one hexagon as the unit whole. After he showed the students, I pointed out that Charles got the same numerical answer doing it that way, but that it was not correct. This led to a discussion regarding how the value of $\frac{1}{6}$ depends on the unit whole. "One-sixth can be very small or very big depending on what it is $\frac{1}{6}$ of," I said. As a class, we generated different examples, like $\frac{1}{6}$ of a large pizza versus $\frac{1}{6}$ of a small pizza and $\frac{1}{6}$ of a farmer's field versus $\frac{1}{6}$ of a backyard garden. One student brought up the fact that store discounts translate into different amounts of savings in real dollars depending on the original price—10% off $100 is a lot more than 10% off $25. I took this opportunity to draw a connection between percents and fractions, noting that both had to be interpreted in terms of the unit whole.

As the students settled back into their pairwork, we had 15 minutes left in the class. As I walked around I didn't see any students starting with the symbolic manipulations. At least they appeared to be aware that the diagrams were important. A high point was when Tamara—the same student who was thinking only in terms of algorithms earlier—made an observation that I thought was really insightful. She commented, "The numbers follow the pictures." When I asked her what she meant, she said, "For #1 you have to divide the shapes into sixths for your answer and that is 2×3 [pointing to the denominators in the multiplication sentence]. For #2 you have to divide the shapes more times—into twelfths—for your answer and that is 3×4 [again pointing to the denominators in the multiplication sentence]." I complimented her, saying that she was beginning to understand why we follow all these silly rules.

With 5 minutes to go in the period, most students had begun to work on problems 4, 5, and 6. Although these were slightly more difficult (for example, they asked students to find $\frac{2}{3}$ of $\frac{1}{4}$), most students appeared to be doing okay. I decided to have them finish the problems for homework and to call their attention to the front of the room for some closing remarks. Once I had everyone's attention, I asked the students to look at the three multiplication sentences they had produced on the first three problems ($\frac{1}{2} \times \frac{1}{3} = \frac{1}{6}$; $\frac{1}{3} \times \frac{1}{4} = \frac{1}{12}$; and $\frac{1}{4} \times \frac{1}{3} = \frac{1}{12}$) and to tell me what they noticed. After discussing how $\frac{1}{3} \times \frac{1}{4}$ was the same as $\frac{1}{4} \times \frac{1}{3}$, we moved on to a discussion of the sizes of the products versus the factors. When the students noted that the products ended up being smaller than the number they started out with, I said, "But I thought that multiplication always made numbers bigger! Could we have made a mistake?" The students sat quietly, but I could tell they were thinking.

"For homework you have one additional question to answer," I said. "Using sketches of pattern blocks and/or words, explain why when we multiply by a fraction that is smaller than one—we get a smaller number than the one we started out with."

DISCUSSION QUESTIONS

Following Fran's Class and the Teacher Meeting

1. Why do you think Fran and Kevin selected the task they did? Do you think the task is capable of bringing out the ideas they thought were important? Why or why not?
2. Describe how you would feel if you were a student in Fran's class. What would you be trying to accomplish? What would you be most worried about? What would you have learned?
3. What do you think was accomplished during the teacher meeting?
   a. Were the teachers, including Kevin, helpful to Fran? Why or why not?
   b. Was she forthright with them? Why or why not?
   c. How could the meeting have gone differently?

Following Kevin's Class

4. How did Kevin deal with the students when they didn't appear to be "getting it"? How was Kevin's way of dealing with students different from Fran's? Discuss the pros and cons of Kevin's versus Fran's approach.
5. Describe how you would feel if you were a student in Kevin's class. What would you be trying to accomplish? What would you be most worried about? What would you have learned?

TEACHING NOTES

Both Fran Gorman and Kevin Cooper are teachers who are motivated to change. They realized that, under the "old" system, their students were building fragile, superficial, and sometimes inaccurate understandings of mathematics. Both of them wholeheartedly endorsed their school's new mathematics project—a project that aimed to teach for understanding and meaning as opposed to focusing solely on the drill and practice of procedures and the memorization of facts.

Fran and Kevin are very fortunate to have time built into their day during which they can meet with each other and with other teachers to discuss their new mathematics program. They used this time to plan the multiplication of fractions lessons discussed in this case. Fran and Kevin discussed some of the big ideas they wanted their students to come away from the lessons with (the notion of a unit whole and the expansion of the definition of multiplication beyond "making something bigger") and they found materials that would help their students develop these ideas. By stressing big ideas, Fran and Kevin were pushing for deeper layers of understanding than what most students typically develop. As argued in NCTM's *Curriculum and Evaluation Standards* (1989, p. 57), an emphasis on conceptual ideas (developed through the use of manipulatives and diagrams) should reduce the amount of time currently spent in correcting students' many misconceptions and procedural difficulties in the domain of rational numbers.

Ideally, the shared meeting times could also be used as a forum for reflecting on one's lessons and getting help from colleagues when things don't go as planned. Whether the meeting in this case served that purpose—and why or why not—will be a matter for discussion.

Cognitive Levels

The same task is used in both classes and is set up in essentially the same manner. In both Fran's and Kevin's classes, we consider the task—as set up—to be at the *procedures-with-connections* level. In general, *procedures-with-connections* tasks focus students' attention on the use of procedures for the purpose of developing deeper levels of understanding of important mathematical concepts or ideas. In this particular task, there is a suggested pathway (or procedure) to follow through the problem space. It involves using pattern blocks to model multiplication as x of y with the unit whole being represented by two hexagons.

To solve this task successfully, students must move back and forth between and among multiple representations of fractions and connect them in meaningful ways. The suggested pathway is a broad procedure that makes transparent the meaning of "a fraction of a fraction." This is very different from algorithms such as "multiply the numerators and multiply the denominators," which mask the underlying structure and concepts. In this task, students have the opportunity to connect the symbolic representation of fractions (e.g., ½) with the pattern block representation and to connect the symbolic operation of multiplication with the process of physically finding a fractional amount of this fractional quantity (e.g., finding ½ of ½). Although the "way to do this" was modeled during the setup phase by a competent student, students have to think about what their actions mean as they work through the remaining problems. They cannot apply the procedure mindlessly.

The way in which this task was actually implemented differed in Fran's and Kevin's classes. In Fran's class, the procedure of "how to do it" was stressed above all else. As students tried to follow Fran's directions, they appeared to lose—or never really establish—connections to the concepts or meanings associated with the task. They lost track of where they were in the process and why they were doing what they were doing. Not surprisingly, when the elements of the task changed slightly (multiplying with fractions that had numerators greater than one), the students fell apart. This suggests that their knowledge was quite fragile and superficial, connected only to the specific problems and not at all to the underlying ideas. In Fran's class, we classified the task implementation as the "use of *procedures without connections.*"

In Kevin's class, on the other hand, the students appeared to be really thinking as they went about solving the problems. Despite some early missteps (during which some students reverted to algorithms instead of truly working with the pattern blocks), most students appeared to stay in the conceptual realm most of the time, connecting the pattern block configurations with the symbolic representations of the fractional quantities. In Kevin's class, we classified the task implementation as the "use of *procedures with connections.*"

Factors

Despite setting up the lesson in a similar fashion and being confronted with similar problems during the implementation phase, Fran and Kevin chose to handle the problems in very different ways.

Factors in Fran's class. In this section, we discuss the factors that appeared to be responsible for the task's declining into a procedural exercise in Fran's class. These are ideas toward which the discussion should be steered.

1. Challenges become nonproblems. For student after student, Fran "took over" the task, essentially showing the students, step-by-step, what steps to follow and in what order. She did not allow the students to struggle on their own at all. Rather, she performed the thinking and reasoning processes for them. Moreover, her directions were very fragmented. Although she sometimes referred to conceptual entailments (e.g., "What does the 3 in the denominator tell you?"), most often she gave orders without explaining (or getting the student to explain) why they were doing what they were doing.

2. Teacher shifts the emphasis from meaning, concepts, or understanding to the correctness or completeness of the answer. Fran appeared to want students to get the correct answer in the right way, that is, in the way that had been modeled. She appeared to be convinced that imitation and repeated practice of the procedure would ultimately lead to the students' being able to perform the procedure flawlessly and hence get to the right answer. Little if any time was devoted to "smelling the roses along the way." Fran marched her students through the step-by-step procedures, as if the destination were the only thing that mattered. In the process, however, she failed to stop to remind students of what they were doing and why. As a result, the students could work well enough under her micromanaged directions, but lacked the overall conceptual map for locating where they had been and where they were going.

3. Students are not held accountable for high-level products or processes. Fran did not hold her students (or herself) accountable to two of the big ideas that she set out to engage with: the unit whole and the idea that multiplication does not always mean getting bigger. These ideas appeared to get lost in all of the step-by-step attention to details.

4. Not building on students' knowledge. The two student examples that are presented in detail suggest that Fran was more concerned with "telling" her way of thinking than she was with "listening" to the students' ways of thinking. She was quick to ask students to "start over," thereby discrediting any thought or effort they had put into their work to that point. This also deprived Fran of building on students' ways of understanding the problems.

Factors in Kevin's class. In this section, we discuss the factors that enabled the task to remain at a high level in Kevin's class.

1. Building on students' prior knowledge. Overall, Kevin appeared to be more attentive to what the students were or were not learning. Even during the setup phase, he was suspicious about their silence, being careful not to assume that it meant understanding. At the beginning of the implementation phase, Kevin made it a point to spend time "watching and listening" without barging in and solving the students' problems for them. With the students he helped individually, he first asked them to explain what they were thinking (even though it was wrong) and then challenged (as with Charles) or assisted them (as with Maria). In this way, Kevin was able to tailor his response to students' knowledge and their attitudes about their knowledge.

2. Teacher or capable students model high-level performance. As soon as Kevin decided that most of the students were not engaging with the task in the way that he had hoped, he asked two students to come to the front of the room to model the solution to a problem. He took a chance because he did not know whether the two students would present a coherent solution. It worked out quite well, however, because not only did the students model a nice solution, but Charles was also able to explain how he had mixed up the unit whole on an earlier try. This led into a discussion of the importance of the unit whole (see below).

3. *Teacher draws conceptual connections.* Kevin made sure that he drew students' attention to the big ideas. Taking Charles's discussion of his earlier mistake (using one hexagon as the unit whole) as a cue, Kevin got the class to engage in a discussion of the importance of the unit whole. He also made the connection between percents and fractions. Later in the class, he also drew students' attention to the idea that multiplication can give you a smaller number than the number with which you began. For homework, he asked students to explain why.

4. *Sustained press for justifications, explanations, and/or meaning through teacher questioning, comments, and/or feedback.* Kevin always brought discussions back to meaning or concepts. For example, he asked Charles "⅙ of what?" in an attempt to get him to consider the unit whole. He complimented Tamara when she was beginning to draw meaningful connections between the work with pattern blocks and the algorithm of multiplying numerators and denominators.

Additional Layers of Interpretation

An additional issue that this dual case raises for discussion is the process of teacher collaboration. Many reform projects have begun to build in time for teachers to meet with one another during the school day to discuss how things are going and to help each other out. Yet there is little information about what teachers actually do during these times and the extent to which it is useful. Instead of discussing instructional practice in a deep way, teachers may politely listen, taking what they can from the meetings, but never risk the interpersonal confrontation that—it is often feared—will accompany critical questioning of another teacher's decisions and actions (Little, 1990). This type of teacher collaboration follows long-established norms in the teaching profession of not intruding on a colleague's classroom practice.

NOTES

1. Pattern blocks are brightly colored wooden or plastic two-dimensional geometric shapes that are used by students as they work on fraction problems. They come in a variety of shapes (e.g., triangles, parallelograms, trapezoids, hexagons) and the sizes are calibrated to each other, thereby allowing students to see, for example, that six triangles (or three parallelograms) comprise one hexagon.

CHAPTER 7

Giving Meaning to Measures of Central Tendency

FIGURE 7.1. Opening activity to be completed prior to reading the case of Trina Naruda and Ursula Hernandez.

Using the data sets given below, make conjectures about the meaning of the following terms: mean, median, mode, and range.

Set A: 5, 12, 16, 10, 2 Mean: 9 Median: 10 Mode: none Range: 14	*Set E: 8, 6, 7, 8, 9, 10* Mean: 8 Median: 8 Mode: 8 Range: 4
Set B: 1, 2, 2, 6, 7, 18 Mean: 6 Median: 4 Mode: 2 Range: 17	*Set F: 8, 0, 5, 0, 12* Mean: 5 Median: 5 Mode: 0 Range: 4
Set C: 7, 6, 8, 10, 9, 11 Mean: 8.5 Median: 8.5 Mode: none Range: 5	*Set G: 6, 9, 9, 6, 8, 5, 9, 4* Mean: 7 Median: 7 Mode: 9 Range: 5
Set D: 1, 20, 5, 8, 1 Mean: 7 Median: 5 Mode: 1 Range: 19	*Set H: 3, 15, 21, 9, 18, 12* Mean: 13 Median: 13.5 Mode: none Range: 18

THE CASE OF TRINA NARUDA AND URSULA HERNANDEZ

Trina Naruda teaches seventh and eighth grade in a large urban school district in the Southwest currently engaged in several educational reform efforts, including an innovative mathematics program. The district has the highest percentage of Spanish Limited English Proficient (LEP) students in the state and a growing number of LEP students of Asian descent. This is Trina's second year of teaching mathematics. She has a strong background in mathematics and her pre-service preparation reflected a strong endorsement of the kind of instruction and curriculum advocated by the NCTM Standards. When Trina came to this school, she was delighted to find out that she would have the freedom to use what she had learned in her certification program.

One of the things Trina enjoys most about her job is interacting and collaborating with her colleagues. This year, Trina has spent a great deal of time working with one of the new teachers, Ursula Hernandez.

Like Trina, Ursula is bilingual (Spanish and English) and has a strong orientation toward teaching and learning with understanding. This is Ursula's first year teaching mathematics, but she has taught social studies before at the middle-school level. Like Trina, Ursula is very adept at classroom management and has developed a good rapport with her students. Ursula and Trina like working together and they often use a floating substitute teacher available to the department to spend time observing one another's instruction and providing one another with feedback.

Trina Talks About Her Class

Last year I had been frustrated because I didn't think my students really understood the concepts of mean, median, mode, and range, and they seemed to be confusing the terms and how to calculate them. I think this is because I was just giving them definitions and having them apply the definitions to numbers. This approach did not allow the students to construct any meaning for measures of central tendency on their own. This year I wanted to find some way of presenting the topic so it would be more meaningful for the students and so they might retain more of the information after the unit ended. I am a firm believer that students understand more when they are involved in constructing or discovering things for themselves, so I was looking for a way to do that with this topic.

This year two of my seventh grade classes are full—inclusion classes. That means that I team teach with a special education teacher because the classes contain a number of special education students. I teach this particular class with Ms. Edwards. She and I get along very well and we have worked hard to have all the students think of us as co-teachers. The special education students are integrated into the groups and we both think it is important that the regular education students don't see the special education students as different or separate. In this class we also have another adult helper, Mr. Ezoto, who works primarily with a group of Vietnamese students who communicate mainly in French or Vietnamese. In addition to the Vietnamese students, I have several different levels of LEP students in the class. Since I am fluent in Spanish, this isn't really a big problem for me. The primary language of instruction, however, is English, and I use my Spanish as extra support for the students who need it. Altogether, there are 41 students in the class.

Ms. Edwards and I worked together to develop a group project for the students in which they would have to figure out the meanings of mean, median, mode, and range by looking at and exploring several sets of data. We wanted students to make their own conjectures about how mean, median, mode, and range should be defined based on their exploration across several data sets. Conjecture, or informed guessing, is a very important mathematical process with which Ms. Edwards and I both think our students need more experience. It's a discovery process in which the students will be reasoning based on data. Students also need to have experiences with testing their conjectures and convincing themselves whether or not a conjecture is valid. So this lesson is as much about mathematical and logical reasoning processes as it is about measures of central tendency. Once the students understand the meaning of these concepts, then our hope is that they will be able to apply the concepts to real data sets. Ways of calculating the measures of center arise naturally from how they are defined. We also needed a project that was rich enough for students of a variety of ability levels, including special education, to get engaged. I hoped that it would all work out well because Ursula was going to be observing and then trying it out with her own class later.

Trina's Setup

Ms. Edwards and I had decided to begin the lesson by talking with students about the nature of the discovery process they were going to engage in for this project. We wanted students to see the activity as a process of looking through the data sets for patterns and clues to the meanings of mean, median, mode, and range. Ms. Edwards opened the lesson by writing the word *discovery* on the overhead projector. I translated it aloud in Spanish. She asked students to tell her what that word meant to them. As students gave ideas, she wrote them down on the overhead:

Look for something
Treasure
Look for gold
Use what you know to find out something you don't know
Information

Ms. Edwards drew attention to the last two ideas. She told students they should look for clues when they are discovering something and in mathematics, many times that means looking for patterns in the information that you have and making conjectures about what you see in the data. This exercise was an attempt to help students understand the nature of what they would be doing during the lesson since they had not done anything like this recently. This discussion lasted about 5 minutes at the most and Mr. Ezoto quietly translated much of it for the Vietnamese students.

I then took over explaining the task and began by writing a set of numbers on the chalkboard: 10, 14, 12, 10, 10, 16. I explained that each group would be getting an index card with a set of numbers like this, along with the mean, median, mode, and range for each set. I showed them an example of what a card would contain (see Figure 7.2).

I told students that the first thing they should do is look at the numbers. Before I could get on with my instructions, Geraldo thought the next thing to do would be to put the numbers in order. Even though it had been a while, obviously some of the students were remembering their past experiences with pattern finding. So taking Geraldo's cue, I put my set of numbers in order from least to greatest and I asked the students if they thought it might be easier to see patterns this way. The students seemed to agree that this way of arranging the numbers might be good for seeing patterns.

FIGURE 7.2. Example of an index card containing a data set given to students in Trina's and Ursula's classes.

10, 14, 12, 10, 10, 16

The mean is 12.
The mode is 10.
The median is 11.
The range is 6.

I explained that there were eight different cards or sets of numbers and that it would be important for each group to record and graph the data from each set they reviewed so that their card could be passed along to another group and they could get a new card (Ms. Edwards, Mr. Ezoto, and I would make sure the cards circulated around to as many groups as possible). I told the students they would have to examine at least four different sets of numbers but that they should look at more if possible. This was just to make sure they looked at more than one or two sets. I told the students they would have two jobs: First, I asked them to use grid paper to make a graph of each number set and to record the other information found on the card (this would serve as a record of what sets each group had seen and allow them to look across sets, since they only had one set at a time); second, I said they would have to write conjectures, or informed guesses, about what the four words meant based on the sets of numbers on the cards they reviewed. I again reminded them that they would be looking for clues and patterns. The number sets are shown in Figure 7.1.

Ms. Edwards and I deliberately selected these sets so that if we looked across all the sets, students could not overgeneralize a faulty conjecture. For example, some sets had an even number of elements and some had an odd number; some had no repeated elements, while others had two or three repeated elements. I had asked Ursula to check over all the sets ahead of time to make sure Ms. Edwards and I had not missed something important. Once all the sets were distributed, we told the students to begin working. They had about 40 minutes to work on the task.

Trina's Implementation

After 5 minutes, I sensed that the students seemed confused about what to do. Ms. Edwards, Mr. Ezoto, and I circulated around the room to help everyone get started with their first set of numbers. As groups finished with one card set, they would be given another. We encouraged the groups to make conjectures from their first data set and then to revise the conjectures as they looked at more sets of numbers. I noticed that some groups didn't have a good idea of how to go about analyzing the data sets and they were not really sure what to write. After a few more minutes, I stopped the class briefly, asked two groups to share their early conjectures with the class, and recorded them on the board. Marta's group had this set: 1, 1, 5, 8, 20. For their first conjectures they wrote the following: "Range shows how much distance from the smallest number to the largest number; Mode is the one that happens two times; Median is the middle number; Mean is in the middle, but it's not the middle number." I asked if any group had a different first conjecture for the mode. Rigoberto's group had the set 4, 5, 6, 6, 8, 9, 9, 9. They had the following conjecture: "The mode is the one that is there three times." I asked those two groups if they might need to revise their conjectures a little. Rigo said, "Could be it's not a certain number. Maybe it's just the one that shows up the most." I told him that maybe they could test that idea on some other sets of data. Again, it was important for the students to test their conjectures and refine them based on examples and counterexamples found in the data. All this took about 5 or 6 minutes and seemed to be helpful for the other groups who were struggling early on. After they got past their first set of numbers, most groups seemed to understand what they were supposed to be doing and they began writing their conjectures. I was really excited to see the groups looking over their graphs and working hard to find the patterns and make good conjectures.

Obviously, not every student was engaging at the same deep level, but I think all the groups were definitely on-task and the students were paying attention to one another. Most of the students seemed to be doing well. Some of the special education students needed extra coaching by Ms. Edwards or me, but they seemed to be doing all right, too. For example, sometimes they were not quite keeping up with the rest of the group and so we had to review with them what the group had done so far. In other cases, they had trouble with writing (some have severe literacy problems), so we would record on paper what they dictated to us. Usually, other members of their groups were trying to be helpful to these students as well. Mr. Ezoto was working very closely with the Vietnamese students scattered around in different groups. I am never quite sure whether he is telling them too much or whether they are getting all the help they need, but most of the time I just can't worry about it. I'm fluent in Spanish, but I don't understand a word of Vietnamese and there are 35 other students who need attention.

Ms. Edwards, Mr. Ezoto, and I continued to circulate from group to group, spending anywhere from 1 to 5 minutes with each group. Whenever I saw a new conjecture, I asked the students to explain why they thought it was accurate. I really wanted them to be able to show me evidence for how they got the conjectures from the data sets they had seen. One group said the mode was "the one that's there the most often." They explained that in every set they looked at, the mode was the number with the highest frequency. They told me that it's really easy to find the mode if you look at the frequency graph because it would have the highest bar. I asked them if there was always a *highest* bar. They thought for a second and then they grinned and responded, "So far!" I left that group with a big smile on my face. I was glad to see that they were reasoning by looking across all the sets and not just basing their ideas on a single example. This is an important mathematical process that students need to understand.

Next I came across a group that initially had a conjecture for the median stating that it was "half way between the two middle numbers [when you order them by size]." They clearly had an even-numbered set. I asked them for an example. They referred to 1, 2, 2, 6, 7, 18. Students said the median would be 4 because "it's in the middle of 2 and 6," "you subtract 2 from 6 and the difference is 4 and half of that is 2 so you have to be two more than 2 and 2 less than 6. That's 4. It's right in the middle." I asked them if they were sure that would work for every set of numbers. They still needed to check other sets. After they saw an odd-numbered set, they revised their conjecture so it would work for even- and odd-numbered sets. This was just the kind of process I was hoping would happen from looking at more than one data set.

Toward the end of the class, I noticed that two groups had different conjectures for what the median was. Both conjectures were only partially correct. Within each group, the students had reached a point of agreement and they were not questioning themselves any further. They needed some kind of outside challenge in order to make progress. So I decided to have those two groups look across all their data sets together to see if they could resolve the difference. It was a little chaotic at first, but once they laid down all their graphs from both groups onto one table, they were able to get down to business. Eventually, a couple of students were able to see how both conjectures were not quite right and they revised their conjectures accordingly. Those groups were very pleased with themselves!

By the end of the period, all groups had accurate conjectures for at least two of the terms, *range* and *median*. I was a little surprised that more of them didn't have *mode* figured out. I think some groups got into the median and ended up spending a lot of time with it, so they didn't get to the mode. But since I expected to have another day of this, I was not too worried about their pace. A couple of groups had conjectures for all four terms, but they still needed to look at more data sets in order to refine their conjectures. By the end of tomorrow I hope we will have established the definitions of all four terms and that by having students develop the definitions in this way, students will retain them, not confuse them, and be able to apply the definitions more accurately to describe and interpret sets of data. Ms. Edwards and I were both happy with how things were going. With 5 minutes left in the period, I asked students to put all their records into their group folders. I complimented the students on how well they were working on this project and I told them we would work on it more tomorrow. After class, Ursula and I arranged to spend some time at lunch talking about what she had just observed in my class. Ursula was then going to try the lesson with her fifth-period class.

STOP

Discuss Trina's class

Ursula Reflects on Her Conversation with Trina

Trina and I spent half an hour at lunch talking about how her lesson went. I had jotted down a few notes about her questioning strategies and about how she, Ms. Edwards, and Mr. Ezoto seemed to be working with the groups. Trina and I talk about questioning a lot because I think she is pretty good at getting the students to make progress without telling them everything. For example, in the beginning of class when students were not sure what to write, she found a way to help them get started without actually telling them anything. I think this is so hard to do, but I keep trying. The nice thing is that I know I can trust Trina. She doesn't ever judge me for my mistakes, so I don't mind her pointing them out to me. I use group work quite a bit with my students, so I was not really concerned about that aspect of the lesson. Mainly, I was worried about whether the students would be able to come up with good conjectures. I know Trina does a lot more investigations like this with her students than I do, so I knew it might be a little rocky getting my students to understand the point of the task. After watching Trina's class, though, I thought it was a great lesson so I was kind of excited about trying it out and I was glad Trina agreed to observe my class and give me feedback.

Ursula Talks About Her Class

My class is not quite as diverse as Trina's. I don't have any Asian LEP students and my class is not an inclusion class for special education. All the students in this class are Spanish LEP students, but they do represent several different language-ability levels. This is not a problem for me since I speak Spanish fluently. Also, my class is a little smaller than Trina's, with only 35 students. Funny, I never imagined that I would come to think of a class of 35 as small. But I guess you just get used to having so many students. Anyway, I have a bilingual assistant because this is considered to be an LEP class just like Trina's. My assistant is Diana Cortes. She just started working with this class a couple of months ago and I like her very much. She attends our math department meetings and retreats regularly like Mr. Ezoto. I know she has a pretty good background in math since she used to be a teacher in Colombia. I can trust her to work with the groups in the same way that I would.

Ursula's Setup

I watched very closely as Trina and Ms. Edwards set up the activity in their class because I wanted to make sure that I did everything exactly the same. I wanted my students to have the same opportunity to deal with the task as Trina's students had. So I also started with a little discussion about the discovery process and looking for patterns and then I gave them the instructions for the activity. I basically set it all up the same way Trina did except I didn't have any interruptions, so it went a little faster. So my students had about 45 minutes to work on the task. I used the same materials as Trina and Ms. Edwards had used, and Trina helped me distribute the data set cards to each group. Other than that, Trina just sat back and observed the class.

Ursula's Implementation

At first, I thought the students seemed a little confused about what to do. Ms. Cortes and I circulated around the room to make sure everyone was getting started with their first set of numbers. As the lesson progressed, we also had to make sure the index cards were circulating around to as many groups as possible. Just as Trina had done, we encouraged the groups to make conjectures from their first data set and then to revise the conjectures as they looked at more sets of numbers. With many of the groups it took longer than I thought it should to get through the first set of numbers. We ended up having to repeat parts of the directions as we visited each group. This took a lot of time, but at least the students were still trying to work on the task and not just fooling around while they waited for me or Ms. Cortes to come and help.

I realized at this point that it might have been helpful to take one set of numbers and do it together as a whole class. I did not start the task that way because I wanted the students to do it on their own and not just copy what I did. I could see that some of the students weren't sure how to go about analyzing the data sets for clues or patterns, even though they knew this was what they were supposed to do. As I visited groups, sometimes I ended up walking them through a process with their first data set. I noticed Ms. Cortes was doing the same thing. Because of this, many groups spent too much time on the first data set. This was a problem because I knew from Trina's class that in order to make progress, the students really needed to look at several data sets. The students were working hard on the activity. As I walked around, I tried to notice what conjectures were being recorded and I tried to make sure all the students were participating in the discussion or in the recording. Obviously, not every student was engaging at the same deep level, but I think all the groups were definitely on-task and that the students were paying attention to one another's ideas.

As I visited each group, I tried to make sure that I asked the students to explain why they thought their conjectures were good ones. Juan's group said the mode was "the one that's there the most." I asked them to show me how they got that conjecture and they picked up one graph and said, "See, the green card says the mode is 2, and 2 is there the most times, so that's it!" I told them to keep up the good work and I moved on to another group. A few minutes later, while I questioned Rosa, Luz, and Maria, I realized that Juan's group hadn't really given me a good explanation, but I was already on to another group at that point. I just hoped Juan's group really knew they were supposed to be looking across lots of sets of numbers to get generalizable definitions.

About halfway through the class, I visited Tomas's group. They initially had a conjecture for the median stating that it was "half way between the two numbers in the middle if they are in order." They clearly had an even-numbered set. I asked them for an example. They referred to 6, 7, 8, 9, 10, 11. Students said the median would be 8.5 because "you take the middle two numbers," "you see there's 1 between 8 and 9 and when you cut in half that's a half. So it's 8 and a half. It's right in the middle." I told them they needed to check some other sets of numbers to make sure their method worked all the time.

I was hoping they would find an odd-numbered set and see that their conjecture was good, but limited. Instead, they looked at another data set, but they didn't look at the median again. I noticed that several groups were just getting the first conjecture for one term and moving on to another term without evaluating the validity of all their conjectures across sets. I was disappointed with this, but I wasn't sure what to do about it since I was trying to avoid being too directive.

Toward the end of the class, I noticed that two groups had different conjectures for what the median was. I remembered something like this also happened in Trina's class. I pointed out to each of the groups that I had seen a different conjecture in another group and maybe they needed to do some more testing and look at some more data sets. Unfortunately, this didn't have the effect I was hoping for. One group did look at more data sets and revise their conjecture, but the other group quickly decided that they were right and the others were wrong and did not do anything more with it. I wanted to get back to them and work with them more, but I simply ran out of time.

By the end of the period, all groups had some conjectures for at least two of the terms, *range* and *median*. Some groups also had conjectures written for *mode* and *mean*. Still, I was pretty unsatisfied with how things had gone in this task, but I couldn't quite put my finger on why.

DISCUSSION QUESTIONS

Following Trina's Class

1. From Trina's perspective, what issues was she facing in the lesson?
2. What were Trina's mathematical goals for the students in the task? Were Trina's goals accomplished?
3. What was happening in Trina's classroom that supported student engagement with the task at a high level?

Following Ursula's Class

4. What was the same and what was different about Ursula's and Trina's classes? Was Ursula facing the same issues as Trina? Different issues?
5. Were Ursula's mathematical goals for her students the same as Trina's? Did Ursula's goals change during the task? Were Ursula's goals accomplished?
6. What classroom-based factors might have contributed to the different levels of student engagement in the two classes?
   a. Were there differences in the kind of support Trina and Ursula provided the students in their respective classes?
   b. What, if anything, did they do that was the same?
   c. Were there differences in the ways in which the students behaved that might have affected their own level of engagement with the task?

TEACHING NOTES

Trina Naruda and Ursula Hernandez are both relatively new to teaching mathematics and they are both oriented toward the idea that students understand more about mathematics when they are actively engaged in learning. Trina and Ursula think that students who are more actively involved are more likely to construct meaningful understandings about the mathematics they are learning. Both teachers are obviously very committed to trying to implement the NCTM Standards recommendations in their classrooms, and they are very comfortable collaborating with one another in those efforts.

In the lessons presented in the case, Trina and Ursula hope to help students gain a solid understanding of different measures of central tendency by exploring their meaning in the context of numerical data sets, rather than memorizing definitions of terms. According to the NCTM Standards, students should be engaged in activities that will enable them to relate concepts of center and dispersion of data to numerical and non-numerical data sets. Also, students should be given opportunities to explore several different measures of central tendency, not just the mean (NCTM, 1989, pp. 108–109). In addition, Trina and Ursula wanted to engage students in the process of making and testing conjectures, another important foundational process for mathematical reasoning and proof.

We recommend spending time working on the task prior to reading the case in order to give participants an opportunity to explore all the features of the task that students are faced with in the case. The presentation of mean, median, mode, and range in this task is an uncommon approach, and having the participants explore the task may enhance their understanding of the various issues that arise in the case.

Cognitive Levels

The task used in both classes is the same and is set up in essentially the same way. In both classes, we consider the task to be an example of *doing mathematics* as it was set up. In this particular task, students are required to access relevant knowledge and experiences and make appropriate use of them in the task. There is not a predictable solution path suggested by the task and students are being asked to explore the concepts of mean, median, mode, and range in a meaningful way by an inductive reasoning process using several sets of data.

To solve this task successfully, students have to explore a series of data sets; construct a graphical representation of each data set; and look for patterns with respect to how the mean, median, mode, and range for each data set were derived from the data. Students then have to make conjectures based on their exploration of multiple data sets about the possible meanings of each concept. This is different from the way these concepts are often presented in middle-school curricular materials. Usually, students are given acceptable definitions of these terms and then asked to apply the definitions to calculate the mean, median, mode, and range given a set of data. The teachers in this case elect not to present these concepts in the usual way because they think, based on past experience, that students will not necessarily understand how the definitions connect to the data. Also, they think that without these connections, students tend to confuse the terms or how to calculate them. By forcing students to analyze the structure of several different sets of data in relation to measures of central tendency and to look for patterns across data sets, the teachers hope that students will construct more meaningful knowledge of these concepts.

Implementation of the task plays out differently in each of the two classes. In Trina's class, most of the students work productively in their groups for most of the class, analyzing the data sets and recording conjectures for definitions of at least some of the terms. Students are able to provide evidence in the data sets to justify their conjectures. Many groups initially record conjectures based on only one data set, but then are able to revise their conjectures when they inspect different sets of data. Also, some groups with conflicting conjectures combine their efforts and question one another in order to resolve the apparent contradictions. Thus, we considered the implementation in Trina's class to have remained at the level of *doing mathematics*.

In Ursula's class, the task plays out a little differently. Although the teacher, instructional assistants, and students all work in earnest on the task throughout the class and do produce conjectures, they do not make as much progress toward understanding the target mathematical ideas and processes as Trina's class. We consider the implementation of the task in Ursula's class to be at the level of *unsystematic exploration*. The students in Ursula's class seem to be much more confused about how to approach the task and, in particular, how to go about analyzing the data and looking for patterns. Students are less articulate about the justifications for their conjectures—that is, what they are using as evidence to support their conjectures. Also, many students do not understand the importance of testing their initial conjectures with more than one data set. Some students appear to be focused on getting through all four terms rather than making sure their definitions are generalizable across data sets.

Factors

Even though Trina and Ursula use the same initial task and set it up in similar ways, the implementation of the task differs in the two classes.

Factors in Trina's class. In Trina's class, the task demands appear to remain high for most of the students in the class, while in Ursula's class, the students do not seem to be engaging with the task in a way that progresses toward increased understanding of the target mathematical ideas or of the process of making and testing conjectures. In this section, we discuss the factors that appear to contribute to the maintenance of high-level engagement in Trina's class. *These are ideas toward which the case discussion should be steered.*

1. Building on students' prior knowledge. Both Trina and Ms. Edwards are attentive to what students understand about the mathematical content and processes from the setup of the task through the implementation of the task. From the very beginning, they talk with the students about the nature of the processes they should engage in during the lesson (looking for patterns and clues in the data, and forming conclusions) since they had not done anything like it recently. During the setup, Trina capitalizes on Geraldo's articulation of his prior experience with a way to arrange the numbers so it is easier to look for patterns. Trina builds on Geraldo's idea when she introduces the task to the rest of the class.

2. Scaffolding. Trina is very skillful at listening to students, assessing the sources of their difficulties or confusions, and then suggesting a course of action that might help them resolve their confusions on their own. For example, late in the lesson, Trina comes across two groups who have contradictory conjectures for the meaning of median. Both conjectures are partially correct. Trina thinks that both groups need to see something that would challenge their original thinking about the median and move them toward a more general definition. Trina asks the two groups to compare their conjectures, look across all their data sets, and see if they can resolve the problem this way.

3. Appropriate amount of time. Trina's class unfolds at a fairly leisurely pace, as she does not expect students to complete the task entirely in one class period. Students have plenty of time to explore multiple data sets (a crucial part of the process).

4. Sustained pressure for explanation and meaning. Trina and Ms. Edwards consistently press students to give evidence for their conjectures and to continually test their conjectures on multiple data sets. For example, when Trina approaches a group with a limited conjecture for the median as "half way between the two middle numbers [when you order them by size]," she presses them to show her an example that illustrates their definition. She also asks them if they are sure it would work for every set of numbers. Trina has similar interactions with several of the groups.

Factors in Ursula's class. In Ursula's class, the high-level demands of the task were not maintained. Some of the reasons for this are discussed below.

1. Challenges become nonproblems. The students are not tuned in to the full scope of the processes involved in the task. Most of the students are able to make conjectures from particular data sets and feel very good about their accomplishments, but the students do not seem to fully realize the importance of finding definitions that apply across *all* sets of data. They often look at one or two sets of data and stop there. Hence, many of their conjectures are limited by the few examples they explore, but the students do not seem to realize that this is problematic or that they are not engaging with the task as Ursula had intended.

2. Students not held accountable for high-level processes. Ursula often does not hold students accountable for the high-level processes she had hoped they would engage in. For example, when she questions Juan's group, she does ask them to give evidence to justify their conjecture, but she accepts an inadequate explanation and does not press the students for more information. It is unclear whether the students realize they are supposed to be aiming for definitions that can be applied to any data set (even though Ursula later realizes she has not pressed Juan's group enough, she is unable to bring this concern out in the way she interacts with the students). Later in the lesson, Ursula has an occurrence similar to one in Trina's class in which two groups generate contradictory conjectures for the median. Ursula tries Trina's strategy of putting the two groups together to give them more data sets to examine. The groups do not persist in trying to resolve their conflict and Ursula does not press them to do so.

3. Time. Ursula seems to be concerned about the students' having enough time to look at multiple data sets. Because of this, she does not often take the time to query students extensively about what they are doing or press the students to explore their conjectures more deeply.

4. Absence of modeling of high-level performance. When Ursula and Ms. Cortes found themselves having to repeat the initial task instructions for each group, Ursula realizes that students might have been able to make more progress if they had worked through an example together with the whole class. One reason that Ursula seems to be reluctant to model high-level performance for the students is her fear of being too directive, or having students simply copy what she does. Still, students might have benefited from some modeling of how to at least get started in the process of making and testing conjectures about the sets of data. This modeling could have been done by Ursula or by a group of students who seemed to be navigating the task successfully.

Additional Layers of Interpretation

This case raises at least two other issues in addition to what has been discussed regarding the Mathematical Tasks Framework. One issue raised in this case is the potential benefit of teacher peer collaboration. Trina and Ursula have the opportunity to collaborate regularly in their instruction because of the availability of a floating substitute teacher, which enables them to spend time observing one another teach. Trina and Ursula are able to try out similar activities and lessons and then spend time talking with each other about how things are working in both their classes. This enables them to spend time both reflecting on their own instruction and providing useful feedback to a colleague.

Another issue raised in this case is the challenge of teaching in a multilingual setting in which English is a second language for the majority of students. Both Trina and Ursula speak Spanish. However, in Trina's class, there are not only native Spanish speakers but also native Vietnamese speakers who speak very little English. An important aspect of this challenge is the way in which the teacher and the bilingual instructional assistant communicate with one another and coordinate their efforts. Both Trina and Ursula work toward increasing their bilingual assistants' understanding of the mathematics and the kind of thinking in which they are aiming to engage their students, and the bilingual assistants are expected to be a resource for all the students in the classroom.

NOTES

1. The mathematics department chairperson was released half-time to allow him to provide instructional support to the teachers at Tyler Middle School. In some cases, teachers could ask him to substitute in their classes, enabling them to observe another colleague's teaching.

CHAPTER 8

Using Algebra Tiles to Multiply Monomials and Binomials

FIGURE 8.1. Opening activity to be completed prior to reading the case of Monique Butler.

Use algebra tiles to show these multiplications and make a sketch of your model. Write the product.

1. $2x(x - 1)$
2. $(x + 1)(x + 2)$
3. $(x - 2)(3x + 3)$
4. $(x - 3)(x + 3)$
5. $(2x + 2)(2x - 2)$
6. $(x + 3)(x + 3)$

THE CASE OF MONIQUE BUTLER

Monique Butler teaches eighth-grade mathematics in a middle school in a large southeastern urban school district. The students come primarily from two large public housing projects and have a history of low standardized test achievement. In reaction to this situation, school administrators and mathematics teachers initiated a 5-year project to reform the mathematics instructional program for all students in the school. A basic tenet of the reform effort was that the school would prepare all students to successfully complete any high school mathematics course, including algebra and other college-prep courses. Monique and her colleagues were committed to providing students with instruction that focused on thinking, reasoning, and problem solving rather than memorizing and performing procedures with speed and accuracy. However, the district still required that they administer assessments that were heavily oriented toward "basic skills" and contained almost no items assessing students' conceptual understanding of mathematics.

The first year of the reform effort at the school was Monique's first year as a teacher. She had worked as an information systems analyst for a large corporation for 4 years before returning to college to obtain her certification to teach. Having spent several years working in the corporate world, Monique valued teamwork and wanted to give her students opportunities to develop that important life skill. Monique was glad to be teaching in an urban district and she felt she could be a positive role model for her students because she came from a similar background.

Monique Talks About Her Class

The eighth-grade semester exam is coming up and it will cover material up through operations using algebraic expressions, so I have to at least get through the four basic operations with monomials and binomials with my students. We cover algebra topics in the eighth grade even though it is not an algebra course. Although the district-mandated semester exam has mostly computational problems on it, I also want my students to understand what they are doing and be able to explain it. In other words, I want them to know more than just how to move the symbols around. I always give my own semester exam in addition to the one the district gives. That way, I can ask about the things I think are important and I can get a better idea of what they know, not just how fast they can get through a test booklet.

This year our school bought algebra tiles—classroom sets and overhead versions—for each eighth-grade math teacher. The pieces are great for showing a visual representation of what is happening with the abstract symbols. For example, x is represented by a rectangle (1 by x) and x^2 is represented by a square (x by x). Here are the pieces we needed for this lesson (see Figure 8.2). One side of each is *red* and the flip side is *black*, so we can represent positive terms with one color and negative terms with the other. A couple of weeks ago, we used them to do polynomial addition and subtraction and most of the students seemed to get it pretty easily. Although they'd never seen the algebra tiles before this year, the sixth- and seventh-grade teachers use things like fraction pieces, so the students had had some practice using manipulatives to represent operations with numbers.

FIGURE 8.2. The algebra pieces used in Monique's lesson.

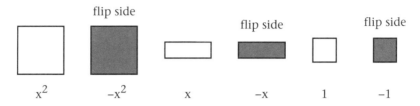

Because the semester exams stress symbol manipulation and because time is getting short, yesterday, I showed the students how to multiply monomials and binomials using the symbolic expressions such as $3w(5w + 3)$. We talked about how when you multiply something like $3w$ and $5w$, you multiply the numbers and then for the variable you add the exponents to get the degree of the product. The most they'll have to do on the exam is multiply two binomials and so we went through the FOIL method—First, Outside, Inside, Last (see Figure 8.3).

We also talked about how the formula for the area of a rectangle was length times width and how you could think of binomials as the measures of sides of a rectangle and the area as the product of the lengths of the sides. This part was especially important in preparing them to use the tiles successfully in the lesson we did today. Even though I didn't really have the time, what I wanted to do in today's lesson was to get the students to use the tiles to really be able to see how multiplication of binomials can be thought of as creating a rectangle with the two factors representing the length and width. I wanted them to model the multiplication with the tiles and look at the symbols and tiles side-by-side so that they could see where the terms in the product come from. I thought this would help students remember the procedures and give some meaning to them.

FIGURE 8.3. The example $[(2x + 1) (x + 3)]$ completed using the FOIL method.

$$(2x + 1)(x+3)$$

First		Outside		Inside		Last
(2x)(x)	+	(2x)(3)	+	(1)(x)	+	(1)(3)
$2x^2$	+	6x	+	x	+	3

$$2x^2 + 7x + 3$$

Setup

After going over the homework, which asked students to find the values of various expressions by substituting certain values for variables, I told the students they would be working on finding the products of monomials and binomials as they had done the day before, but this time they'd be using the tiles. They got in their groups and I passed out the group job assignment cards and told them to look on the board for their assignments based on the color of the card they got. We reviewed what the jobs were: Architect (design, arrange tiles); Timekeeper (keep group on task, use time adequately); Group Leader (raise any questions the group has, keep group on task); and Domestic Engineer (get and put away materials, make sure group area stays clean). I had developed this system of roles to help the students become more productive team members. I think it is important for each student to have a well-defined responsibility in the group. After the Domestic Engineers got the tiles for their groups, I went through an example. The Architects in each group were supposed to build for their group what I was building at the overhead.

We did $(3x + 2)(2x-1)$ all together as a class (see Figure 8.4). The Architects followed what I was doing and put $3x + 2$ along the left side and $2x-1$ along the top (these wouldn't be part of the rectangle; we used these as a way to remember what the dimensions were).

Then I showed them how we would fill in the area of the rectangle that had these dimensions. I placed one tile at a time, beginning with the x^2 in the top left corner, creating three rows of two x^2 tiles. I had the students tell me which tile I should use, based on the factors I was multiplying. So, for example, when I was doing the $3x$ times negative 1, they had to know to represent a

FIGURE 8.4. The example $[(3x + 2)(2x-1)]$ completed jointly by the whole class prior to beginning work on the task.

$$(3x + 2)(2x - 1) = 6x^2 - 3x + 4x - 2 = 6x^2 + x - 2$$

negative x using the shaded side of an x tile. In order to show them how the rectangle related to the product using symbols as we went along I had them figure out the product using the FOIL method. They got $6x^2–3x + 4x–2$. I then pointed to each symbol and its corresponding piece in the rectangle. For example, we looked at the six x^2 tiles and showed how they were derived from multiplying the x terms in the dimensions. We also looked at how the x tiles came from multiplying the constant terms (unit tiles) in one dimension by the x terms in the other dimensions, and so on.

I also paired up each -x piece with an x piece to show how negative terms and their opposites added to zero. I had the students draw lines between positive and negative paired terms to help keep track of how many were left when all the pairs had been made. This, we decided, was the same as -3x + 4x. We saw that the rectangular area formed by the tiles with these two dimensions was equivalent to the symbolic expression we found using the FOIL method. I think most of the students were watching me and the Architects were trying to do the same thing in their groups with the tiles. I saw lots of heads nodding and expressions like "Oh, I see it now." After this demonstration, I asked the groups to do the problems that appeared on a worksheet that was available in the middle of each group table. The worksheet contained six multiplication problems with the following directions:

> Use the tiles to show these multiplications. Make a sketch of your model. Label the dimensions clearly. Draw arrows to show any tiles that add to zero. Write the product.

    1. $2x(x–1)$
    2. $(x + 1) (x + 2)$
    3. $(x–2) (3x + 3)$
    4. $(x–3) (x + 3)$
    5. $(2x + 2) (2x–2)$
    6. $(x + 3) (x + 3)$

The problems were either a monomial times a binomial or a binomial times a binomial. The students were each given an individual sheet on which to record the solutions to each problem. I reminded them that, as always, I would expect all of them to be able to explain how and why they did what they did to solve each problem. I told the students to collaborate to figure out with the tiles what the answer was, but that the Architect should be the one building the solution. I have to designate one person as the builder in each group, or we would probably have chaos. After they had found an answer together, group members were to draw the tile solution on their individual worksheets and then write the solution in symbols. I gave them about half an hour to work on the six problems.

Implementation

As the students started to work in their groups, I walked around so that I could observe what they were doing. Students were engaged with the problems, and most of them seemed to be working cooperatively. One student, Kwali, was working on his own, drawing pictures and writing the symbols without paying attention to what his group was doing with the tiles. I didn't comment, since Kwali hasn't liked to work in groups all year. In the past, when I've tried to make him participate in a group, it was more disruptive than helpful. I choose my battles carefully, and this one did not seem important at the moment.

Most students did not have difficulty getting the tiles that represented each factor in a problem, even when there was a negative number or variable. However, I began to notice that they were having trouble figuring out what should go inside the rectangle to represent the product. After about 8 minutes of working on the problems, students in several groups had their hands raised and asked me to help them. What they really wanted was for me to tell them exactly what to do, step-by-step. I didn't want to just give them the answer, so at this point I told them to look again at the example we had done together. Then I told them to think harder and talk it over within their groups.

After several more minutes, things were not getting any better. It was then that I noticed that most of the Timekeepers were sitting back keeping time and not contributing to the group effort. I made an announcement telling all the students that their roles meant that they had special responsibilities, but that *everyone* had the responsibility to contribute to the group's mathematical work.

Several groups had what looked like the correct tiles down for the products but not in any form that looked like a rectangle. For example, on the first problem [2x (x–1)], I saw that the group with Brianna, Henry, Tyrone, and Whitney had a sketch in which they had not formed a rectangle (see Figure 8.5).

FIGURE 8.5. Brianna, Henry, Tyrone, and Whitney's sketch for 2x(x–1).

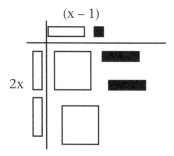

This was kind of an easy one, but if they didn't put it in a rectangle now, this would surely be a problem later on. So I pushed the tiles together into a rectangle for them and told them that they needed to pay attention to how the tiles on the dimensions were related to the tiles forming the product. As I rearranged the pieces, I told them it was like a puzzle and to think about it. I wasn't sure they knew what I was talking about, but at least they had a rectangle now. I told them to write the symbols for the tiles they had forming the product. I went through it with them step-by-step until they had the right answer recorded. Other groups were asking for me so I had to move on.

I was beginning to get nervous. The groups had been working for about half the period and I saw only one group that had completed more than half of the problems with the correct picture and symbol solutions on their worksheets. My hints did not seem to be getting them moving in the right direction. I thought, if I could get a student to go through the solution to one of the problems on the overhead, that would give the students a chance to see the process again. When I asked the group that was farthest along if they could explain to the class how they got their answers, Malcolm, the group leader, explained to me that they had worked the problems using the FOIL method from yesterday and then figured out by trial and error how to fit the tiles together to make a rectangle. Part of me wanted to scream when I heard that. They weren't using the tiles in the way that I had hoped. I told them to think some more about how they could have gotten the pictures without knowing the product ahead of time. They looked at me like I was from outer space. I thought to myself, "Oh, great, the one group that I thought was making connections is totally clueless!"

We had about 15 minutes left in the period; we were running out of time. At that point, I asked for everyone's attention and reported to the students that I was seeing lots of nice drawings of tiles but that they didn't seem to be using the pieces to get the solutions as they were supposed to. Vanetta raised her hand and asked if I would show them the steps for what to do again. At least 15 other students were mumbling in agreement, so I decided to give in and do another example with them and show them how to do it.

I decided to do problem 5 since most of the groups hadn't looked at it yet. The problem was $(2x + 2)(2x-2)$. So I asked the students what I should do first. Hakeem said, "First you gotta get all the pieces for 2x plus 2 and for 2x minus 2." So I put the proper pieces on the overhead and told everyone to do as I did. I then asked what was the next step. Tonya shouted out that I should put the pieces on the edges: "Put the first parentheses down the side and the second one across the top." I did this and then asked what the third step would be. Malcolm raised his hand and he was practically jumping out of his chair.

He said, "Ms. Butler, I just figured this out. Can I show it, can I, can I?" So I let Malcolm come up and complete the example.

I told him to hurry because the bell was going to ring in about 5 minutes. He said, "Look, you can figure out what pieces to use just by matching up the lengths going down and going across." He picked up an x^2 tile and an x tile and he matched up their lengths and said, "See, you need this much going down and this much going across so it has to be one of these square ones. And you just do that until you got 'em all." He then proceeded to fill in the rectangle (see Figure 8.6, first sketch).

Malcolm then announced that the answer had to be $4x^2 + 8x + 4$. I asked him if the +2 and the -2 meant you should do something different. He said, "Oh, yeah, these ones have to flip over because they are underneath the shaded blocks." He then flipped over the four x tiles and the four unit tiles below the two negative unit dimension tiles (see Figure 8.6, second sketch).

I asked him if he wanted to change his final answer now and he said, "Yeah, these four shaded ones cancel these four so it's $4x^2$ and negative 4 left." Vanetta corrected him by saying, "Four x^2 minus 4." I asked if everyone understood that, and most of the students nodded yes. I told the class to give Malcolm a round of applause for being brave enough to get up in front of the class. Since the period was about to end, I asked the Domestic Engineers to gather up the tiles and told everyone to take the worksheets home and to see if they could finish them for homework.

When I thought about this lesson later, I had mixed feelings. On the one hand, I was happy to see Malcolm get up in front of the class, especially since he actually came up with the right answer. On the other hand, when I really thought about what he had said in his explanation, I had to ask myself, "How mathematical was it? Was he making any of the connections I was hoping for? Was anyone else?"

FIGURE 8.6. Malcolm's solutions to $(2x + 2)$ $(2x-2)$.

DISCUSSION QUESTIONS

1. What issues was Monique concerned about in this lesson?
    a. What were the mathematical issues Monique was concerned about?
    b. What do you think Monique wanted her students to learn?
    c. Were there any nonmathematical issues of concern to Monique?
2. What do you think Monique's students were learning in the lesson?
    a. Were they making connections between the area representations and the symbolic procedures?
    b. Was Malcolm's explanation at the end of the class a good mathematical explanation? Why or why not?
3. What factors may have influenced whether students were making the connections Monique was hoping they would make?
    a. Were there things Monique was doing to support or inhibit the students' engagement in high-level thinking?
    b. What were the students doing that might have influenced their own learning?
4. What do you think Monique should do next? (Or if Monique had more time in the lesson, how do you think she should have responded to Malcolm?)

TEACHING NOTES

The content covered in the lesson presented in the case is the multiplication of monomials and binomials, a traditional algebra topic related to factoring polynomials. The *Curriculum and Evaluation Standards for School Mathematics* (NCTM, 1989) recommends a decreased emphasis on memorization of rules and procedures, in addition to a decreased emphasis on symbol manipulation in algebra. Monique's goal for her students is that they should understand the concepts underlying the common algorithm for multiplying monomials and binomials. She hopes the students will then be able to give meaning to the procedures they use for multiplication.

She also wants her students to connect the process of multiplication in this context with an area model through the use of algebra tiles and pictorial drawings of the tiles. These are important goals and are consonant with the current calls for reform. According to the NCTM Standards (1989), "Relating models to one another builds a better understanding of each" (p. 104). In Monique's case, she is hoping that through the use of the algebra tiles, students will understand how the monomial and binomial factors can represent the dimensions of rectangles with the areas of the rectangles corresponding to the symbolic products of the monomial and binomial terms.

Monique wants her students to build their understanding of algebraic operations using algebra tiles. However, she succumbs to the pressure of an upcoming district test and tries to expedite the students' learning process by first showing them a shortcut algorithm (FOIL) for multiplying binomials prior to their experiences with the manipulatives. At the end of the lesson, Monique wonders whether the students were making the connections she hoped they would. This aspect of Monique's case is similar to what happened in the case of Ron Castleman. Ron also introduced symbolic algorithms prior to having students work with nonsymbolic representations in the hope that this approach would make it easier for the students to make the connections between the symbols and the pictorial diagrams.

Cognitive Levels

In the setup of the task, Monique asks the students to work in groups to use algebra tiles for modeling areas in order to find products of monomials and binomials. Specifically, students are asked to follow a general process that involves the following:

- model the symbolic monomial or binomial factors in the product using the algebra pieces;
- arrange these models on an area chart so they form the dimensions of a rectangle;
- fill in the area of the rectangle with the appropriate algebra pieces and record the algebra piece solution onto a diagram;
- determine the area and show pictorially how it is determined (e.g., use arrows to indicate how positive and negative pieces are combined); and
- transform the rectangular area representation of the product into the corresponding symbolic representation of the product.

We consider this task—as setup—to be at the level of *procedures with connections*. In the setup of the task, Monique gives students a general pathway to follow in completing the task. Along the way, students are expected to connect multiple representations (symbolic, physical, and pictorial) of monomial and binomial products. During implementation, however, we consider the cognitive demands of the task to be lower than at setup. The majority of students in the class do not appear to be making the connections Monique is targeting and, therefore, we consider the implementation of the task to be at the level of *procedures without connections.* The students do not understand how the symbolic expressions with which they are working relate to the dimensions and area of a rectangle and they do not even engage in the multiplication process using the tiles. Many of the students obtain their answers through trial and error or by first performing the symbolic multiplication procedure and then finding the appropriate tiles to match, as though they are trying to fit the pieces of a puzzle together with no concern for what the puzzle pieces represent.

Factors

When the cognitive demands of a task decline between setup and implementation, it is important to reflect on the classroom factors that contributed to the change in cognitive demands. The presence or absence of these factors can make the difference between a task's being implemented as intended or being reduced to a form that has less potential for engaging students in high-level processes. *These are ideas toward which the case discussion should be steered.*

Building on students' prior knowledge. This is a case where students' prior experiences, including some provided by Monique, may be interfering with their ability to make the connections Monique is hoping they will make. Monique thought that first exposing students to the FOIL algorithm for multiplying binomials would facilitate their understanding of the multiplication process using the tiles. During the lesson, many of the students are unable to follow through an entire solution using the tile representation because they want to start with the FOIL method instead. Also, many students did not have previous experience with an area model for multiplication and have difficulty understanding how the rectangles are relevant to solving the problems in the task.

Challenges become nonproblems. Because many of Monique's students do not really understand how the factors and products relate to the area model for multiplication, they are unable to form the rectangular areas and use them to find solutions. Instead, they engage in symbol manipulation only, without spending time thinking about the connections between the symbols and the algebra tiles or their drawings of the tiles. For example, many of the students generate arrangements of isolated groups of tiles, rather than forming rectangular areas needed to see the relationships between the factors and the dimensions. Thus, this crucial part of the task ceases to be problematic for them. Also, many of the students use the FOIL method to solve the binomial products, rather than working with the rectangular areas first. Once they obtain the product using the symbolic algorithm, they simply use trial and error to form the rectangles. Therefore, they are not making any connections between the tiles, the rectangular areas, and the symbolic algorithm.

Students press the teacher to simplify the task. There are several points during the lesson at which the students seem to be pressing Monique to simplify the task for them. Monique resists this pressure successfully for most of the lesson by redirecting the students' attention to reviewing examples or by asking them to think harder. However, as time goes on, Monique begins to lose her resolve. For example, with 15 minutes left in the lesson, several students ask Monique to show them the steps again for solving the task. Since many of the students are not really focusing on the solution process Monique had hoped they would, she "gives in" and quickly goes through another example with the students, with little time spent justifying or explaining the underlying meaning of the solution steps. This action changes the emphasis of the task from focusing attention on exploring with the tiles and rectangular areas to working through a step-by-step process for successfully solving the task.

Students not held accountable for high-level processes. Monique does not always hold students accountable to make the connections among representations she is hoping they will when they explain their solution strategies. During the whole-class discussions, she often asks students to state procedural steps without necessarily asking them to articulate any connections among the symbols, tiles, and drawings. When Monique presses students for further elaborations, they often stop short of answering in a way that would reveal what they understand about the relationship between multiplication and the area of a rectangle.

Time. Monique starts out by giving students plenty of time to explore the problems in the task, but as time marches on she begins to grow nervous about whether the students will complete the task. The rushed nature of the last 15 minutes of the lesson may discourage the kind of exploration of the solution strategies presented that might have illuminated some of the connections Monique is hoping to bring to the forefront with her students. For example, Monique wonders at the end of the case whether Malcolm's explanation was mathematical enough or whether he was actually making the connections between the symbolic process and the dimensions and area of the rectangle. Because time was running out, she encouraged him to hurry through his explanation, and there was no time to ask Malcolm to provide elaborations or justifications that might have provided answers to Monique's questions.

Additional Layers of Interpretation

An additional issue that this case raises is how teachers can balance the pressures of preparing students for externally mandated tests that are heavily oriented toward basic skills with their goals of providing students with adequate time to explore mathematical concepts in depth and to develop high-level thinking and reasoning skills. In Monique's case, she was required to keep pace with semester exams administered across the district. Because she did not think the results of these exams would give her adequate assessment information about her students' conceptual understanding, she chose to create her own semester exams that were oriented more toward the kinds of mathematical activities in which she was trying to engage her students.

Another issue that could be discussed in the context of this case is Monique's approach to organizing her students into groups or cooperative learning. In Monique's case, students are assigned specific roles within their groups and with each role comes a set of responsibilities. One advantage to this approach is that each student has something to do; therefore, participation in the group activity across the class is potentially increased. One disadvantage to giving students preassigned roles within groups is that the roles can sometimes be overspecified such that some students limit the ways in which they participate in the group. For example, the group recorder may not participate in the discussion fully because the preassigned role is to record, not to discuss.

Another issue raised in this case is the manner in which students should be provided with opportunities to learn both deep-seated mathematical ideas and concepts *and* algorithmic procedures. Like Ron Castleman, Monique teaches the procedural algorithms first and then moves on to a more conceptual approach. Participants may suggest that Monique should instead have begun with the algebra tiles and then used those experiences to develop symbolic algorithms for multiplying the symbolic expressions. This approach might have helped to alleviate the problem that many students have in the case because the symbolic algorithm interferes with their ability to use the tiles meaningfully.

CHAPTER 9

Organizing Data

FIGURE 9.1. Opening activity to be completed prior to reading the case of Nicole Clark.

> *Part 1*
>
> You and the members of your class have just completed a unit on data analysis. As a culminating project for the unit, you and the members of your small group are to design a data collection activity to answer the question "What Is Your Favorite—?" Once you have collected the data, you need to analyze the data and create a graph.
>
> *Part 2*
>
> The graph assigned to Part 1 has been completed. You and the members of your group have now been asked to make a presentation to the class about your work. The goal of the presentation is to communicate to the class the most important mathematical ideas in your graph. What points should be addressed in your presentation?

THE CASE OF NICOLE CLARK

Nicole Clark is a teacher at a middle school that recently opened in a small city. The entire curriculum at the school is enriched by the arts, although students are recruited not on the basis of their talents, but rather on their expressed interest in learning through arts-centered ideas and projects. A major focus of the school's instructional program is the enhancement of student confidence and self-esteem. Students can gain self-confidence through the school's emphasis on bilingualism and the commitment to provide every student with the opportunity to learn and use both Spanish and English. This was particularly important given that the majority of students were Latino and many were English Language Learners.

Nicole taught at several elementary schools prior to accepting the position at the new school. She is a warm and caring person who believes deeply that all children can learn; she was eager to work in a school that was committed to providing opportunities to students who had been previously underserved. This was of particular importance to her since as a student she had felt that many of her mathematics teachers did not believe that she could succeed. As a result, she did not have the mathematics and science background needed to pursue her dream of being a pediatrician. Nicole saw her ability to develop curriculum that would foster positive self-esteem and to address students' social and emotional needs as among her greatest strengths as a teacher.

Nicole Clark Talks About Her Class

My sixth-grade class recently began a unit on data analysis. Early this week I gave my students the assignment to conduct a survey in the school, completing the question, "What is your favorite—?" The project consisted of three components: (1) determining the question and designing the data collection; (2) organizing the data and creating a graphic display; and (3) presenting the completed graph to the class. I asked students to work in their groups and provided several class periods for the project.

Up to this point, we had discussed different ways of representing data, using the graphs from *USA Today*. During these discussions, we talked about the type of representation that was used (e.g., pictograph, pie graph, histogram, line graph), how the graph helped one understand a data set, what could be learned about the data set from the graph, and issues of scaling (e.g., how to represent the number of people who were included in the sample). I thought that the students had a basic understanding of graphs and my goal for this assignment was to give them a meaningful experience in data collection and organization. By having students collect data on a topic of their choice, I thought that the project would be more interesting to them. Also, since all groups would have different data sets, the discussions about the graphs would be open-ended and unpredictable but would provide a rich opportunity for the entire class to reflect on the meaning of the data. Although I knew that the open-endedness of the assignment would raise some issues for students (e.g., How should we select a topic? How should we decide who should be included in the sample? What type of graph should we use?), I thought that they had sufficient experiences to draw on and that the group collectively should be able to work through these issues. By creating their own graphs, I thought that they would better understand the issues involved in representing data and, hence, would be better able to read and interpret data from a variety of sources. In addition to being part of the curriculum, I saw this as an important life skill.

The third component of the project, presenting the graphs to the class, was very important to me since it fit with my goal for the students to become more comfortable with public presentation and discussion. I had been trying during the first month of school to create an atmosphere of trust and mutual respect in the classroom that was safe for thinking and speaking. Many of my students arrived at middle school with the assumption that it was acceptable to criticize fellow students for doing something they characterize as "dumb" or "stupid." I had been encouraging students to question each other's ideas, yet demanding that they respect each other as persons. Discussion in my classroom has been further complicated by the fact that many of my students speak English as a second language and tend to be self-conscious and somewhat nervous about talking in class. Since I speak a little Spanish myself, I try to provide some explanation in both languages and encourage students to respond to or ask questions in either language. This sends the message that both languages are valued, and I think it helps students learn vocabulary in the language with which they have less experience, whether it is English or Spanish. I also thought that working collaboratively in a small group of peers and using graphic displays to communicate information would support both students' mathematics learning and communication skills.

The task seemed accessible to my students, and they were engaged for several days selecting the topic, surveying students in the school, compiling data, and creating graphs. Since I wanted my students to do their own mathematical thinking, I did not want to guide their observations or let them think that their job was to second-guess what I had in mind. I answered questions throughout the process, and provided guidance to keep students on track, but left students to develop and implement a plan without interference from me.

The graphs that my students created were works of art. They had used markers, colored pencils, water colors, and crayons to create visual displays that would have made the art teacher proud. Some students took great care with labeling the graphs, using stencils and calligraphy rather than relying on their own handwriting. A few students created graphs that were unique in design (e.g., a television served as a border for the graph on favorite TV shows). All in all, I was very impressed with the creativity that my students had demonstrated.

Setup

Today, students were to make presentations about their graphs. I gave each group 10 minutes to choose the spokesperson for the group, to decide whether they wanted to present at the board or at their table, and to determine the most important mathematical ideas they wanted to communicate about their chart. I did not want to be too prescriptive about the presentation and therefore decided not to identify key elements that should be included. It was my hope that the group members would communicate their ideas with one another and reach consensus about what was most important.

Implementation

As the groups began their discussion, I circulated around the room, stopping for a few moments at each group to ask what they had decided and to ensure that they were attending to the task. The overriding concern among the groups seemed to be selecting a presenter. At one table where the discussion seemed to be at an impasse, I suggested that members of the group vote for their choice for presenter. When this resulted in a tie, the students decided to have those who wanted to be group spokesperson write their names on a piece of paper and then randomly select one of the papers. I was anxious for the students to get down to what I considered to be the most important part of what I had asked them to do—deciding on the ideas that they wanted to convey. I looked at my watch to make sure that we were on schedule. I wanted to have enough time for at least two groups to present their graphs.

It had occurred to me that since this was the first time my students would be making presentations, they might be reluctant to volunteer. Therefore, I decided to assign each group a number and to put each number in the "winner's envelope" and randomly select the group that would make the first presentation. When 10 minutes had passed, I called the students together and indicated that we were ready for the first presentation. I reached into the envelope, pulled out one paper, and announced that "cuatro" (group 4) would go first. The group indicated that Juan would be the spokesperson, and the entire group—Maria, Carlos, Jennifer, Juan, and Mark—moved to the front of the room. I had worked hard to create a sense of shared ownership of the project and I was thrilled that the group wanted to support Juan. I explained to the class that our job was to be good listeners and to try to understand the information that was being presented.

Juan indicated that his group had conducted a survey on students' favorite television programs and listed the names of the programs that were shown on the graph—*The Simpsons*, *The Fresh Prince of Bel-Air*, *In Living Color*, and *Teenage Mutant Ninja Turtles* (see Figure 9.2).

FIGURE 9.2. Juan's group's graphical representation of data they collected about students' favorite television programs.

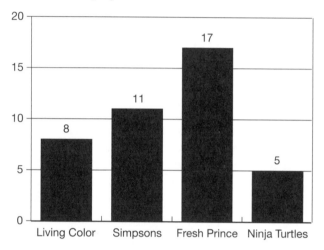

At this point, I expected Juan and the members of the group to report what they had concluded from their survey, but instead they began to whisper quietly among themselves, forming a small circle in the front of the room. I was a bit puzzled by this, since I thought that they had had sufficient time to work out what they planned to present. I was anxious for them to continue, but wanted to give them enough time to work through things on their own without my interference. The students in the class were very quiet during this time, showing respect for the group and their apparent struggle to figure out what they wanted to present. After 3 minutes, which seemed like an eternity to me, I asked if the group was having trouble moving forward. I wanted to be supportive yet not controlling or directive, while at the same time ensuring that all students in the class remained engaged. I thought that perhaps the group needed some assistance and I pointed out that asking for help was always positive and invited members of the class to provide assistance to the group. Kevin, one of the students in the class, suggested that the group tell the class how many students had voted for each TV program. Juan eagerly responded by reading the numbers off the graph. When Juan and his groupmates continued their whispered discussion, I suggested that they invite the class to ask questions about the graph. I hoped that by opening the discussion up to the students, the important ideas that I wanted to bring out for discussion would be raised (e.g., Why had they chosen a bar graph to represent the data? What question were they trying to answer with the survey they conducted? How was the sample selected? What was the relationship between the scaling they used and the responses to each category?).

Hands shot up all over the classroom and Juan began calling on students. I was ecstatic to see my students actively participating. Students asked questions such as: "How did you decide which TV shows to include?" "How long did it take to design the graph?" "How did you divide the work?" "Whom did you ask to complete the survey?" Juan began answering the questions, at first with some hesitation, but growing in confidence with each successive question. At times, he referred a question to another member of the group, hence recognizing the contributions of group members. The group was elated. I was pleased to see my students engaged, but I thought that they were focusing too much on the design of the chart and the process by which the group constructed the chart and not enough on the mathematics. I asked Juan how I could tell which was the favorite program by looking at the graph. He indicated that I could tell by looking at the numbers along the top of the bars. Since I was trying to get at the relationship of the height of the bar to the frequency of the response, I asked if the numbers corresponded to the rectangles. The group responded in unison, "Yes!" but did not provide further elaboration. I thought that I had pressed enough on this point and decided to move on. I thanked the group for their presentation, and was thrilled when the class broke out in applause as the first group took their seats. This had been very difficult for them and they were beaming with pride.

We were now 30 minutes into the class. The first presentation had taken longer than I had expected, but it would still be possible to get in one more presentation before the period ended. I went back to the winner's envelope to select the next group. Following the lead of the first group, all members of the second group—Susan, Juanita, David, Miguel, and Edwardo—went to the front of the room. Susan, as spokesperson for the group, explained that they had asked students in the red, blue, and green barrios (subdivisions within the sixth-grade class) which of four movies—*Robo Cop, Die Hard, Lethal Weapon,* and *Teenage Mutant Ninja Turtles*—was their favorite (see Figure 9.3).

Susan indicated that each small square in the graph represented six people and the half square represented three people. Carlos, who was a member of the first group that presented, immediately asked how they had come up with this idea. Susan indicated that it had been Edwardo's suggestion that they do this. Edwardo smiled broadly, obviously pleased at Susan's recognition of his contribution to the project. Without urging, Susan turned to the class and asked if there were additional questions. I was pleased to see her take the initiative. Martina asked how many people there were all together in the chart. Susan repeated that one square equaled 6 people so that meant that 33 people had voted for *Robo Cop,* 21 for *Die Hard,* 24 for *Lethal Weapon,* and 9 for *Teenage Mutant Ninja*

FIGURE 9.3. Susan's group's graphical representation of data they collected about students' favorite movies.

Turtles. Since Susan had failed to answer the question that had been raised, I urged Martina to ask her question in another way. This time Martina asked, "How many do you have for a total?" Susan looked to the other members of the group and they responded in unison with "87."

Students in the class continued to ask questions of the group, most of which were nonmathematical in nature. For example, Ramon asked how the group had decided on the colors to use in representing each of the movies. Susan responded that the group had tried to pick a color that was tied to the movie in some way. The main character in *Ninja Turtles,* she explained, wore a red shirt. Therefore, they decided to make the squares that represented *Ninja Turtles* red. While I wished that students would focus on more than the surface features of the graph, I was reluctant to challenge them or to appear to criticize the graphs they had produced. I wanted my students to feel empowered and capable of doing mathematics, and, at this point, I did not think that pushing too hard would be helpful toward that end. Realizing that I had drifted away from the conversation for a moment, I took a quick look at my watch. Where had the time gone? I felt good about the engagement of students in the discussion and the respect they showed for each other. They were making progress and were feeling pretty good about themselves.

DISCUSSION QUESTIONS

1. How would Nicole Clark evaluate the class?
   a. Do you agree with her perspective?

   b. What was going on in her classroom?
   c. What do you suppose Nicole's students were learning?
   d. What mathematics could have been learned?
2. What was Nicole's purpose in asking her students to make
   presentations to the class?
   a. Do you think this was a worthwhile goal?
   b. Was her goal accomplished?
   c. How could Nicole have "struck a balance" between her affective and
      cognitive goals?
3. What classroom-based factors influenced what did or did not occur in
   the class?
   a. What teacher actions influenced the way the students engaged with
      the task?
   b. What student actions influenced the way the students engaged with
      the task?
4. How do you think Nicole should proceed the next day when the four
   remaining groups are asked to make their presentations to the class?

TEACHING NOTES

   Nicole Clark is a teacher who has two interrelated goals: mathematics
learning and the development of students' self-esteem. Self-esteem is important to Nicole because she knows that, without it, her students won't have a
chance. Thus, she has worked hard to create an environment where students
feel comfortable and are beginning to feel safe enough to present ideas and
question each other.
   The content she was covering in the lesson presented in the case—data
collection and analysis—has been recommended for inclusion in the middle-
school curriculum in recent years. According to the *Curriculum and Evaluation Standards for School Mathematics* (NCTM, 1989), "because of society's
expanding use of data for prediction and decision making, it is important that
students develop an understanding of the concepts and processes used in analyzing data" (p. 105). In addition, her emphasis on communication is consistent with current thinking about how students develop deep understandings
of mathematical ideas.
   Hence, her goals for this lesson in terms of content, process, and affect are
appropriate. In this case, however, Nicole finds herself faced with a dilemma.
The students are talking, but most of the talk is not about mathematics. She is
afraid to push too hard on the mathematics, since this may negatively impact

students' fragile egos, yet if she allows students to stay in a less mathematical, presumably safer space, students will not have the opportunity to learn what was intended. She ultimately decides not to push too hard and, as a result, students engage in very little mathematics.

Cognitive Level

The task at the heart of this case is the public presentation of graphs that various groups had created over the previous few days. The teacher instructed the groups "to determine the most important mathematical ideas that they wanted to communicate about their chart." We consider this task—as set up—to be at the *doing-mathematics* level. The complexity of the task is largely derived from its open-ended nature. There was not a predictable, well-rehearsed approach or pathway suggested by the task or task instructions, nor was an example provided by the teacher. In fact, the teacher was intentionally vague about what should be included in the presentation so as to encourage students to explore the nature of the graphs and question each other. Thus, students were left to determine what the important mathematical ideas were.

Although the majority of students were actively engaged throughout the lesson, they were not engaged in mathematical activity. Therefore, we consider the implementation of the task to be at the level of *no mathematical activity*. The presentations, and the discussions that preceded them, focused on nonmathematical aspects of the charts and graphs and organizational issues such as who was going to make the presentation. Although there were several references to more mathematical components of the charts (e.g., in the first presentation, when the teacher asked Juan how he could tell which was the favorite program; in the second presentation, when Martina asked how many people there were all together in the chart), the opportunities were not pursued. Follow-up questions could have been directed at the importance of a scale, how the scale was chosen, whether the scale was appropriate, and how the scale was indicated on the chart or graph.

There were other "missed opportunities." For example, there was no discussion by the presenters, the teacher, or the other students in the class about how the "favorites" were selected for inclusion in the graph (i.e., were these the shows that were identified most frequently by the students surveyed or did the graph represent a rank ordering of four preselected shows), the extent to which this sample of favorites provided any information about a larger segment of the population, or why bar graphs were selected to display the data. The assignment had the potential to engage students mathematically, but the potential of the task was not realized during implementation.

Factors

When a task declines between setup and implementation, it is important to consider the classroom factors that contributed to the change in cognitive demands. The presence or absence of these factors can make the difference between a task's being implemented as intended or being reduced to a form that has less potential for engaging students in high-level processes. *These are the ideas toward which the case discussion should be steered.*

Task expectations not clear enough. In this situation, it is likely that the task expectations were not clear enough to put students in the right cognitive space. The initial directions given by the teacher at setup may have been too open-ended for students. The teacher might have picked up on this as she traveled from group to group and noted that the students were focusing more on who should present the graph than on the content of the presentation itself. While the teacher did not want to be too directive with students, more guidance might have helped move their thinking into a more mathematical space.

Students not held accountable for high-level products or processes. Although the task as stated at setup clearly articulated that the presentation was to focus on "the most important mathematical ideas," this was never stressed by the teacher again during the discussions that preceded the presentations or during the presentations themselves. At some point, we might have expected the teacher to refocus the group on the mathematical aspects of the graphs, but this did not occur in an explicit way. Presumably, she was trying to do this by occasionally framing a question that was mathematical, but this was apparently too subtle a cue for students to pick up on. Reminders that, while there were many interesting questions that could be asked about the graphs, the goal was to focus on the *mathematical* questions might have helped refocus student efforts on the important mathematical ideas embedded in the task.

Modeling high-level performance. The *absence* of this type of support contributed to the decline in the task from setup to implementation. Once students started asking questions related to the design and construction of the graphs, and these questions were not challenged by anyone in the classroom (i.e., teacher, students, or presenters), the nonmathematical questions appeared to serve as models for low-level (and acceptable) performance. In the absence of *mathematical* questions posed by students, teacher modeling of high-level performance might have moved students into the intended cognitive space. For example, the question posed by the teacher concerning how to tell which was the favorite program by looking at the graph could have served as a catalyst for "getting into the mathematics." If she was concerned about pressing students too hard, she might have taken this as a "teachable moment," pointing out things that she had observed or questions that the graph had raised for her.

Scaffolding of student thinking. The absence of this kind of support of student thinking also contributed to the decline of the task from setup to implementation. Keeping the overall goal of a coherent mathematical explanation of the graph in mind, Nicole could have provided supports to assist students' realization of this goal. For example, during the first group presentation the teacher asked a question about how the students decided to represent the information in a particular way. Despite a nonelaborate answer to the question, the teacher didn't assist the students toward the construction of a better explanation. She could have, for example, asked the students whether they considered alternative representations, what the pros and cons might have been, and what features of a bar graph were particularly useful.

Additional Layer of Interpretation

Another issue that is raised in this case is the importance of student self-esteem. While the teacher may not have accomplished her mathematical goal, she accomplished much in the way of creating an atmosphere in which students learned to respect each other's ideas and to participate in discussions related to mathematical tasks. By allowing the class discussion to proceed as it did, she clearly succeeded in building a sense of mutual trust and safety for the students to participate in public discussion, but in so doing, she also allowed many mathematical issues to go largely unexplored.

It is important to make the point that while building a sense of mutual trust and safety may be a reasonable short-term goal, the long-term goal should be to place the exploration of mathematical ideas in the foreground of the discussion rather than in the background. It is crucial that the teacher ensure that the mathematics does not always get lost in the talk. Progress must be made toward building a trusting community and toward increased mathematical proficiency of students. After students become sufficiently comfortable with themselves as participants in classroom discourse, it is essential that their continued growth in self-confidence result from a perceived and actual increase in being able to do mathematics.

CHAPTER 10

Solving Problems

FIGURE 10.1. Opening activity to be completed prior to reading the case of Jerome Robinson.

Solve the following problems:

1. A man entered an orchard that had 7 guards and picked some apples. When he left, he gave the first guard half his apples and 1 apple more. To the second guard, he gave half his remaining apples and 1 more. He did the same to each of the remaining five guards and left the orchard with 1 apple. How many apples did he gather in all? Explain how you solved the problem.

2. Find the sum of numbers from 1 to 25 *without* using a calculator, just adding the numbers. Describe the strategy you used and why you think it worked.

3. There were there stacks of bills, one of $5, one of $10, and one of $20. If the total was $1,000 and no two stacks could have the same number of bills, what is a possible solution for the number of bills in each stack? Explain how you could find many solutions to this problem.

THE CASE OF JEROME ROBINSON

Jerome Robinson is a teacher at Thurston Middle School, which is part of a large urban district beset with financial problems. It is a school that for years was regarded as one of the worst in the district, with high staff turnover, poor attendance, low achievement of students, limited parental support for education, and lack of resources (e.g., outdated textbooks, limited numbers of calculators and computers). Teachers' vision for students had been based on low expectations and was limited to students' mastery of basic skills. Because Thurston was considered a school that was not expected to produce the best and the brightest students in the district, most teachers did not volunteer to teach there and opted for assignments in less-blighted sections of the city.

Jerome was different. He chose to come to Thurston 4 years ago to work with the principal and a small number of mathematics teachers who had a vision of turning things around and making Thurston the math and science center in the cluster of schools in which it was located. Jerome and his colleagues believed that the students at Thurston brought with them an array of problem-solving skills that helped them cope with the daily demands of urban living and that were not being tapped by the current mathematics program. They vowed to make a difference in student achievement by shifting the focus of mathematics instruction from drill-and-practice to developing conceptual understanding and problem solving.

Jerome is a 15-year veteran teacher who is certified in both early childhood and secondary mathematics education and holds a master's degree in elementary education. Although he has taught mathematics during his 4 years at Thurston, the majority of his prior experience was in self-contained elementary classrooms where he taught all subjects. As a result of his education and experiences, he is passionate about mathematics and at the same time is deeply concerned about educating the whole child. He wants desperately to improve the life chances and opportunities of the students he serves and sees his interaction with students as his greatest strength as a teacher.

Jerome Robinson Talks About His Class

I want my students to become competent and confident problem solvers. Being able to apply procedures and recall facts is simply not enough. They need to be able to think and reason so that they can tackle new problem situations they encounter, not only in the classroom but in life. They need to see mathematics as something more than mind-numbing repetitive exercises. At the beginning of the year when my seventh-grade students told me that they had never been good at math, I told them that they have never had math—they have had 6 years of arithmetic. I told them that if they hung around I would show them mathematics.

The place that I have moved to in terms of my thinking is that problem solving is not just another thing to teach in math; problem solving is the *only reason* to teach math. Students need to work on problems that are open to more than one solution method, that involve more than one step, and that allow them to draw on a range of strategies. They need to experience problems for which a solution path is not transparent and for which a procedure is not always available. They need to think and reason on a daily basis. These are the skills that will serve them best in the long run.

When I was working on my secondary math certification about 5 years ago, I took a course in problem solving that had a big impact on my view of mathematics teaching. We spent a lot of time in that course working on problems and discussing problem-solving strategies. Polya's (1985) four-step method for problem solving became an important guide for me and it is something that I have since used in all my classes. A poster on the wall of my classroom serves as a constant reminder of the four steps—THINK, PLAN, SOLVE, LOOK BACK.

One concern I have is that the seventh-grade curriculum is really full. I have to cover each of the 10 distinct content units since the citywide test that is given to all students in January and June is based on this material. The test is "high stakes" because it is used to determine placement into special programs (e.g., gifted and talented, Chapter 1) and high school mathematics courses. So problem solving has to be taught in addition to everything else. To make matters worse, I am using a new book this year that doesn't integrate problem solving very well. As a result, I am torn between marching through the material in the book in order to prepare my students for the test and doing problem solving. I finally decided to spend the entire class period each Monday doing problem solving and then to do a warm-up activity at the beginning of each class Tuesday through Friday that focuses on problem solving.

Since this is Tuesday, we will begin class with a problem-solving warm-up and then move on to the main lesson of the day, which will focus on comparing negative numbers and locating them on a number line. Although the warm-up problems are not necessarily connected to the topic of the lesson, they are always selected for a reason. In both of the problems selected for class today (the first two problems in Figure 10.1) I am trying to focus on the PLAN phase of the problem-solving process by getting students to consider different strategies that we have discussed such as thinking of a simpler problem, drawing a diagram, looking for a pattern, or working backward. In addition, unlike many of the textbook exercises, the warm-up problems require students to think. There is no predictable, well-rehearsed approach or algorithm explicitly suggested by the problems. Hence, students have to expend considerable effort to figure them out.

Setup

Students entered the classroom and found the first two problems in Figure 10.1 on the overhead. They knew that they should begin working on the problems as soon as they settled into their chairs.

Implementation

I took attendance and then visited the groups, checking to see what answers they had found for the two problems. I told students whether their answer was correct or incorrect and went on to the next group. I did not want to interfere with their discussion, but I wanted them to know whether or not they were on the right track. Students appreciated this feedback. Having the incorrect answer was not considered "bad"; it just signaled that there was more work to be done.

I looked at my watch and noted that students had been working for about 8 minutes. Although this was not much time, I had a lot I wanted to do during the period. I know I have a tendency to pack too many things into a 42-minute lesson, but there is so much to do and so little time!

I asked if anyone had an answer to the first problem. A very enthusiastic Tamika volunteered her answer of 8 apples. This wasn't the answer I was looking for. I asked what strategy she had used. She explained that she used "guess and check." I told Tamika that I did not think that her solution would work out. I asked the class if there was a better strategy that could be used for this problem. Students started offering suggestions such as "look for a pattern" and "build a table." No one had hit on the strategy that was likely to be most helpful. Finally, Jamal suggested "working backward." I agreed that this was the best strategy, but that it could be used in conjunction with "building a table." I proceeded to make the following table to keep track of the apples given to each of the guards (see Figure 10.2).

FIGURE 10.2. The table Jerome constructed to help solve the Apples and Guards Problem.

Guard	After	Work Backward	Before
7	1	$(1+1) \times 2$	4
6	4	$(4+1) \times 2$	10
5			
4			
3			
2			
1			

We did the first entry together. I explained that the problem stated that there was one apple left after giving apples to the guards, and entered 1 in the "After" column for guard seven. Since you gave "half the apples plus one to the seventh guard," I explained, then the apple that was left over plus the extra apple that you gave to the guard must be half of the apples. Therefore, 2 is half of the apples. So if you multiply 2 by 2, you would get the number of apples you had before giving any apples to the seventh guard. We recorded our calculation in the "Work Backward" column and entered a 4 in the "Before" column. We went on to do the next entry. I asked students what number should go in the "After" column. They enthusiastically responded "4." I then asked what should happen next. Michael volunteered that you needed to add 1 and multiply by 2 as we had done for guard seven. He went on to explain that the "Work Backward" column for guard six should be "$4 + 1 = 5$ and $5 \times 2 = 10$" and the "Before" column should be 10. Since it was now 15 minutes into the period, I needed to pick up the pace so that we could get through the next problem and onto the discussion of negative numbers. I told students to fill in the rest of the table for homework.

I then asked if anyone had an answer to the second problem. No one responded immediately so I went to the overhead and listed the numbers from 1 to 25 in a column. I drew a bracket connecting numbers 1 and 25 and asked students what the sum of the two numbers would be. They responded in chorus "26." I proceeded to draw brackets between successive pairs of numbers (e.g., 2 and 24, 3 and 23, 4 and 22), asking students to give me the sum of each pair (see Figure 10.3).

As I continued to mark off sets of 26, Hassan apparently recognized how to find the solution and held up his hand excitedly. He explained that you could determine the sum of 1 through 25 by finding out how many 26s there were and then adding that number of 26s. I commented that yes, you could add *or* you could multiply. I checked my watch again and decided that if they finished this problem for homework, we could take a minute or two and revisit one of the problems from yesterday, which I had asked students to complete last night.

I asked students to take out the problem from the previous day about the stacks of bills. *(There were three stacks of bills, one of $5, one of $10, and one of $20. If the total was $1,000 and no two stacks could have the same number of bills, what is a possible solution for the number of bills in each stack?)* I had selected this problem because there were many possible solutions and because the strategies of making a table, guess and check, and look for a pattern, which we had recently discussed, would be useful. The previous day, we had not made much progress, although several incorrect solutions had been offered. I asked if anyone had an answer he or she wanted to share. Anthony said that you could have

FIGURE 10.3. Diagram used by Jerome to show how to find the sum of the numbers 1 to 25.

13 $5 bills, 13 $10 bills, and 40 $20 bills. I told Anthony that he had the same number of $5 and $10 bills, and therefore, this solution would not work. I took this opportunity to remind my students that they needed to *look back* once they had a possible solution and make sure that it did not violate any of the problem conditions. Kyree then offered the solution of 4 $5 bills, 2 $10 bills, and 49 $20 bills. After taking a minute to mentally work through the arithmetic, I told Kyree that she had made a computational error and should review her solution.

At this point, I checked the time again—20 minutes had passed and I had not yet started the lesson. Since there appeared to be no other solutions for the stack-of-bills problem, I asked students to again work on it for homework.

Finally, I was ready to begin the lesson for the day. Problem solving is so important that it is worth the time spent. However, the students rarely take the problems seriously enough to complete them at home. This is pretty frustrating. Oh well, there is not much I can do about that. On to negative numbers!

DISCUSSION QUESTIONS

1. How would Jerome Robinson evaluate the class?
   a. Do you agree with his perspective?
   b. What was going on in his classroom?
   c. What do you suppose Jerome's students were learning?
2. What was Jerome Robinson's view of problem solving?
   a. In what ways did his actions support or contradict his beliefs about problem solving?
   b. In what ways is Mr. Robinson's view of problem solving consistent or inconsistent with the approach to problem solving being recommended by the National Council of Teachers of Mathematics (1989)?
3. In your view, were Mr. Robinson's students on their way to becoming mathematical problem solvers?
   a. What factors supported or interfered with the development of his students' problem-solving expertise?
   b. How could Mr. Robinson determine whether his students were attaining the problem-solving goals he had set for them?
   c. If Mr. Robinson found that his students were not becoming capable problem solvers, how might he alter his approach?

TEACHING NOTES

Jerome Robinson is a veteran teacher with a strong mathematics background and a deep commitment to educating the whole child. He and his colleagues are engaged in an enormous reform effort aimed at capitalizing on students' out-of-school problem-solving skills and knowledge in order to improve their in-school mathematical problem-solving and reasoning capabilities. According to Jerome, problem solving is the only reason to teach mathematics. Jerome wants to enable his students to make use of some problem-solving tools that he has found helpful in his own mathematics learning, such as the Polya (1985) model for problem solving (THINK, PLAN, SOLVE, LOOK BACK) and various useful problem-solving heuristics, such as thinking of a simpler problem, making a table, drawing a diagram, or working backwards.

Jerome's goal for his students—that is, to increase their problem-solving and reasoning capabilities—is an integral part of the calls for reform as reflected in the NCTM Standards (1989). Problem solving is one of the four overarching strands that cuts across all content areas and all grade levels as articulated in the NCTM Standards. According to the standards, students should be given ample opportunities to "develop and apply a variety of strategies to solve problems, with emphasis on multistep and nonroutine problems" (p. 75).

We recommend that participants spend some time exploring the problems in Jerome's task prior to reading the case. The three problems in the task are similar to those commonly found in typical middle-school and some high school textbooks. Later in this section, we have provided a set of possible solution strategies for each problem in the task. Exploring these strategies, as well as those generated by the participants, provides an important context for reading the case and understanding the issues that arise from it with regard to increasing students' problem-solving and reasoning capabilities.

Cognitive Levels

In the setup of the task, we consider this task—as set up—to be at the level of *doing mathematics*. In this case, Jerome is trying to focus his students' attention on mathematical processes, rather than on a specific content area. The problems in the task do not suggest particular algorithms or well-rehearsed approaches to solving them and all of the problems could be solved in multiple ways. In order to solve the problems, students must think about the problem situations and plan an appropriate way to go about finding solutions.

As the task plays out during the lesson, however, the cognitive demands of the task do not appear to remain at the level of *doing mathematics*. Students do not explore the problem situations and they do not reflect on multiple solution strategies. Instead, instruction is focused more on getting the correct answers to the problems using a method considered the most correct by the teacher. Thus, we consider the implementation of this task to be at the level of *procedures without connections*.

Factors

In the case of Jerome Robinson, the high-level cognitive demands of the task do not appear to be maintained as the class goes about working on and talking about the problems and their solutions. In fact, there is little evidence in the case of how the students thought about and solved the problems because most of the explanations about the problems are provided by Jerome, rather than by students. When the cognitive demands of a task decline between setup and implementation, it is important to reflect on the classroom factors that contributed to the change in cognitive demands. The presence or absence of these factors can make the difference between a task's being implemented as intended or being reduced to a form that has less potential for engaging students in high-level processes. These are ideas toward which the case discussion should be steered.

Emphasis on correct answer or procedure. Jerome's interactions with the students are highly focused on correct answers. When he interacts with groups, he does not comment on their solution strategies, but focuses on whether the final answer is correct. During the discussion of the Apples and Guards Problem, Tamika offered an incorrect answer and was not allowed to explain her strategy because Jerome thought it was not likely to work out. This student was essentially cut off from participating in the remainder of the discussion because she had not achieved the correct final answer. When no students offered what Jerome thought was the best strategy for solving the problem, he walked the students through it on the board. No other strategies for solving the problem were discussed. In general, Jerome tended to quickly point out students' errors in reasoning or computation, rather than allowing students to articulate their strategies and possibly detect their own errors either through the process of explaining or with the help of their peers.

Time. Jerome was very concerned about the amount of time spent on the first two problems, partly because the problems were intended as a warm-up activity. With only 8 minutes to work on two nonroutine problems, it was unlikely that many students had enough time to explore the problems fully or to plan more than one solution strategy.

Students not held accountable for high-level products or processes. Most of the explanations of solutions to the problems are provided by Jerome. Thus, Jerome essentially takes over the task for students, providing them with strategies for solving the problem, and he does not hold them accountable for explaining their own strategies or ways of thinking about the problems. The most students are asked to provide in the discussion of the problems is to call out specific problem-solving strategies that might be useful, such as "work backward," "look for a pattern," or "build a table." In other instances, students are asked to provide brief answers to the problems, which often are expected to follow from Jerome's strategy or fill up individual cells in the tables that Jerome set up to solve each problem.

Additional Layers of Interpretation

One additional issue raised in Jerome's case has to do with the role of problem solving in students' learning of mathematics in school. In the NCTM Standards (1989), problem solving is one of the four strands intended to cut across all content areas. At the middle-school level, problem-solving approaches are recommended to be used "to investigate and understand mathematical content" and as a means of helping students to learn to use mathematics meaningfully (p. 23). This suggests that problem solving is a process that is central to the entire mathematics curriculum, rather than a separate mathematical skill or topic. Jerome's stated beliefs about problem solving seem to be consonant with the notion of problem solving as a central mathematical process. However, the practical difficulties that arise make it very difficult for Jerome to teach problem solving in a way that coincides with his belief that problem solving is the only reason to teach mathematics. He is under pressure to keep pace with citywide unit tests, which are used to determine placement into special programs and high school mathematics courses. The curriculum used at his school does not integrate problem solving very well, so he decided to devote one full day per week in addition to daily warm-up exercises to problem solving.

POSSIBLE SOLUTION STRATEGIES

Problem 1

A man entered an orchard that had 7 guards and picked some apples. When he left, he gave the first guard half his apples and 1 apple more. To the second guard he gave half his remaining apples and 1 more. He did the same to each of the remaining five guards and left the orchard with 1 apple. How many apples did he gather in all?

Solution A (Figure 10.4). I started at the bottom of the table and worked my way up. Since there was one apple left after giving apples to the guards, I entered a 1 in the "number of apples left" column for guard seven. Since you gave "half the apples plus 1 to the seventh guard," then the apple that was left over plus the extra apple that you gave to the guard must be half of the apples. So if 2 (1 + 1) is half of the apples, then the number of apples left after giving apples to guard six must have been 4. So I worked my way up the table by adding the number of apples left to the extra one that was given to the guard and doubling this amount. So for guard six, 4 apples left plus 1 extra apple is equal to 5 apples. So the number of apples left after giving apples to guard five is 2 × 5 or 10.

Once I got to guard one and found that I had 190 apples left after giving him (or her) apples, then I must have had (190 + 1) × 2 apples to begin with. This would be 382 apples.

FIGURE 10.4. The table used in Solution A for Problem 1.

	Number of Apples Given Away	Number of Apples Left
Guard 1	½ of what was left + 1	190
Guard 2	½ of what was left + 1	94
Guard 3	½ of what was left + 1	46
Guard 4	½ of what was left + 1	22
Guard 5	½ of what was left + 1	10
Guard 6	½ of what was left + 1	4
Guard 7	½ of what was left + 1	1

Solution B (Figure 10.5). I decided just to focus on the number of apples left and to look for a pattern that would help solve the problem. I figured that the number of apples left after each "giveaway," plus 1, must equal one-half of the apples. Therefore, if I double this amount, I would get the number of apples left after the previous giveaway. So if I had 1 left in the end, then 2 must represent half the apples. Therefore, the number of apples left after the sixth guard got apples would be 4.

FIGURE 10.5. The table used in Solution B for Problem 1.

	Number of Apples Left	Differences Between Number of Apples Current Guard and Previous Guard Received
Guard 1	190	192
Guard 2	94	96
Guard 3	46	48
Guard 4	22	24
Guard 5	10	12
Guard 6	4	6
Guard 7	1	3

Following this logic, I added 4 + 1 and multiplied by 2 to get the number of apples left after the fifth guard got his apples and then $(10 + 1) \times 2$ to get the number of apples left after the fourth guard. I decided that instead of going any further on this, I would look for a pattern. Starting at the bottom of the table, I recorded the differences between the number of apples left after two consecutive guards received apples. There were 4 apples left after guard 6 received his apples and 1 apple left after guard 7 received his apples, for a difference of 3. There were 10 apples left after guard 5 received his apples and 4 apples left after guard 6 received his apples, for a difference of 6. There were 22 apples left after guard 4 received his apples and 10 apples left after guard 5 received his apples, for a difference of 12. The differences were doubling, so I completed the table by doubling the difference. I then figured out the number of apples left by adding the difference to the number of apples left from the previous guard. So for guard 3, the number of apples left was 46—the difference in apples left between guards 3 and 4 plus the number of apples left after guard four. When I got to the last entry, I added 190 and 192 to get 382 apples.

Solution C (Figure 10.6). The way I solved the problem was by working backward. I went through 7 guards. I had one apple at the end, so then I added one more and multiplied it by 2. So that was $2 \times 2 = 4$. I went to guard 6. He ended with 4, so $4 + 1 = 5$ and $5 \times 2 = 10$.

Solution D. I let x represent the number of apples that I had before giving any to a guard. Then ½ x + 1 is equal to the number of apples given away and ½ x–1 is the number of apples left. Since I know that after giving apples to

FIGURE 10.6. The table used in Solution C for Problem 1.

Guard	Ends	Work Backward	Start
7	1	$(1 + 1) \times 2$	4
6	4	$(4 + 1) \times 2$	10
5	10	$(10 + 1) \times 2$	22
4	22	$(22 + 1) \times 2$	46
3	46	$(46 + 1) \times 2$	94
2	94	$(94 + 1) \times 2$	190
1	190	$(190 + 1) \times 2$	382

the seventh guard I have one left, then ½ x – 1 = 1. Solving this equation, I get ½ x = 2 and x = 4. Now I know that the number of apples I have left after giving apples to the sixth guard is 4. I can just keep using the equation, substituting the number of apples left for the x. After I have done this seven times, I will have the answer to the question.

Problem 2

Find the sum of the first 25 consecutive whole numbers.

Solution A (Figure 10.7).

Solution B (Figure 10.8). There are 12 pairs of numbers that add up to 26, so that is 12 × 26 and there is one extra number, 13, for which there is no pair, so it is 12(26) + 13, which is equal to 325.

Solution C (Figure 10.9). Begin by thinking of a simpler problem. Instead of trying to find the sum of the numbers from 1 to 25, try to find the sum of the numbers from 1 to 5. I built a staircase model to show the numbers 1 through 5 (far left figure). Then I made a rectangle out of two similar staircases (middle figure). Then I could observe that the area of the staircase is ½ of the area of the new rectangle. Since the new rectangle is 5 × 6, the area is 30, so the area of the staircase is half of that, or 15. The sum of the numbers 1 to 5 is 15.

Now if I try to use this strategy on the numbers 1 to 25, I realize I would have a staircase that goes from 1 to 25 and a rectangle that is 25 × 26. The area of this rectangle would be 650. So the sum of the numbers 1 to 25 would be ½ of this amount, or 325.

FIGURE 10.7. Calculation method used in Solution A for Problem 2.

$$
\begin{array}{cccccccccccccc}
1 & + & 2 & + & 3 & + & 4 & + & \ldots & + & 22 & + & 23 & + & 24 & + & 25 & = & N \\
25 & + & 24 & + & 23 & + & 22 & + & \ldots & + & 4 & + & 3 & + & 2 & + & 1 & = & N \\
\hline
26 & + & 26 & + & 26 & + & 26 & + & \ldots & + & 26 & + & 26 & + & 26 & + & 26 & = & 2N
\end{array}
$$

$$26(25) = 2N$$

$$\frac{26(25)}{2} = N$$

$$13(25) = N$$

$$325 = N$$

FIGURE 10.8. Diagram used in Solution B for Problem 2.

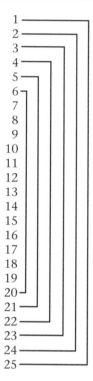

FIGURE 10.9. Diagrams used in Solution C for Problem 2.

Build a staircase
model

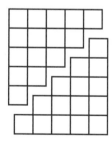

Make a rectangle
out of two staircases

The staircase has
an area that is ½
of the area of the
new rectangle

Solution D (Figure 10.10). I know the formula shown below for finding the sum of a set of numbers from 1 to n, so I just substitute the number 25 for n. This gives me 25(25 + 1)/2, which is equal to $^{650}\!/_2$, or 325.

Solution E (Figure 10.11). I decided to create a table and look at patterns of successive sums. So I made a column that showed the numbers to be added and another that showed the sum of the numbers. I did this for the numbers 1 through 10 so I could look for a pattern in the sums.

I tried to see if I could find a pattern between the "number of numbers" being added and the sum. After trying a few things that did not work, I noticed that if I had eight numbers, the sum was equal to $(8 \times 9) \div 2$. So if I multiplied a number like x by one more than the number (x + 1) and divided the product by 2, I would get the sum of the numbers from 1 to x. I tried this on a few other pairs and found that it worked. So applying this rule to the numbers 1 to 25, I figured that it would be $(25 \times 26) \div 2$, which was 325.

FIGURE 10.10. Formula used in Solution D for Problem 2.

$$\sum_{1}^{n} = \frac{n(n + 1)}{2}$$

FIGURE 10.11. The table used in Solution E for Problem 2.

Number of numbers being added starting at 1	Numbers to be added	Sum of the numbers
1	1	1
2	1 + 2	3
3	1 + 2 + 3	6
4	1 + 2 + 3 + 4	10
5	1 + 2 + 3 + 4 + 5	15
6	1 + 2 + 3 + 4 + 5 + 6	21
7	1 + 2 + 3 + 4 + 5 + 6 + 7	28
8	1 + 2 + 3 + 4 + 5 + 6 + 7 + 8	36
9	1 + 2 + 3 + 4 + 5 + 6 + 7 + 8 + 9	45
10	1 + 2 + 3 + 4 + 5 + 6 + 7 + 8 + 9 + 10	55

Problem 3 (Figure 10.12).

There were three stacks of bills, one of $5, one of $10, and one of $20. If the total was $1,000 and no two stacks could have the same number of bills, what is a possible solution for the number of bills in each stack?

Things I discovered:

- You must have an even number of $5 bills since the sum of the totals of the $10 and $20 bills will always be a multiple of 10.
- The value of the $5 stack plus the value of the $10 stack must be a multiple of 20. If the number of $5 bills has a factor of 4 (e.g., 4), then the number of $10 bills must be even. If the number of $5 bills does not have a factor of 4 (e.g., 10), then the number of $10 bills must be odd.
- The largest number of $5 bills you can have is 192. (If you have 192 $5 bills, then you must have 2 $10 bills and 1 $20 bill.)
- There are many solutions, but there is a pattern for solutions. If you continue this table you will find them all.

FIGURE 10.12. The table used to solve Problem 3.

$5 bills (value 5 × a)	$10 bills (value 10 × b)	$20 bills (value 20 × c)	Total Value
2	1	49	10 + 10 + 980
2	3	48	10 + 30 + 960
2	5	47	10 + 50 + 940
2	7	46	10 + 70 + 920
4	2	48	20 + 20 + 960
4*	4	47	20 + 40 + 940
4	6	46	20 + 60 + 920
4	8	45	20 + 80 + 900

* not a solution since the number of $5 bills and the number of $10 bills is the same.

PART III

USING THE CASES

CHAPTER 11

Assisting the Learning of Teachers

It has been argued that teaching needs to be parsed into a set of core practices that teachers can learn (Grossman & MacDonald, 2008). Professional education could then focus its efforts on developing teachers' ability to engage in the identified practices. Among the core practices, in our view, are the strategic selection and the skillful enactment of high-quality instructional tasks. In this chapter, we provide a rationale for focusing professional development on these aspects of instructional practice along with practical suggestions for using this book as a centerpiece of a professional education program centered on the selection and enactment of worthwhile, cognitively demanding tasks.

Focusing teachers' professional education on the selection and enactment of mathematical tasks makes sense for several reasons. First, classroom instruction is generally organized and orchestrated around mathematical tasks. That is, students' day-to-day work in mathematics classrooms consists of working on tasks, activities, or problems. For example, the TIMSS analysis of 100 eighth-grade lessons revealed that the delivery of content "was accomplished primarily by working through problems" (NCES, 2003, p. 144). Therefore, because the selection and use of mathematical tasks is central to the work that teachers do, it should be a key focus of teacher education.

Second, the tasks with which students engage constitute, to a great extent, the domain of students' opportunities to learn mathematics. According to Doyle (1983, p. 161), "tasks influence learners by directing their attention to particular aspects of content and by specifying ways of processing information." As we have discussed in earlier chapters, tasks that ask students to perform a memorized procedure in a routine manner lead to one type of opportunity for student thinking; tasks that demand engagement with concepts and that stimulate students to make connections lead to a different set of opportunities for student thinking. Hence, "there is no decision that teachers make that has a greater impact on students' opportunities to learn, and on their perceptions about what mathematics is, than the selection or creation of the tasks with which the teacher engages students in studying mathematics" (Lappan & Briars, 1995, p. 138). Therefore, learning to make decisions about which tasks to use to accomplish particular goals for student learning is a critical first step if the goal of instruction is to promote students' thinking and reasoning.

Third, in the TIMSS 1999 video study, the ability to maintain the high-level demands of cognitively challenging tasks during instruction was the central feature that distinguished classroom teaching in countries where students exhibited high levels of mathematics performance when compared with countries like the United States, where performance was lower and teachers rarely maintained the cognitive demands of tasks during instruction (NCES, 2003; Stigler & Hiebert, 2004). The authors concluded that U.S. eighth-grade students spend most of their time in mathematics classrooms practicing procedures regardless of the nature of the tasks they are given. Hence, in order to give U.S. students the same kinds of high-quality opportunities to learn that are provided in many other countries, teachers need to enhance their skill in supporting students' engagement in high-level tasks without taking over the thinking and reasoning for them.

Selecting high-level tasks and using them well will require providing teachers with professional education opportunities that are *transformative* in nature—catalyzing changes in teachers' long-held, underlying beliefs about effective teaching and learning of mathematics (Thompson & Zeuli, 1999). Specifically, teachers will need opportunities to thoroughly overhaul their thinking about what it means to know and understand mathematics, the kinds of mathematical tasks in which their students should engage, and how they can support their students' learning. The remainder of this chapter focuses on how such learning can be accomplished.

TRANSFORMATIVE PROFESSIONAL DEVELOPMENT

For the last decade, we have been using the Mathematical Tasks Framework (MTF) and the materials contained in this book as the focus of our professional work with pre-service and practicing teachers. We, along with our students and colleagues, have used these materials with teachers preparing to teach mathematics at the elementary-, middle-, and secondary-school levels, and also with teachers who are already certified to teach. In teacher preparation programs, this book has been used in methods courses and also in courses whose intent is to teach mathematics content. We have used it with teachers in professional development projects in urban and suburban school settings; in large and small school districts; with veteran teachers and also with novices; and with teachers whose base curriculum is quite innovative, and also with those who are using more conventional mathematics textbooks.

Our work can be characterized as an effort to bridge the divide that often exists between professional development and the improvement of practice. Frequently, teachers learn new ideas and practices in professional development but fail to implement them once they are back in their classrooms. Often, this is because they don't know when to implement them in the real-time, deeply contextualized world of classroom teaching or fail to understand their purpose. In our work, three features of our professional development model address this challenge: (a) all professional development is situated in the actual work of teaching (i.e., it is practice-based); (b) instances of practice are linked to a larger set of ideas about mathematics teaching and learning through the Mathematics Task Framework; and (c) scaffolded field experiences provide opportunities for teachers to apply the ideas and principles that emerge from professional development in their own classrooms. Each of these aspects of our work is discussed in the following sections.

Practice-Based Professional Development

In a seminal paper on this topic, Ball and Cohen (1999, p. 6) argue that "teachers' everyday work could become a source for constructive professional development" through the development of a curriculum for professional learning that is grounded in the tasks, questions, and problems of practice. They propose that teachers' professional practice be seen both as a site for professional learning and as a stimulus for developing inquiry into practice from which many teachers could learn. To accomplish this goal, they argue that records of authentic practice—curriculum materials, narrative or video summaries of teachers planning for and/or engaging in instruction, and samples of student work—should become the core of professional education, providing a focus for sustained teacher inquiry and investigation.

In general, the activities we design for use in professional development sessions are centered on "records of authentic practice" (Smith, 2001, p. 7). The mathematical tasks and cases in this book are examples of practice-based materials. These materials, in particular, are drawn from the lived experiences of urban middle-school teachers and, as such, provide vivid images of life in real classrooms. They serve to ground abstract ideas related to content and pedagogy and help teachers "develop skills of analysis and problem-solving, gain broad repertoires of pedagogical technique, capitalize on the power of reflection, and experience a positive learning community" (Merseth, 1999, pp. xi–xii). Though there remains much to learn about the efficacy of this approach to professional learning (Silver, 2009), there are many reasons to be optimistic about its potential.

Linking Particulars with Generalities Through the Mathematical Tasks Framework

Three key ideas about mathematics teaching and learning emerge from the research on mathematical tasks on which this book is based and provide the underpinnings for our professional development efforts: (1) cognitively challenging mathematical tasks provide critical opportunities for students to develop the capacity to think and reason with and about mathematics; (2) cognitively challenging tasks unfold during classroom instruction in predictable ways, frequently resulting in the decline of the cognitive demands (i.e., a task that starts out as challenging is transformed during instruction to a less rigorous exercise); and (3) a set of classroom-based factors is associated with the maintenance and decline of cognitively challenging tasks during instruction and highlight the classroom actions and interactions that determine the extent to which students were able to maintain a high level of intellectual engagement with challenging mathematical tasks (Stein, Grover, & Henningsen, 1996; Henningsen & Stein, 1997).

The MTF, which is the embodiment of these ideas, serves as a lens through which to examine instruction and provides a way of linking particular classroom events to a larger set of ideas about mathematics teaching and learning. For example, in the case of Fran Gorman and Kevin Cooper (Chapter 6), Fran is faced with a classroom of students who are confused about how to use pattern blocks. Fran's assistance involves having students start over so she can lead them through a series of steps that result in the correct answer. Teachers reading the case see that students are learning to use the patterns blocks but are not developing a conceptual understanding of fraction multiplication as intended. Although this realization may be useful to teachers in a narrow range of situations, viewing this particular event through the lens of the MTF makes salient that although the task was initially set up as a high-level task (*procedures with connections*), the cognitive demands of the task declined during implementation due largely to the fact that the teacher took over the thinking and told students how to solve the problem. As we argue in Chapter 3, by recognizing events as instances of something larger and more generalizable, knowledge can accumulate and "lessons learned" can serve to catalyze changes in teachers' own instructional practices. Hence, in our work, theories or ideas are abstracted from the examination of specific classroom artifacts rather than being learned in advance or outside of practice.

Scaffolded Field Experiences (SFEs)

Scaffolded field experiences (SFEs) provide opportunities for teachers to "experiment with instructional innovation while receiving support" (Borasi & Fonzi, 2002, p. 91). In our work, SFEs serve to bridge the divide between the learning that occurs in professional development settings and the teaching that takes place in real classrooms. Although the term *scaffolded field experience* may suggest pre-service education learning opportunities, we intend it to apply to in-service education as well. In our work with in-service teachers, for example, between any two professional development sessions, teachers are expected to try something out in their own classroom and return to the next session with written reflections and any evidence or artifacts (i.e., student work, lesson plans, transcribed or para-phrased interactions, video- or audio-taped segments of the lesson) that would help them tell the story of how the new ideas played out in their classroom.

Central to our SFEs is a set of tools that provide support for teachers as they seek to test out new ideas in their own classroom. According to the National Academy of Education (1999, p. 35), "tools—including student assessments, curriculum and professional development materials, software programs, questionnaires for probing community attitudes, and protocols for observing classrooms or professional meetings—are powerful carriers of theory and knowledge. Carefully designed tools that educators find useful in their practice can become a powerful means of changing educational practice." In our view, tools provide a scaffold for teachers—a structure that allows them to do something that they would otherwise not be able to do. As such, they provide support to teachers who are developing and refining their instructional practices.

The tools that are central to our work are based on the research on mathematical tasks described in this book and are related to the MTF that was discussed in the previous section. The Task Analysis Guide (TAG) (Figure 1.2) provides a general list of features of mathematical tasks at each of the four levels of cognitive demand, and as such it can be used to analyze the potential of tasks to support students' thinking and reasoning. The Factors Associated with Maintenance and Decline (Figure 2.1) can be used to pinpoint the classroom-based factors that account for the ways in which tasks typically unfold during instruction. Although these tools can be used to analyze the tasks and cases found in this volume, their real value is that they can be flexibly used by teachers to gain greater insights into instruction in their own classrooms.

One additional tool related to the MTF that has been central to our recent work is the Thinking Through a Lesson Protocol (TTLP), shown in Figure 11.1. The TTLP (Smith, Bill, & Hughes, 2008) is intended to make teaching with high-level tasks more "intellectually controllable" (Stein & Kim, in press) and, we argue, more successful. By encouraging teachers to think through key aspects of a lesson (e.g., the range of methods a student might use to solve a task, the misconceptions students might have and the errors they might make, questions that a teacher might ask to assess and advance student thinking) *prior to* the lesson, teachers are better positioned to maintain the demands of a task during instruction and to tie students' diverse ways of thinking to key disciplinary ideas.

FIGURE 11.1. Thinking Through a Lesson Protocol

Part 1: Selecting and Setting up a Mathematical Task

- What are your mathematical goals for the lesson (i.e., what is it that you want students to know and understand about mathematics as a result of this lesson)?
- In what ways does the task build on students' previous knowledge, life experiences, and culture? What definitions, concepts, or ideas do students need to know in order to begin to work on the task? What questions will you ask to help students access their prior knowledge and relevant life and cultural experiences?
- What are all the ways the task can be solved?
  - → Which of these methods do you think your students will use?
  - → What misconceptions might students have?
  - → What errors might students make?
- What particular challenges might the task present to struggling students or students who are English Language Learners (ELL)? How will you address these challenges?
- What are your expectations for students as they work on and complete this task?
  - → What resources or tools will students have to use in their work that will give them entry to and help them reason through the task?
  - → How will the students work—independently, in small groups, or in pairs—to explore this task? How long will they work individually or in small groups/pairs? Will students be partnered in a specific way? If so, in what way?
  - → How will students record and report their work?
- How will you introduce students to the activity so as to provide access to all students while maintaining the cognitive demands of the task? How will you ensure that students understand the context of the problem? What will you hear that lets you know students understand what the task is asking them to do?

Part 2: Supporting Students' Exploration of the Task

- As students are working independently or in small groups:
  - → What questions will you ask to help a group get started or make progress on the task?
  - → What questions will you ask to focus students' thinking around the key mathematical ideas in the task?
  - → What questions will you ask to assess students' understanding of key mathematical ideas, problem-solving strategies, or the representations?
  - → What questions will you ask to advance students' understanding of the mathematical ideas?
  - → What questions will you ask to encourage all students to share their thinking with others or to assess their understanding of their peers' ideas?
- How will you ensure that students remain engaged in the task?
  - → What assistance will you give or what questions will you ask a student (or group) who becomes quickly frustrated and requests more direction and guidance in solving the task?
  - → What will you do if a student (or group) finishes the task almost immediately? How will you extend the task so as to provide additional challenge?
  - → What will you do if a student (or group) focus on nonmathematical aspects of the activity (e.g., spend most of their time making a poster of their work)?

Part 3: Sharing and Discussing the Task

- How will you orchestrate the class discussion so that you accomplish your mathematical goals? Specifically:
  - → Which solution paths do you want to have shared during the class discussion? In what order will the solutions be presented? Why?
  - → In what ways will the order in which solutions are presented help develop students' understanding of the mathematical ideas that are the focus of your lesson?
  - → What specific questions will you ask so that students will:
    - * make sense of the mathematical ideas that you want them to learn?
    - * expand on, debate, and question the solutions being shared?
    - * make connections between the different strategies that are presented?
    - * look for patterns?
    - * begin to form generalizations?
- How will you ensure that, over time, each student has the opportunity to share their thinking and reasoning with their peers?
- What will you see or hear that lets you know that all students in the class understand the mathematical ideas that you intended for them to learn?
- What will you do tomorrow that will build on this lesson?

(Reprinted with permission from *Mathematics Teaching in the Middle School*, copyright © 2008 by the National Council of Teachers of Mathematics. All rights reserved.)

The tools serve to instantiate key aspects of the MTF, thereby bringing the ideas learned in professional development into teachers' classrooms as they engage in the SFEs. For example, an initial SFE might ask teachers to identify a task from their curricular materials that they intend to use in the next few weeks and analyze the cognitive demands of the task using the Task Analysis Guide. This SFE helps teachers take the ideas learned from professional development (i.e., tasks can be characterized in terms of their cognitive demands, and not all tasks provide the same learning opportunities for students) and apply them to their own curricular materials with the aid of the TAG. Over time, SFEs can expand to include the full cycle of teaching activities (e.g., planning, teaching, and reflecting on a lesson). Teachers also need opportunities during professional development sessions to share the results of SFEs with their peers and to receive feedback (see Hughes, Smith, Hogel, & Boston, in press, for additional details on this process). In these conversations, the tools (e.g., TAG) provide a common language for talking about teaching and learning.

Our model of professional development is shown in Figure 11.2. The SFEs (top arrow) and the classroom artifacts that result from enactment of the SFEs (bottom arrow) serve as a bridge between the professional development setting, where new ideas are learned, and the classroom, where new ideas are implemented.

KEY PROFESSIONAL ACTIVITIES RELATED TO MATHEMATICAL TASKS

There are three major activities related to tasks that are, in our view, central to teachers' professional development experience: recognizing that mathematical tasks vary in level of cognitive demand; exploring challenging mathematical

FIGURE 11.2. Professional development model that supports the improvement of practice.

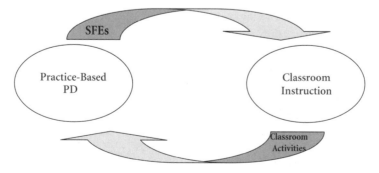

tasks; and analyzing and reflecting on instruction. In this section, we describe and provide examples of each type of task-related activity and show how they support the improvement of practice.

Recognizing That Tasks Vary in Level of Cognitive Demand

By learning to recognize differences between high-demand and low-demand tasks, teachers refine their capacity to think about the kind and level of thinking that various mathematics tasks may require of their students. As we argued in Chapter 1, the goal is not to privilege high-level tasks over all others, nor is it to determine with certainty that a particular task is in the high-level versus low-level category for all students at all times, but rather to ensure that teachers can appropriately match their goals for student learning with tasks that have the potential to reach the desired goal.

Comparing two tasks. We generally begin our work by presenting teachers with two tasks and asking them first to solve each task and then to consider how the two tasks are the same and how they are different. The tasks selected for this comparison should have some surface level similarity, but they should differ with respect to the level and kind of thinking required to solve them, the range of ways in which they can be solved, and the access they provide to students with a range of prior knowledge and experience.

For example, the Carpeting and Fencing tasks (Figures 1.1 and 1.2) provide a good basis for this activity. Each involves finding the area of rectangle, yet they differ with respect to the way in which the area formula is used, the number of ways the problem can be solved, and the need to generalize beyond a specific case. We have also found that two patterns, as shown in Figure 11.3, can also be used to set up the desired contrast. (Note that the Square Pattern Task is one of the tasks included in the task sort in Figure 1.3.)

Analyzing a set of tasks. After teachers have had a chance to consider the demands of two tasks, we provide them with a larger, more diverse set of tasks and ask them to separate the tasks into two categories (high-level and low-level) and to develop a set of criteria to describe the tasks in each category. This process is described in some detail in Chapter 1, and a more detailed discussion can be found in Chapter 12. (Additional details on orchestrating this activity, as well as task sets that focus on elementary-, middle- , and high-school mathematics that can be used in the sort, can be found in Smith, Stein, Arbaugh, Brown, & Mossgrove, 2004. In addition, tasks in the middle-school sort can be found at *http://www.tcpress.com.*)

FIGURE 11.3. Two tasks with surface-level similarities that differ with respect to cognitive demand.

Square Pattern Task	Hexagon Pattern Task
Using the side of a square pattern tile as a measure, find the perimeter (i.e., distance around) of each train in the pattern block figure shown below. [The edge of the square has a length of one.]	For the pattern shown below, compute the perimeter for the first four trains, determine the perimeter for the tenth train without constructing it, and then write a description that could be used to compute the perimeter of any train in the pattern. [The edge of the hexagon has a length of one.]

Note: Hexagon Pattern Task published by the Math Learning Center, *www.mathlearningcenter.org.*

After teachers have had a chance to consider the characteristics of high- and low-level tasks at a general level, finer level distinctions can be made (e.g., high-level tasks include both *procedures-with-connections* tasks and *doing-mathematics* tasks) and the Task Analysis Guide can be introduced as a tool for analyzing tasks. Teachers might be asked about the characteristics on the TAG that were the same as or similar to ones that they had identified and whether or not they agreed with those they had not identified previously. This will help teachers see the TAG not as something imposed on them but rather as a tool that reflects, in large measure, their own thinking.

These activities are intended to highlight two key ideas: (1) not all tasks are created equal—different tasks promote different levels and kinds of student thinking; and (2) the level and kind of thinking in which students engage determines what they learn (Hiebert et al., 1997). As George Polya (1973/1945) stated:

> A teacher of mathematics has a great opportunity. If he fills his allotted time with drilling his students in routine operations, he kills their interest, hampers their intellectual development, and misuses his opportunity. But if he challenges the curiosity of his students by setting them problems proportionate to their knowledge, and helps them to solve their problems with stimulating questions, he may give them a task for, and some means of, independent thinking. (p. v)

Analyzing tasks used for instruction. Our goal through this set of experiences is for teachers to see the great opportunity presented to them as they make decisions regarding the tasks in which their students will engage. Toward this end, it is important to have them move from characterizing tasks that are not directly related to their work to analyzing tasks that are (or could become) part of their curriculum. To accomplish this, one or more SFEs (used in conjunction with the TAG) are critical. For example, as suggested in Chapter 1, teachers might be asked to collect the tasks used during classroom instruction over a defined period of time, categorize the tasks using the TAG, and determine the extent to which students have been given sufficient opportunities to engage in high-level thinking and reasoning and to practice procedures. Alternatively, teachers might be asked to identify a high-level task from a broader set of resources that could be used for instruction, analyze the task in terms of the features that make it high-level, and contrast the identified task with a task that was previously used to teach the same content. Two popular websites that are good resources for teachers who are looking for challenging mathematical task are the National Council of Teachers of Mathematics (*http://illuminations.nctm.org*) and the Ohio Resource Center (*http://www.ohiorc.org*). Regardless of the SFE that is assigned, teachers need to bring the tasks they have collected with them to a subsequent professional development session to discuss with their colleagues.

Exploring Challenging Mathematical Tasks

Exploring mathematical tasks involves engaging teachers at three levels: as mathematics learners, as analyzers and interpreters of students' mathematical work, and as planners of mathematical activity. In this way, teachers are able to experience firsthand a form of mathematics teaching that facilitates and supports learning, to consider student learning in the context of their own learning, and to begin to plan lessons to facilitate the learning of others.

Teachers as doers and learners of mathematics. The exploration of mathematical tasks provides teachers with the opportunity to construct or reconstruct their own understanding of what mathematics is and how one does it. Since "teachers' understanding of mathematics is a critical part of the resources available which comprise the realm of pedagogical possibilities in teaching mathematics" (Ball, 1991, p. 38), helping teachers develop this resource is critical.

The tasks that are at the heart of the cases in this book provide a rich resource for engaging teachers in mathematical activity for several reasons. First, the tasks are all high-level but include both those characterized as *procedures-with-connections* (e.g., multiplication of fractions using pattern blocks in Chapter 6) and those characterized as *doing-mathematics* (e.g., linking fractions, decimals, and percents in Chapter 5). This gives teachers an opportunity to experience tasks that are more (*procedures-with-connections*) and less (*doing-mathematics*) constrained and to discuss the contributions of each in helping students develop mathematical proficiency.

Second, as a collection, the tasks use a range of different representations and tools, some of which may be unfamiliar to teachers. For example, in our work, we have found that many teachers have no prior experience with patterns blocks (Chapter 6) or algebra tiles (Chapter 8). Engaging teachers in the use of these materials to solve specific tasks helps them see how these manipulatives can help students make sense of algorithms and develop a deeper understanding of why things work the way that they do. It is important, however, to ensure that teachers have the background knowledge and experience needed to engage with these materials productively. For example, prior to presenting the multiplying binomial task posed by Monique Butler (Chapter 8), we engage teachers in a set of introductory activities (shown in Figure 11.4) in which they explore the area model of multiplication with whole numbers using tiles and base-10 blocks. This experience helps teachers make connections between multiplication and area and between whole-number multiplication and multiplication of binomials. For an expanded example of teachers learning mathematics from experience with the materials in this book and closely related resources, see Silver, Clark, Ghousseini, Charlambous, and Sealy (2007).

Finally, having teachers complete and reflect on the task that is at the heart of the case they are going to read is critical to a rich and successful case discussion. Teachers go on to read the case with much more interest and confidence

Figure 11.4. Activities that are used to prepare teachers for the multiplication of binomials task.

> Create a model for each of the following expressions using any of the materials available at your table:
>
> 3×4
> $3 \times n$
> 6×13
> $6 \times (n + 3)$
> 26×12
> $(2x + 6)(x + 2)$
>
> *Available materials include: square tiles, base-10 blocks, algebra tiles, grid paper*

if they first engaged with the mathematical ideas themselves. Also, engaging in the tasks allows the teachers' own misconceptions to surface. Further, teachers are "primed for" and able to recognize many of the solution strategies put forth by students in the case. This way, teachers' understanding of the multiple pathways to solving the problems becomes strengthened and their perception of student thinking becomes sharper. Finally, Steele (2008) argues that working on the task and then engaging in a discussion of the case provides teachers with the opportunity to integrate their knowledge of mathematics with their knowledge of pedagogy and "create a more powerful learning experience than either activity might have afforded individually" (p. 15).

Our work on mathematical tasks proceeds through three phases. We begin with 5 minutes of private think time during which teachers work individually on the task. This provides teachers with the opportunity to make sense of the situation and to consider possible solution paths. The goal is not to complete the task but rather to determine what resources you can bring to the subsequent small-group discussion of the task. Next, teachers work in small groups and share ideas and strategies, eventually deciding which pathway to pursue. Finally, we orchestrate a whole-group discussion during which different solutions are shared on posters, transparencies, or on a document projector (see Stein, Engle, Smith, & Hughes, in press, for more details on how a facilitator might orchestrate a productive discussion of a mathematical task). It is important to note, however, that teachers' participation in a productive discussion in which multiple solution methods are carefully selected, sequenced, and discussed may not be sufficient for teachers to apply these practices in their own classroom. Teachers may need considerable support to make the transition from discussion participant to discussion facilitator, and this issue may need explicit attention in professional development sessions. (See Silver, Ghousseini, Gosen, Charalambous, & Strawhun, 2005, for more on the challenges embedded in this aspect of teaching practice and how practice-based professional development might be used to address these issues; see also Smith, Hughes, Engle, & Stein, in press, for a model intended to help teachers orchestrate productive discussions.)

Teachers as analyzers and interpreters. In addition to solving tasks themselves, teachers need the opportunity to make sense of the work produced by students on challenging mathematical tasks—particularly on tasks that they themselves have solved. Examining students' work affords the opportunity for teachers to move from their own understanding of a task to a broader consideration of what students' responses might reveal about their thinking. Through this work we are developing what Moon (1997) refers to as *professional judgment*, that is, moving beyond intuitions and grounding interpretations of student work in evidence.

In our work, we have used student responses from many different published sources (e.g., Parke, Lane, Silver, & Magone, 2003; Brown & Clark, 2006), actual work produced by students featured in the cases contained in this volume (e.g., the solution created by Antonio in Fran Gorman's class described in Chapter 6), as well as responses to tasks in this volume collected by teachers with whom we have worked. Consider, for example, the student responses to the fraction, decimal, and percent task featured in the case of Ron Castleman (Chapter 5) shown in Figure 11.5. A close examination of these responses might raise questions regarding the difference between procedural fluency (demonstrated by student A) and conceptual understanding (demonstrated by student B in part A); whether arriving at the correct answer (as in the case of student A) implies understanding; and how to interpret and remediate student misconceptions (e.g., student D's response to parts A and B). The student responses also provide an opportunity for teachers to consider what questions they would ask each student to gain additional insight into what they currently understand and to help them move beyond their current understandings.

Teachers as planners of mathematical activity. Our goal through this set of experiences is to help teachers recognize the potential for learning afforded by cognitively challenging mathematical tasks and the insight into student thinking that such tasks provide so that they will endeavor to use more challenging tasks in their own classrooms. Toward that end, the SFEs in which we engage teachers focus on collaboratively planning lessons that feature high-level tasks. Although teachers may, at times, decide to use one of the professional development tasks (e.g., multiplying binomials; linking fractions, decimals, and percents) with their own students, we encourage teachers to select or adapt tasks from their own curricular resources as the basis of the SFEs they complete related to lesson planning.

The TTLP, discussed previously and shown in Figure 11.1, is central in the planning process. The TTLP guides teachers through a set of questions that focus on students (e.g., What do they know now? What will they do? What will they learn? How will you know what they learn?) and how their learning can be supported (e.g., What will you do with students' misconceptions? How will you challenge students who finish early? What will you do for students who can't get started? How will you support students as they work?). Even when teachers are fortunate enough to have a base curriculum that offers an ample supply of cognitively demanding tasks for their students, the challenges of effectively

FIGURE 11.5. Student responses produced in response to task featured in the case of
Ron Castleman.

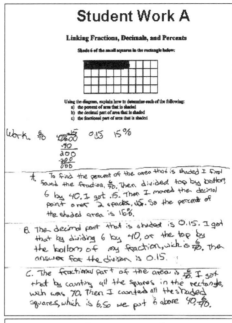

Student Work A

Linking Fractions, Decimals, and Percents

Shade 6 of the small squares in the rectangle below:

Using the diagram, explain how to determine each of the following:
a) the percent of area that is shaded
b) the decimal part of area that is shaded
c) the fractional part of area that is shaded

Work. $\frac{6}{40}$ $\frac{.15}{40\overline{)6.00}}$ 0.15   15%
         $\frac{-40}{200}$
         $\frac{-200}{000}$

A. To find the percent of the area that is shaded I first found the fraction, $\frac{6}{40}$. Then divided top by bottom, 6 by 40. I got .15. Then I moved the decimal point over 2 spaces, 15. So the percent of the shaded area is 15%.

B. The decimal part that is shaded is 0.15. I got that by dividing 6 by 40, or the top by the bottom of my fraction, which is $\frac{6}{40}$. Then answer for the division is 0.15.

C. The fractional part of the area is $\frac{6}{40}$. I got that by counting all the squares in the rectangle, which was 70. Then I counted all the shaded squares, which is 6. So we put 6 above 40. $\frac{6}{40}$.

Student Work B

Linking Fractions, Decimals, and Percents

Shade 6 of the small squares in the rectangle below:

_10%_

Using the diagram, explain how to determine each of the following:
a) the percent of area that is shaded
b) the decimal part of area that is shaded
c) the fractional part of area that is shaded

a.) When 6 squares filled, I counted 40 squares for the entire area. That must be 100%. First I noticed the 10 columns, so four squares are 10%. I have 2 more squares so that is half. I have 10% + 5% = 15%

b.) The decimal part is .15 What I did was move the .15% over 2 places.

c.) The fraction part is $\frac{1}{20}$. I found this by simply reducing $\frac{6}{40}$ to $\frac{1}{20}$ giving me the lowest term fraction.

Figure 11.5. (cont'd)

Student Work C

Linking Fractions, Decimals, and Percents

Shade 6 of the small squares in the rectangle below:

Using the diagram, explain how to determine each of the following:
a) the percent of area that is shaded
b) the decimal part of area that is shaded
c) the fractional part of area that is shaded

A.) There's 40 squares in all and there's 6 squares shaded in the one rectangle. I know that the rectangle = 100%. I counted the rows, 4 total. So, a row = 25%, but I have 10 squares. So a square = 2.5%

Six squares = 2.5% × 6 = (15%)

B.) Same as above except each row = .25
So a square = 2.5
Six squares = 2.5 × 6 (1.5)

C.) Same but I have $\frac{\text{Shaded Squares}}{\text{Total Squares}} = \frac{6}{40} = \frac{3}{20}$

Student Work D

Linking Fractions, Decimals, and Percents

Shade 6 of the small squares in the rectangle below:

Using the diagram, explain how to determine each of the following:
a) the percent of area that is shaded
b) the decimal part of area that is shaded
c) the fractional part of area that is shaded

a) $6.4 = 64\%$ $\overset{100\%}{(36\%)}$ $\Big|$ $6.2 = 62\%$ $\overset{100\%}{(38\%)}$

B) $3\overline{)20}$ $\frac{18}{2}$ $\Big|$ $6\overline{)40}$ $\frac{36}{4}$

C) $\frac{6}{40}$ reduced $\frac{3}{20}$

We first solved c then went to B then went to a. To solve c we just took the shaded area then counted all the squares. Then reduced it. Then we divided the numerator by the denominator. Then we moved the decimal for a, then subtracted it by 100% to get our answers.

enacting these tasks are many, and the TTLP can be a valuable tool to assist in both the planning and debriefing of lessons. (See Silver, Ghousseini, Charlambous, & Mills, 2009, for an example of some of the challenges of teaching with a curriculum base of cognitively demanding tasks and how the TTLP was used by professional developers and teachers to address the challenges.)

In each professional development session, time for joint planning is allocated as appropriate. Likewise, in subsequent sessions, teachers are given time to debrief on what occurred during their teaching of the coplanned lesson and to share with colleagues any artifacts they collected. Generally, we introduce teachers to the TTLP gradually by first focusing on a subset of questions and then moving, over time, to include the entire protocol. Smith, Bill, and Hughes (2008) provide more details regarding how the TTLP might be used for collaborative planning, and Silver, Mills, Castro, and Ghousseini (2006) offer a general argument for and a specific example of the synergy achieved in professional development that employs case analysis and discussion together with collaborative lesson planning.

The teachers with whom we have worked have used the TTLP periodically (and collaboratively!) to prepare lessons so that, over time, they grow a collection of carefully designed lessons. In addition, as teachers become more familiar with the TTLP, they begin to ask themselves questions from the protocol as they plan lessons *without explicit reference to the protocol*. This sentiment is echoed in the comment made by one middle-school teacher:

> I may not have it sitting on my desk, going point to point with it, but I think: What are the misconceptions? How am I going to organize work? What are my questions? Those are the three big things that I've taken from the TTLP, and those are the three big things that I think about when planning a lesson. So, no, I'm not matching it up point for point but those three concepts are pretty much in every lesson, essentially. (Smith, Bill, & Hughes, 2008, p. 137)

Analyzing and Reflecting on Instruction

According to the *Principles and Standards for School Mathematics* (NCTM, 2000), in order to improve their instructional practices, teachers must be able to analyze their classroom actions and interactions and consider how those actions impact students' learning opportunities. In our work, there are three ways in which we help teachers develop this capacity to reflect on and learn from instruction: reflecting on their experience as learners, analyzing the teaching of others, and analyzing and reflecting on instruction in their own classrooms.

Reflecting on their experience as learners. Following the discussion of a task in which they have engaged as learners, teachers are asked to consider the following question: What did the facilitator do to support or inhibit your learning of mathematics? The question engages teachers in reflecting on their own learning and the particular pedagogical moves that the facilitator made that impacted their learning in some way. The intent is to make visible what often is left invisible so that pedagogy—what the facilitator did and why— becomes an object of inquiry. The first time this question is posed, the "moves" that emerge from the discussion are charted on newsprint. If there is more than one facilitator present during the session, the facilitator who is not leading the session often takes on the role of "the shadow," taking notes on what the lead facilitator does and says as teachers work on the task. If the "shadow" observed something that was not brought out by teachers, this move is raised for discussion and added to the list if the teachers deem it appropriate. The factors of support and decline (shown in Figure 2.1) can then be introduced, and the list can be analyzed in light of those factors. This tool serves to highlight the generalizability of these moves across a range of teaching situations.

Analyzing the teaching of others. Analyzing the teaching of others through the examination of video and narrative cases can help teachers explore important mathematical ideas, to analyze and critically reflect on a teacher's actions and interactions in the classroom, and to consider the different courses of actions open to the teacher. By learning how to analyze "messy and complex situations," teachers can learn to make well-informed decisions in their own classrooms (Barnett & Ramirez, 1996, p. 11). Toward that end, the cases in this volume are a valuable resource. Each case embodies an empirical pattern of mathematics teaching and learning and the associated factors that influence students' opportunities to learn. Figure 11.6 shows the pattern that is highlighted in each case. Hence, each case is connected, through the mathematical tasks framework, to a larger set of ideas that teachers can ultimately apply to their own classrooms.

We generally begin our exploration of these cases with Chapter 5, the case of Ron Castleman. This dual case is a particularly good starting point since it juxtaposes two different classes taught by the same teacher and allows for comparisons of how instruction unfolded in these two classes. There are three questions that we have used to guide this analysis (and the analysis of other dual cases): (1) How are the two classes the same and how are they are different?; (2) Do the differences matter?; and (3) In terms of the Mathematical Tasks Framework, what is Ron Castleman a case of? In answering the first question, teachers must identify specific events that occur during one class and compare

FIGURE 11.6. The empirical pattern of task setup and implementation exemplified in each of the case chapters. (Shading indicates cases where the cognitive demands of the task were maintained during implementation.)

Chapter	Teacher	Task Setup	Task Implementation
5	Ron Castleman—2nd	Doing Mathematics	Procedures without Connections
	Ron Castleman—6th	Doing Mathematics	Doing Mathematics
6	Fran Gorman	Procedures with Connections	Procedures without Connections
	Kevin Cooper	Procedures with Connections	Procedures with Connections
7	Trina Naruda	Doing Mathematics	Doing Mathematics
	Ursula Hernandez	Doing Mathematics	Unsystematic Exploration
8	Monique Butler	Procedures with Connections	Procedures without Connections
9	Nicole Clark	Doing Mathematics	No mathematical activity
10	Jerome Robinson	Doing Mathematics	Procedures without Connections

them to events in the other class. Through this analysis, key differences emerge—most notably the way in which Castleman handled students' confusion (i.e., in the second-period class suggesting that they start with part C, and in the sixth-period class suggesting that they look at the 4 × 10 grid and think about how it could be used). This leads nicely into a discussion of the second question, where teachers consider the connection between teaching and opportunities for student learning, eventually coming to the realization that by suggesting a pathway for solving the task in the second-period class, students were left with nothing more than a procedure to follow and, thus, had no opportunity to engage in thinking and reasoning.

   Although cases such as Ron Castleman's provide rich detail about particular situations, it is important to see beyond the details instead of becoming caught up in them. Toward this end, the final question (i.e., What is this a case of?) is critical, since it connects the specific events of the case with more general patterns of task setup and implementation embodied in the MTF. To move from the particulars of a case to generalities, facilitators must stimulate teachers "to move up and down, back and forth, between the memorable particularities of cases and the powerful generalizations and simplifications of principles and theories" (Shulman, 1996, p. 201). With the cases in this book, it is critical to use the MTF (Figure 1.3), the factors (Figure 2.1), and the patterns (Figure 2.2) to provide coherence across cases and a set of generalizable principles. For a discussion of how one might strategically select cases for specific professional development goals, see Silver, Clark, Gosen, and Mills (2008).

Analyzing and reflecting on one's own teaching. The process of examining instructional cases can become so analytical that it loses its connection to the work of teaching. The goal of these analyses is to help teachers develop a knowledge base for teaching that will improve their ability to make decisions during live instruction *not* to become more skillful at analysis for its own sake. Therefore, it is important to have teachers continue to teach and reflect on their own lessons, using the frameworks and tools that have guided their analysis of the cases.

We begin the process of reflecting on one's own teaching right after our analysis of the first case—Ron Castleman. Through this discussion, teachers become aware of the factors that impact students' learning opportunities in the classroom and how the teacher's actions within the classroom are a major influence on what students ultimately learn. We ask teachers to identify some issues that the case raised for them and that they want to explore in their own practice.

In some situations, we asked teachers to pick a factor (from the list in Figure 2.1) that they would like to work on in their own classroom during the year. There are two factors that are frequently selected—scaffolding of student thinking (#1 in right column of the figure) and reducing the complexity of the task (#1 in the left column of the figure). These choices are not surprising since these factors account in large measure for the differences in what occurred in Castleman's sixth- and second-period classes, and they are critical to the success (right column) or failure (left column) of a lesson. A sequence of SFEs (all focused on planning, teaching, and reflecting on a lesson involving a high-level task) might begin by asking teachers to describe how the factor identified played out during a lesson, continue with requests for descriptions of the progress being made on the factor, and conclude with a discussion of the areas that the teacher still needs to work on.

Over an extended period of time, teachers are asked to focus on different aspects of their instruction (e.g., asking questions, orchestrating discussion) and to bring in artifacts to share with colleagues that provide insights into the nature of activity in their classrooms.

CONCLUSION

A recent report from the American Institutes for Research (Ginsburg, Cooke, Leinwand, Noell, & Pollock, 2005) that analyzed the performance of students in 12 countries who participated in both the Trends in International Mathematics and Science Study (TIMSS) and Program for International Student Assessment (PISA) in 2003 suggests that students in the United States need to improve their ability to use cognitively demanding skills (e.g., reasoning) and to apply facts and procedures in order to achieve at the level of higher-performing countries. In order to improve students' capacity to engage in high-level cognitive activity, the nature of tasks that are selected and used in our nation's classrooms must change. Students must have more opportunities to engage in mathematical tasks that require them to reason and make sense of the mathematics they are learning.

The model of mathematics task-focused professional development described herein is intended to help teachers' develop the knowledge and skills needed to select and enact challenging tasks in their classrooms. Using mathematical tasks as the lever for change narrows the focus of instructional improvement efforts to what research has shown matters most: the nature of the mathematical activity in which children are asked to engage.

Over the last several years, we have engaged in several studies aimed at determining the efficacy of this approach. For example, Boston and Smith (in press) report that following their participation a yearlong workshop (six 6-hour sessions between September and May), secondary mathematics teacher-participants significantly increased: (1) their ability to distinguish between tasks based on their level of cognitive demand; (2) the level of cognitive demand of the main instructional tasks used in their classrooms (as indicated by the tasks submitted for three 1-week periods during the year); and (3) their ability to maintain high-level cognitive demands (as indicated by the student work samples collected). Furthermore, as compared to a contrast group of secondary mathematics teachers who did not participate in the professional development workshop, the teacher-participants had significantly higher task and implementation mean scores for classroom observations. This research supports and extends Arbaugh and Brown's (2005) findings that engaging high school teachers in learning about the levels of cognitive demand influenced their task choice over the course of a school year, thus serving as a catalyst for change in their instructional practice.

CHAPTER 12

Assisting the Learning and Professional Practice of Principals

The call for instructional leadership has grown louder over the past decade. Yet, what is meant by instructional leadership and how it is actually carried out remain vague. Most textbooks used in the training of principals now include several chapters on instructional leadership; a quick scan of some of the most popular, however, reveals that advice on how to improve instruction typically fails to include attention to the content of instruction. In this chapter, we illustrate how the Mathematics Task Framework (MTF) and the cases depicting various enactments of high-level tasks can provide a solid base for principals who want to become leaders of mathematics instruction.

Our approach stems from a view of instructional leadership that recognizes the important role that subject matter plays in effective leadership. Mathematics classrooms are different from literacy classrooms: Their goals vary, the kinds of student thinking and reasoning that one is apt to observe in them diverge, and the improvement challenges that teachers face are not the same (Stein & Nelson, 2003). A principal who is equipped to "instructionally lead" must be aware of these differences. In mathematics, she must be aware of the big ideas that students should be learning, the agreed-upon instructional strategies for assisting students in learning those ideas, and the challenges that teachers face as they attempt to enact those strategies. She must be able to guide the selection of curriculum materials that will challenge students to learn important and worthwhile mathematics and make decisions that support appropriate professional development for teachers. And she must be able to defend her mathematical choices to a variety of constituencies, including parents and school board members.

Why should principals focus on mathematical instructional tasks? As leaders of their buildings, principals are held responsible for student achievement. There is no better way to boost student achievement than by shaping the kinds of instructional tasks used in a school's classrooms (Lappan & Briars, 1995). The tasks in which students engage and how they engage with them determine their opportunities for learning (Doyle, 1983; Hiebert & Wearne, 1996; Stein & Lane, 1996). If principals want their students to learn how to think and reason and to make conceptual connections, they must encourage and support the selection of high-level, cognitively demanding tasks that support that kind of learning.

Recent international comparisons suggest that most U.S. principals *should* be focused on the development of students' high-level thinking and reasoning skills. From international comparisons, we know that U.S. students do not perform at the level of our economic competitors (Lemke, Sen, Pahike, Partelow, Miller, Williams, Kastberg, & Jocelyn, 2004; Mullis, Martin, Gonzalez, & Chrostowski, 2004) and that their performance on cognitively demanding tasks is especially low in comparison to other countries (Ginsburg et al, 2005).

Ensuring that teachers select high-level tasks would be a first step in addressing students' limitations in this area. Research suggests, however, that it is only the first step. For example, the TIMMS video study (NCES, 2003; Stigler & Hiebert, 2004) highlighted the difficulty U.S. teachers have in maintaining the rigor of tasks during instruction. Although 17% of the tasks used by teachers in the United States were judged to be high-level (making connections), none of these tasks was implemented as intended. Instead, most of the *making connections* problems were transformed into procedural exercises. Thus, focusing on the classroom teaching practices that surround the use of high-level tasks is essential for helping students improve their capacity to think and reason in mathematics.

Professional development has a key role to play in improving teachers' instructional practice, and principals can play an important role in providing resources of time and money for high-quality professional development that focuses on core issues of mathematics teaching and learning. Moreover, research tells us that teachers also need the support of their building administrators in order to implement the practices learned in professional development. For example, they need to be held accountable for implementing the new practices—and *not* held accountable for practices that are orthogonal or in direct contradiction to what they have learned in professional development. In addition, principals can align their observational approach to support teacher enactment of high-level tasks. Too often, the observations conducted by principals are brief and focus on superficial features of the lesson, such as whether or not students are engaged in "hands-on" activities. Teachers quickly learn that what is focused on is what is valued and will "stage" lessons that they believe will be favorably evaluated.

Principals can also create conditions in the school that are conducive to teacher and student learning around high-level tasks. This includes arranging for resources to support a focus on complex thinking and reasoning. For example, principals can ensure that curricula are selected that feature cognitively complex tasks, that time is available (and well spent) for teachers to work together to grapple with the challenges of implementing high-level tasks, and that higher levels of administration as well as parents and community members are on board with a focus on developing students' capacity to think and reason.

Over the past decade, we have worked with principals to introduce them to the MTF and to suggest ways in which they might instill a focus on mathematics instructional tasks in their schools. We have found that, similar to teachers, principals' understanding of mathematical tasks, student learning, and pedagogical practice is important. However, equally important is principals' understanding of the challenges *that teachers face* as they work with high-level tasks and the school-level supports that are required to support teachers as they cope with these challenges.

The purpose of this chapter is to describe ways in which principals can learn to support teachers as they struggle to enact high-level tasks. In particular, we focus on (a) conducting classroom observations and arranging for tailored professional development; and (b) providing schoolwide resources for ongoing teacher development.

This chapter can serve as a resource for principals or for those who educate principals. Even without a trained facilitator, we believe that principals themselves can benefit from reading this chapter (either alone or in groups) and enacting its suggestions. We have used the ideas discussed herein in preservice courses for individuals who are enrolled in a university-based principal preparation program as well as in professional development workshops for principals in large urban districts.

CONDUCTING OBSERVATIONS AND ARRANGING FOR TAILORED PROFESSIONAL DEVELOPMENT

The centerpiece of instructional leadership is frequent classroom observation. To be effective, classroom observations require, first and foremost, principals who know good instruction when they see it and know how to identify and encourage it when they don't. Toward this end, many of the tools discussed in Chapter 11 (e.g., the Task Analysis Guide, the Factors) can be used with or by principals. In fact, we encourage principals to sit in on the professional development that their teachers receive surrounding mathematics instructional tasks so that they will be able to reinforce the messages that teachers receive and hold teachers accountable for accomplishing the

Scaffolded Field Experiences that are intended to occur in their classrooms between professional development sessions.

Although many principals report that "sitting in" on teacher professional development is useful, we believe it is equally important for principals to prepare for the specific challenges that they will face in their roles as instructional leaders of teachers who are learning to enact cognitively challenging tasks. One of these challenges involves learning to differentiate high-level instruction from instruction that looks high-level on the surface, but—in reality— provides little opportunity for student thinking and reasoning.

The capacity to differentiate high- from low-level instruction is rooted in principals' ability to identify high- versus low-level instructional tasks. Although teachers must learn this also, principals—because they have been out of the classroom and because they may not have been mathematics specialists in the first place—have a particularly steep learning curve. Thus, we have found that spending more time on this foundational skill to be time well spent.

Learning to Differentiate High- versus Low-Level Tasks

When working with principals we typically begin—as we do with teachers—with Martha's Carpeting Task and the Fencing Task (Figures I.1 and I.2), followed by having them sort a set of tasks (see *http://www.tcpress. com*) using the Task Analysis Guide (Figure 1.2). These 16 middle-school tasks (also found in Smith et al., 2004) have been targeted for use with principals because they contain both low-level tasks that have been "dressed up" to resemble high-level tasks and high-level tasks that, at first glance, may appear to be very conventional, even "textbook-like." For example, Task J (see Figure 12.1) is a high-level task that may strike many principals as very textbook-like and overly abstract, in part because it does not have a "real-world" context. Yet we consider it to be a *procedures-with-connections* task because of the thinking and reasoning that it elicits. In order to complete part A of this problem, students have to conceptualize multiplication as finding the area of a rectangle and identify 27 and 3 as dimensions of that rectangle (partitioning 27, the length, into 20 and 7). Finally, they must multiple both 20 and 7 by 3 (to calculate the areas of the two "sub-rectangles") and sum the products for the total area. In doing this, students are meaningfully using the distributive property, distributing the factor 3 across 20 and 7. Overall, students cannot go through the motions of setting up and solving this task without thinking about the fundamental meaning of area and of multiplication.

Task C (see Figure 12.2), on the other hand, is a low-level task that many principals initially think is high-level because it asks students to use pattern tiles to figure the perimeter of three diagrams (this task was also seen in Figure 11.3). Many principals have been led to believe that "manipulative use" means

FIGURE 12.1. A high-level task that superficially resembles a low-level task.

TASK J

Manipulatives or Tools Available: None

One method of mentally computing 7 × 34 is illustrated in the diagram below:

7 × 30 = 210   4 × 30 = 28

Mentally compute these products.
Then sketch a diagram that describes your methods for each.

a) 27 x 3

b) 325 x 4

(Adapted from *Visual Mathematics Course I*, Lesson 37, Focus Teacher Activity, pp. 457–463. *Copyright © 1995 The Math Learning Cente*r.)

that students are thinking conceptually. Other principals may be swayed by the "nontraditional" look of the problem in that it contains a diagram and does not contain any symbols or formulas. However, the problem is very procedural, only requiring that students use one tile as a unit of measure to figure the perimeter (which is defined as the "distance around") by counting. Students can do this without understanding what perimeter means and without recognizing the developing pattern between number of squares and perimeter in the three diagrams, a recognition that would allow them to generalize to larger numbers of squares.

In our experience, principals are especially vulnerable to being derailed by these kinds of superficial task features. We trace this vulnerability to their role as teacher evaluators in which they are expected to visit classrooms only briefly and then make a judgment regarding the quality of instruction. Not surprisingly, many principals have learned to focus on easy-to-spot features of lessons (e.g., whether or not students are working in groups, whether manipulatives are on the table) rather than taking the additional time and effort that would be required to identify the extent to which students are being provided with the opportunities to think and reason deeply about important mathematical ideas.

FIGURE 12.2. A low-level task that superficially resembles a high-level task.

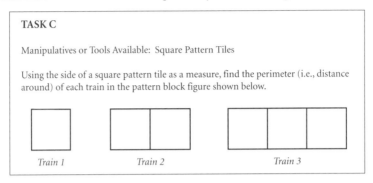

We have found this task sort to be extremely useful in addressing this vulnerability. In order to classify the tasks correctly, principals must read each task carefully and think about the kind of thinking that is required to solve it (often by solving it themselves) rather than relying on "key words" or "props" often associated with high-level tasks. Most principals are surprised when they learn they've misclassified several of the tasks and redouble their efforts to more meaningfully distinguish between high- and low-level tasks. (See *http://www.tcpress.com* for the correct cognitive-level classification and the identification of the surface features of each task.)

Differentiating Variable Classroom Enactments of High-Level Tasks

After principals have become comfortable with categorizing tasks, the next step is to learn how to differentiate high- from low-level enactments of tasks in the classroom. As an introductory activity, we have principals read and analyze a set of six brief, one-paragraph scenarios of classroom enactments of high-level tasks (see *http://www.tcpress.com*). These scenarios build off of the patterns of task setup and implementation established by our research and articulated in Chapter 2. In fact, four of the scenarios expand on the general descriptions found in Chapter 2 of the ways in which the Fencing Task (Figure I.2) might play out (see Figure 12.3 for an example of one of these scenarios). These scenarios can be read and analyzed in one 2-hour session.

Reviewing the scenario in Figure 12.3 in light of the patterns identified in Figure 2.2, principals can begin to see how, although beginning as a *doing-mathematics* task, by providing the table to the students, Ms. Fagan has proceduralized

FIGURE 12.3. Example of a scenario illustrating a classroom enactment pattern.

Ms. Fagan has posted the following problem on the blackboard. As they arrive in the classroom, her students begin to work on the problem immediately with their partners.

"Ms. Brown's class will raise rabbits for their spring science fair. They have 24 feet of fencing with which to build a rectangular rabbit pen to keep rabbits. If Ms. Brown's students want their rabbits to have as much room as possible how long would each of the sides of the pen be?"

One-third of the way into a 40-minute period, Ms. Fagan notices that students have made little or no progress. She puts the following table on the blackboard and tells students they should complete it.

	Length	*Width*	*Perimeter* 2(1 + w)	*Area* lx × w
11 × 1				
10 × 2				
9 × 3				
8 × 4				
7 × 5				
6 × 6				
5 × 7				
4 × 8				
3 × 9				
2 × 10				
1 × 11				

Students busily complete the table, relieved that they now know "what to do." With ten minutes left in the period, Ms. Fagan asks a pair of students to come to the overhead projector and explain their answer.

the problem, in essence, doing all of the thinking for the students (i.e., the task declined into *procedures-without-connections*). All the students are left to do is to "fill in the blanks" and then check to see which configuration has the largest area. Indeed, students can obtain the correct answer and still not understand why it is correct or be able to generalize to another similar problem.

The first objective of these scenarios, then, is to bring home the fact that identifying and setting up high-level tasks is only a beginning step. Keeping high-level demands "alive" during a lesson is the real challenge, illustrated by the fact that only two out of the six enactments portrayed in the scenarios illustrate a classroom in which high-level cognitive demands are maintained throughout the lesson.

The second objective is to illustrate the variability with which high-level tasks are enacted and to help principals learn that the variability that they are likely to encounter in classrooms is predictable. Toward this end, the scenarios are read and analyzed through the lens of the MTF and Figure 2.2, which illustrates the six common ways in which high-level tasks typically play out during a lesson. Principals read each scenario and then decide which of the six patterns depicted in the table it represents. We have found that this activity allows principals to quickly grasp the variable enactments that are possible and also often leads to a recognition that many of the declines portrayed in the scenarios are occurring in classrooms in their buildings, thereby motivating them to do something about it!

Once comfortable with a broad overview of the possible enactments—and usually after exploring at least one case in some depth (see below)—principals can use Figure 2.2 as a tool for observing teachers in their buildings. Principals will find that the table directs them to attend to what students are actually thinking about during the lesson—and whether their thinking represents worthwhile mathematical activity. The figure also provides a list of factors (see column 3 of Figure 2.2) that are typically associated with each of the patterns of decline or maintenance. Some principals actually prefer (at least initially) "looking for" the factors because the factors can help them to identify the pattern. The factors are also important because they provide "actionable" foci for improvement efforts.

Arranging for Tailored Professional Development

After a principal has observed each of the teachers in her building several times using Figure 2.2, she might begin to see natural "groupings" of teachers. There may be some teachers who are regularly struggling with "losing the connection to meaning" that is built into *procedures-with-connections* tasks; others may be frequently allowing *doing-mathematics* tasks to decline into unsystematic and nonproductive exploration. These groupings, in turn, could be used to arrange professional development that is tailored to individual teachers' needs. If there is a coach in the building, the principal should discuss her perceptions of the groupings with the coach in order to (a) determine whether they are on the same page, and (b) provide a starting point for resolving differences if they are not. Once the principal and coach agree on which teachers are doing well and which teachers are having similar struggles, the principal could arrange for the coach to work with them in ways that are appropriate to their needs. If there is not a coach in the building, the principal might ask for another "set of eyes" to observe her teachers (e.g., a department chair, a district mathematics supervisor) and then discuss their assessments. Once the principal feels confident, she can either try to assist the teachers herself (individually or in groups comprised of teachers who share similar struggles) or she could arrange "buddies," teacher partners comprised of a teacher who has worked through a particular challenge and a teacher who is currently struggling with that same challenge. Carefully constructed partnerships can lead to tremendous teacher growth for both parties involved.

Going More Deeply into Selected Cases

An important tension that underlies this work is deciding the depth to which principals must understand the mathematics embedded in instructional tasks and the specific differences in opportunities for student learning afforded by different instructional enactments. In order to increase principals' awareness of the mathematical thinking required by high-level tasks, we recommend that they delve deeply into two of the cases: the case of Ron Castleman and the case of Fran Gorman and Kevin Cooper. Both are "dual cases" that comprise contrasting examples of two lessons on the same topic, thereby highlighting the important features that distinguish high-level enactments from those that decline. The case of Ron Castleman is a good place to begin. Principals can analyze it in the same way as teachers are asked to engage with the case (see Chapter 11).

The case of Fran Gorman and Kevin Cooper is a particularly good case for principals because Fran and Kevin are two teachers in the same building who implement the same instructional task in very different ways. As discussed in Chapter 11, in Fran's class, the cognitive demands of the "multiplication of fractions" task declined as students learned to simply follow a set of procedures to get the right answer, while in Kevin's class, the cognitive demands were maintained. Despite the fact that Fran and Kevin share a common daily meeting time, the discussion in the meeting directly after Fran's unsuccessful lesson did not help her much. This unfortunate event speaks directly to the principal's responsibility to not only provide time for teacher collaboration, but also to set expectations regarding how that time is used.

Principals who participate in a discussion of the Fran and Kevin case can be asked to hypothesize how the meeting could have been more useful to Fran, ultimately leading to a discussion of the importance of meeting structure (Should teachers be simply "reporting" on lessons?), meeting norms (How can critique and intellectual risk taking be encouraged and supported?), and accountability (What does the principal expect to see in classrooms as a result of the shared meeting time?). We discuss how principals can ensure good use of common meeting time in more depth below.

PROVIDING SCHOOLWIDE RESOURCES
FOR ONGOING TEACHER DEVELOPMENT

A schoolwide environment that supports teacher development is the soil in which effective instructional practice grows. Research shows that conditions ranging from the existence of teacher professional communities (Elmore, Peterson, & McCarthey, 1996) to the effective deployment of good curricular materials (Stein & Kaufman, 2008) make a difference in teachers' implementation of improved practice. Here, we discuss three roles that a principal can play to support teachers' implementation of high-level tasks and how the materials contained herein can help principals to begin to enact these roles.

Provision of Time

As noted above, time is an important resource for teachers who are trying to enhance the levels of cognitive demand in their instruction. Since scheduling is usually under the purview of the principal, this is a direct way in which principals can support improved instruction. Many schools now have shared planning periods (weekly or daily) for teachers who teach mathematics at the same or adjacent grade levels. However, time alone will have no impact. Rather, the principal must establish a culture of professional learning in the school and expectations for the content and conduct of teacher meetings.

One obstacle to establishing a learning culture is most teachers' reluctance to open their instructional practice to their peers. The teachers in Fran's and Kevin's school did share their practice, but they did so using only verbal descriptions and copies of handouts. This is much safer—but much less effective—than sharing authentic artifacts such as samples of student work or a videotape of the lesson. When teachers share these more authentic representations of practice, they open themselves to risk but they also stand to gain more useful forms of assistance through targeted feedback and critique.

We have found that principals can support the deprivatization of teacher practice by using our materials in two ways. First, if their teachers are not ready to open up their practice, principals can encourage teachers to use the tools discussed in Chapter 11 when they are discussing their practice verbally with colleagues. For example, principals can encourage teachers to co-plan and reflect on lessons using the Teaching Through a Lesson Protocol (TTLP; Smith, Bill, & Hughes, 2008). Not only will the TTLP provide structure to teacher discussions, but it also will encourage teachers to focus on opportunities that students have to think and reason in their classrooms. Along these same lines, if the principals monitor their teachers' Scaffolded Field Experiences (another tool introduced in Chapter 11), they will be helping teachers to more effectively analyze, improve, and talk about their practice with colleagues.

Second, after their teachers begin to share videotapes of their practice, the principal can model respectful and effective ways of critiquing practice. Principals can prepare to do this by role-playing with each other after reading the cases in the book. One individual pretends to be the teacher depicted in the case while another plays the role of the principal who has just finished observing the lesson depicted in the case. The task is for the person who is playing the principal to lead a critical, but respectful and productive, post-observation discussion. Some effective ways to do this might involve the following:

- I noticed that . . . (as a warm-up; to show careful attention; to engage in respectful dialogue)
- I was wondering how you might have . . . (to open the door to something that could have been done differently and perhaps better)
- I really like how you . . . (to reinforce a practice that the principal doesn't want the teacher to drop)
- For the next time that I observe, it would be great if you tried . . . (to encourage experimentation with a new practice)

Employing the above stems in post-observation discussions helps to maintain a problem-solving stance toward teaching by focusing on specific practices and their implications for how students cognitively engage in classroom activities and by raising questions that implore teachers to think through alternative practices. The focus, then, is not on what is going wrong; instead, the focus remains on how to get it right.

Provision of a Cognitively Complex Curriculum

Providing students with the opportunity to think and reason is much easier when teachers start out with curricula comprised primarily of cognitively challenging tasks. Principals who take an active role in guiding the process of curriculum selection in their building can provide this foundational resource for encouraging high-level teacher practice.

The principal can invite a few teacher-leaders who are knowledgeable about the MTF to co-design with her a curriculum-selection process that calls attention to the nature of the cognitive demands in the textbooks that are being reviewed. In the past, we have found it productive to use the Task Analysis Guide (Figure 1.2) to examine one common topic (e.g., ratio and proportion) across all of the textbooks under consideration. After the process has been designed, other teachers can be asked to join the design group in evaluating the texts. Asking at least three teachers to rate each textbook helps to ensure consistency in how the Task Analysis Guide is applied.

In our experience, this exercise will uncover significant differences among the most popular curricular materials on the market. For example, the NSF-supported standards-based curriculum materials primarily consist of high-level tasks while conventional curricula contain predominantly *procedures-without-connections* tasks. However, not all conventional curricula have solely low-demand tasks; some texts have tasks with mixed levels of cognitive demand. In addition, all standards-based curricula are not exactly the same; some contain more *doing-mathematics* tasks, while others contain more *procedures-with-connections* tasks (Stein & Kim, in press).

Engaging principals (and teachers) in such in-depth analyses of curricular materials is essential because adopted curricular materials often are the primary resource from which teachers draw the mathematical tasks that they use in the classroom. If principals are to be leaders in curriculum and task selection processes, they must understand clearly the implications of the choices that are made and be able to explain them clearly to others.

Convincing Important Stakeholders That High-Level Tasks Are Important

In order to do their best work, teachers need to know that administrators at all levels of the system, as well as the external community, are behind them and supporting their efforts. Parents, in particular, often need convincing because many of them were not exposed to high-level tasks in their own mathematics learning experiences, and they are often not sure why their children need a different mathematics education from the one they experienced. School board members are often skeptical as well and will ask for "proof" that this approach is capable of raising students' test scores.

Principals must be ready to respond to these concerns. We have provided a PowerPoint presentation that principals can make to stakeholders at *http://www.tcpress.com*. The presentation includes a rationale for focusing on high-level tasks, the ways in which instructional tasks often play out in classrooms, and a brief summary of research that connects high-level tasks with increased student learning. It also includes a list of additional references that can be accessed to provide more information about mathematical instructional tasks and research related to the use and impact of high-level mathematics instructional tasks.

CONCLUSION

We have seen principals who have engaged in the activities described in this chapter develop into articulate and convincing spokespersons for the importance of high-level tasks. Those who speak from experience—from having worked through the mathematical tasks in this book, from reading and discussing the cases, and from spending hours observing in classrooms—have become the most passionate leaders of reform in their buildings and communities.

References

Arbaugh, F., & Brown, C. A. (2005). Analyzing mathematical tasks: A catalyst for change? *Journal of Mathematics Teacher Education, 8*, 449–536.

Ball, D. L. (1991). Research on teaching mathematics: Making subject matter knowledge part of the equation. In J. Brophy (Ed.), *Advances in research on teaching: Volume 2, Teachers' knowledge of subject matter as it relates to their teaching practices* (pp. 1–48). Greenwich, CT: JAI Press.

Ball, D. L., & Cohen, D. K. (1999). Developing practice, developing practitioners: Towards a practice-based theory of professional education. In L. Darling-Hammond & G. Sykes (Eds.), *Teaching as the learning profession: Handbook of policy and practice* (pp. 3–32). San Francisco: Jossey-Bass.

Barnett, C., Goldenstein, D., & Jackson, B. (Eds.). (1994). *Fractions, decimals, ratios, and percents: Hard to teach and hard to learn.* Portsmouth, NH: Heinemann.

Barnett, C., & Ramirez, A. (1996). Fostering critical analysis and reflection through mathematics case discussions. In J. Colbert, K. Trimble, & P. Desberg (Eds.), *The case for education: Contemporary approaches for using case methods* (pp. 1–13). Boston: Allyn & Bacon.

Boaler, J., & Staples, M. (2008). Creating mathematical futures through an equitable teaching approach: The case of Railside School. *Teachers College Record, 110 (3),* 608–645.

Borasi, R., & Fonzi, J. (2002). Engaging in scaffolded instructional innovation. *Foundations: Professional development that supports school reform* (pp. 83–98). Washington, DC: National Science Foundation.

Boston, M. D., & Smith, M. S. (in press). Transforming secondary mathematics teaching: Increasing the cognitive demands of instructional tasks used in teachers' classrooms. *Journal for Research in Mathematics Education.*

Brown, C. A., & Clark, L.V. (Eds.). (2006). *Learning from NAEP: Professional development materials for teachers of mathematics.* Reston, VA: National Council of Teachers of Mathematics.

Doyle, W. (1983). Academic work. *Review of Educational Research, 53*(2), 159–199.

Doyle, W. (1988). Work in mathematics classes: The context of students' thinking during instruction. *Educational Psychologist, 23,* 167–180.

Doyle, W., & Carter, K. (1984). Academic tasks in classrooms. *Curriculum Inquiry, 14,* 129–149.

Elmore, R. F., Peterson, P., & McCarthey, S. (1996). *Restructuring in the classroom: Teaching, learning, and school organization.* San Francisco: Jossey-Bass.

Fey, J. T. (1981). *Mathematics teaching today: Perspectives from three national surveys.* Reston, VA: National Council of Teachers of Mathematics.

Ginsburg, A., Cooke, G., Leinwand, S., Noell, J., Pollock, E. (2005). *Reassessing U.S. international mathematics performance: New findings from the 2003 TIMSS and PISA.* Washington, DC: American Institutes for Research.

Grossman, P., & McDonald, M. (2008). Back to the future: Directions for research in teaching and teacher education. *American Education Research Journal, 45* (1), 184–205.

Henningsen, M. A., & Stein, M. K. (1997). Mathematical tasks and student cognition: Classroom-based factors that support and inhibit high-level mathematical thinking and reasoning. *Journal for Research in Mathematics Education, 29*(5), 524–549.

Hiebert, J., Carpenter, T. P., Fennema, E., Fuson, K. C., Wearne, D., Murray, H., Olivier, A., & Human, P. (1997). *Making sense: Teaching and learning mathematics with understanding.* Portsmouth, NH: Heinemann.

Hiebert, J., Gallimore, R., Garnier, H., Givven, K. B., Hollingsworth, H., Jacobs, J., Chui, A. M.-Y., Wearne, D., Smith, M., Manaster, A., Tseng, E., Etterbeek, W., Manaster, C., Gonzales, P., & Stigler, J. W. (2003). *Teaching mathematics in seven countries: Results from the TIMSS 1999 Video Study.* Washington, DC: U.S. Department of Education, National Center for Education Statistics.

Hiebert, J., & Wearne, D. (1996). Instructional tasks, classroom discourse, and students' learning in second-grade arithmetic. *American Educational Research Journal, 30,* 393–425.

Hughes, E. K., Smith, M. S., Hogel, M., & Boston, M. D. (2009). Case stories: Supporting teacher reflection and collaboration on the implementation of cognitively challenging mathematical tasks. In F. Arbaugh & P. M. Taylor (Eds.), *Inquiry into mathematics teacher education* (AMTE Monograph Series No. 5; pp. 71–84). San Diego, CA: Association of Mathematics Teacher Educators.

Lane, S. (1993). The conceptual framework for the development of a mathematics performance assessment instrument. *Educational Measurement: Issues and Practice, 14*(1), 16–23.

Lane, S., & Silver, E. A. (1995). Equity and validity considerations in the design and implementation of a mathematics performance assessment: The experiences of the QUASAR project. In M. Nettles & A. L. Nettles (Eds.), *Equity and excellence in education testing and assessment* (pp. 185–219). Boston: Kluwer.

Lappan, G., & Briars, D. J. (1995). How should mathematics be taught? In I. Carl (Ed.), *75 years of progress: Prospects for school mathematics* (pp. 131–156). Reston, VA: National Council of Teachers of Mathematics.

Lappan, G., Fitzgerald, W., Friel, S., Fey, J., & Phillips, E. (1998). *Connected mathematics.* White Plains, NY: Cuisenaire Dale Seymour Publications.

Lemke, M., Sen, A., Pahike, E., Partelow, L., Miller, D., Williams, T., Kastberg, D., & Jocelyn, L. (2004). *International outcomes of learning in mathematics literacy and problem solving: Pisa 2003 results from the U.S. perspective* (NCES 2005-003). U.S. Department of Education. Washington, DC: National Center for Education Statistics.

Little, J. W. (1990). The persistence of privacy: Autonomy and initiative in teachers' professional relations. *Teachers College Record, 91*(4), 509–536.

The Mathematics in Context Development Team. (1998). *Mathematics in context.* Chicago: Encyclopedia Britannica Education Corporation.

Merseth, K. K. (1999). A rationale for case-based pedagogy in teacher education. In M. A. Lundeberg, B. B. Levin, & H. Harrington (Eds.), *Who learns what from cases and how? The research base for teaching and learning with cases* (pp. ix–xv). Mahwah, NJ: Lawrence Erlbaum Associates.

Moon, J. (1997). *Developing judgment: Assessing children's work in mathematics.* Portsmouth, NH: Heinemann.

Mullis, I. V. S., Martin, M. O., Gonzalez, E. J., & Chrostowski, S. J. (2004). *TIMSS 2003 International Mathematics Report: Findings from IEA's Trends in International Mathematics and Science Study at the Fourth and Eighth Grades.* Chestnut Hill, MA: Boston College.

National Academy of Education. (1999). *Recommendations regarding research priorities: An advisory report to the National Educational Research Policy and Priorities Board.* National Academy of Education. Available at http://www.naeducation. org/1NAEd_Publications

National Center for Education Statistics. (2003). *Teaching mathematics in seven countries: Result from the TIMSS video study.* Washington, DC: U.S. Department of Education.

National Council of Teachers of Mathematics. (1989). *Curriculum and evaluation standards for school mathematics.* Reston, VA: Author.

National Council of Teachers of Mathematics. (1991). *Professional standards for teaching mathematics.* Reston, VA: Author.

National Council of Teachers of Mathematics. (1995). *Assessment standards for school mathematics.* Reston, VA: Author.

National Council of Teachers of Mathematics. (2000). *Principles and standards for school mathematics.* Reston, VA: Author.

Parke, C. S., Lane, S., Silver, E. A., & Magone, M. (2003). *Using assessment to improve middle-grade mathematics teaching and learning: Suggested activities using QUASAR tasks, scoring criteria, and students' work.* Reston, VA: National Council of Teachers of Mathematics.

Polya, G. (1973/1945). *How to solve it: A new aspect of mathematical method.* Princeton, NJ: Princeton University Press.

Polya, G. (1985). *How to solve it: A new aspect of mathematical method* (2nd ed.). Princeton, NJ: Princeton University Press.

Putnam, R., & Borko, H. (1997). Teacher learning: Implications of new views of cognition. In B. J. Biddle, T. L. Good, & I. F. Goodson (Eds.), *The international handbook of teachers and teaching* (Vol. II) (pp. 1223–1296). Dordrecht, The Netherlands: Kluwer.

Resnick, L. B. (1987). *Education and learning to think.* Washington, DC: National Academy Press.

Richardson, V. (1990). Significant and worthwhile change in teaching practice. *Educational Researcher, 19*(7), 10–18.

Romagnano, L. R. (1994). *Wrestling with change: The dilemmas of teaching real mathematics.* Portsmouth, NH: Heinemann.

Shulman, L. S. (1986). Those who understand: Knowledge growth in teaching. *Educational Researcher, 15*(2), 4–14.

Shulman, L. S. (1992). Toward a pedagogy of cases. In J. Shulman (Ed.), *Case methods in teacher education* (pp. 1–30). New York: Teachers College Press.

Shulman, L. S. (1996). "Just in case": Reflections on learning from experiences. In J. Colbert, K. Trimble, & P. Desberg (Eds.), *The case for education: Contemporary approaches for using case methods* (pp. 197–217). Boston: Allyn & Bacon.

Silver, E. A. (2009). Toward a more complete understanding of practice-based professional development for mathematics teachers. In D. L. Ball & R. Even (Eds.), *The professional education and development of teachers of mathematics* (pp. 245–247). New York: Springer.

Silver, E. A., Clark, L. M., Ghousseini, H. N., Charlambous, C. Y., & Sealy, J. T. (2007). Where is the mathematics? Examining teachers' mathematical learning opportunities in practiced-based professional learning tasks. *Journal of Mathematics Teacher Education, 10,* 261–277.

Silver, E. A., Clark, L., Gosen, D., & Mills, V. (2008). Using narrative cases in mathematics teacher professional development: Strategic selection and facilitation issues. In M. S. Smith & S. Friel (Eds.), *Cases in mathematics teacher education: Tools for developing knowledge needed for teaching* (AMTE Monograph Series No. 4) (pp. 89–101). San Diego, CA: Association of Mathematics Teacher Educators.

Silver, E. A., Ghousseini, H., Gosen, D., Charalambous, C., & Strawhun, B. T. F. (2005). Moving from rhetoric to praxis: Issues faced by teachers in having students consider multiple solutions for problems in the mathematics classroom. *Journal of Mathematical Behavior, 24,* 287–301.

Silver, E. A., & Lane, S. (1993). Assessment in the context of mathematics instruction reform: The design of assessment in the QUASAR project. In M. Niss (Ed.), *Cases of assessment in mathematics education* (pp. 59–69). Dordrecht, The Netherlands: Kluwer.

Silver, E. A., Ghousseini, H., Charlambous, C., & Mills, V. (2009). Exploring the curriculum implementation plateau: An instructional perspective. In J. Remillard, B. Herbel-Eisenmann, & G. Lloyd (Eds.). *Mathematics teachers at work: Connecting curriculum materials and classroom instruction* (pp. 245–265). New York: Routledge.

Silver, E. A., Mills, V., Castro, A., & Ghousseini, H. (2006). Blending elements of lesson study with case analysis and discussion: A promising professional development synergy. In K. Lynch-Davis & R. L. Ryder (Eds.), *The work of mathematics teacher educators: Continuing the conversation* (AMTE Monograph Series No. 2) (pp. 117–132). San Diego, CA: Association of Mathematics Teacher Educators.

Silver, E. A., & Smith, M. S. (1996). Building discourse communities in mathematics classrooms: A worthwhile but challenging journey. In P. Elliott (Ed.), *Communication in mathematics, K–12 and beyond* (pp. 20–28). Reston, VA: National Council of Teachers of Mathematics.

Silver, E. A., Smith, M. S., & Nelson, B. S. (1995). The QUASAR project: Equity concerns meeting mathematics education reform in the middle school. In W. G. Secada, E. Fennema, & L. B. Adajian (Eds.), *New directions for equity in mathematics education* (pp. 9–56). New York: Cambridge University Press.

Silver, E. A., & Stein, M. K. (1996). The QUASAR Project: The "revolution of the possible" in mathematics instructional reform in urban middle schools. *Urban Education, 30,* 476–521.

Smith, M. S. (2001). *Practice-based professional development for teachers of mathematics.* Reston, VA: National Council of Teachers of Mathematics.

Smith, M. S., Bill, V., & Hughes, E. K. (2008). Thinking through a lesson protocol: A key for successfully implementing high-level tasks. *Mathematics Teaching in the Middle School, 14(3), 132–138.*

Smith, M. S., Hughes, E. K., Engle, R. A., & Stein, M. K. (in press). Orchestrating discussions of challenging tasks: Keeping your eye on the mathematics to be learned. *Mathematics Teaching in the Middle School.*

Smith, M. S., Silver, E. A., & Stein, M. K. with Boston, M., Henningsen, M., & Hillen, A. (2005). *Using cases to transform mathematics teaching and learning (Volume I: Improving instruction in rational numbers and proportionality).* New York: Teachers College Press.

Smith, M. S., Silver, E. A., & Stein, M. K. with Henningsen, M., Boston, M., & Hughes, E. (2005). *Using cases to transform mathematics teaching and learning (Volume 2: Improving instruction in algebra).* New York: Teachers College Press.

Smith, M. S., Silver, E. A., & Stein, M. K. with Boston, M., & Henningsen, M. (2005). *Using cases to transform mathematics teaching and learning (Volume 3: Improving instruction in geometry and measurement).* New York: Teachers College Press.

Smith, M. S., Stein, M. K., Arbaugh, F., Brown, C.A., & Mossgrove, J. (2004). Characterizing the cognitive demands of mathematical tasks: A sorting activity. *Professional development guidebook for perspectives on the teaching of mathematics* (Companion to 2004 yearbook of the National Council of Teachers of Mathematics) (pp. 45–72). Reston, VA: National Council of Teachers of Mathematics.

Smith, M. S., & Stein, M. K. (1998). Selecting and creating mathematical tasks: From research to practice. *Teaching Mathematics in the Middle School, 3(5),* 344–350.

Steele, M. D. (2008). Building bridges: Cases as catalysts for the integration of mathematical and pedagogical knowledge. In M. S. Smith & S. Friel (Eds.), *Cases in mathematics teacher education: Tools for developing knowledge needed for teaching* (AMTE Monograph Series No. 4) (pp. 57–72). San Diego, CA: Association of Mathematics Teacher Educators.

Stein, M. K., Engle, R. A., Smith, M. S., & Hughes, E. K. (2008). Orchestrating productive mathematical discussions: Helping teachers learn to better incorporate student thinking. *Mathematical Thinking and Learning, 10*(4), 313–340.

Stein, M. K., Grover, B., & Henningsen, M. (1996). Building student capacity for mathematical thinking and reasoning: An analysis of mathematical tasks used in reform classrooms. *American Educational Research Journal, 33*(2), 455–488.

Stein, M. K., & Kaufman, J. (2008). *Examining the relationship between teacher human capital, curriculum use, and quality of implementation.* Paper presented at the annual meeting of the American Educational Research Association, New York.

Stein, M. K., & Kim, G. (2009). The role of mathematics curriculum materials in large-scale urban reform: An analysis of demands and opportunities for teacher learning. In J. Remillard, B. Herbel-Eisenmann, & G. Lloyd (Eds.), *Mathematics teachers at work: Connecting curriculum materials and classroom instruction* (pp. 37–55). New York: Routledge.

Stein, M. K., & Lane, S. (1996). Instructional tasks and the development of student capacity to think and reason: An analysis of the relationship between teaching and learning in a reform mathematics project. *Educational Research and Evaluation, 2*(1), 50–80.

Stein, M. K., Lane, S., & Silver, E. A. (1997). *Classrooms in which students successfully acquire mathematical proficiency: What are the critical features of teachers' instructional practice?* Paper presented at the annual meeting of the American Educational Research Association, New York.

Stein, M. K., & Nelson, B. S. (2003). Leadership content knowledge. *Educational Evaluation and Policy Analysis, 25*(4), 423–448.

Stein, M. K., & Smith, M. S. (1998). Mathematical tasks as a framework for reflection: From research to practice. *Mathematics Teaching in the Middle School, 3(4)*, 268–275.

Stigler, J., & Hiebert, J. (1997). Understanding and improving classroom mathematics instruction: An overview of the TIMSS video study. *Phi Delta Kappan, 79*(1), 14–21.

Stigler, J. W., & Hiebert, J. (2004). Improving mathematics teaching. *Educational Leadership, 61*(5), 12–16.

Stodolsky, S. (1988). *The subject matters: Classroom activity in mathematics and social studies.* Chicago: University of Chicago Press.

Thompson, C. L., & Zeuli, J. S. (1999). The frame and the tapestry: Standards-based reform and professional development. In L. Darling-Hammond & G. Sykes (Eds.), *Teaching as the learning profession: Handbook of policy and practice* (pp. 341–375). San Francisco: Jossey-Bass.

Zulie, M. E. (1988). *Fractions with pattern blocks.* Chicago: Creative Publications.

Index

Accountability
    and Butler case, 99
    for high level products/processes, 99, 110, 120
    of students, 70, 85–86, 99, 110, 120
    of teachers, 152, 153–54
Algebra tiles
    and professional development of teachers, 141
    to multiply monomials and binomials, 88–100
Algorithms
    and Butler case, 96, 97, 98, 99, 100
    and Castleman case, 51–52
    and Cooper case, 68–69, 71
    and Gorman case, 58, 68–69
    and professional development of teachers, 141
    and Robinson case, 119
American Educational Research Association (AERA), 23
American Institutes for Research, 149–50
Arbaugh, F., 8, 138, 150, 154
Area model
    and Butler case, 96, 98, 141
    linking fractions, decimals and percents using, 37–55

Ball, D. L., 133, 140
Barnett, C., 23, 147
Bilingualism, 101
Bill, V., 135, 146, 160
Binomials
    Butler's use of algebra tiles to multiply, 88–100, 141
    and professional development of teachers, 141

Boaler, J., 17
Borasi, R., 134
Boston, M. D., 36, 137, 150
Briars, D. J., 131, 151
Brown, C. A., 8, 138, 143, 150, 154
Butler, Monique (single case)
    Castleman case compared with, 97, 100
    and cognitive levels, 97–98
    discussion questions for, 96
    and factors, 98–99
    goals of, 88–89, 96
    implementation of tasks by, 93–95, 98
    and layers of interpretation, 100
    opening activity for, 88
    overview about, 88–89
    and patterns of decline, 31
    and professional development of teachers, 141
    as role model, 89
    setup of tasks by, 91–92
    as single case, 31
    as talking about her class, 89–90
    and teachers as doers and learners, 141
    teaching notes for, 96–100
    and using algebra tiles to multiply monomials and binomials, 88–100

Carpenter, T. P., 139
Carter, K., 14
Cases. *See also* specific case
    connecting practice with, 36
    dilemma driven, 23
    discussion of, 34–35, 36
    dual, 31, 35
    and follow up activities, 36

Cases (*cont'd*)
function/role of, 23, 24
importance of, 24–25
introduction to, 31–36
learning from, 23–28, 33–36
and objectives, 34
paradigm, 23
and questions, 33, 35, 36
and reflection, 25–27, 36
selection of, 149
single, 31
and tasks, 32–33
and teaching notes, 33, 35
and theoretical considerations, 23–25
and tools for enhancing discourse, 34
types of, 31
using the, 33–34, 131–63
Castleman, Ron (dual case)
and analyzing and reflecting on one's
own case, 149
and analyzing the teaching of others,
147–48
background of, 37–38
Butler case compared with, 97, 100
and cognitive levels, 47–48
dilemmas of, 47, 51
discussion about classes of, 38–39, 49
discussion questions for, 46–47
and factors, 48–51
goals/objectives of, 42, 51
implementation of tasks by, 40–42,
43–46, 48–51
and layers of interpretation, 51
and learning and professional practice of principals, 159
and linking fractions, decimals, and
percents using an area model,
37–55
opening activity for, 37
and possible solution strategies, 51–55
and professional development of
teachers, 143, 147–48, 149
questions about, 147–48
reflection of, 42, 43–46, 47, 51
second-period class of, 39–42, 46, 148
setup of tasks by, 39–40, 42–43, 47–48

sixth-period class of, 42–47
and teachers as analyzers and interpreters, 143
teaching notes for, 33, 47–51
and type of case, 31
Castro, A., 146
Central tendency, giving meaning to
measures of, 72–87
Challenges
and exploring challenging tasks, 140–46
as nonproblems, 69–70, 85, 98–99
of teaching in multilingual settings,
86–87
Charalambous, C., 141, 142, 146
Chrostowski, S. J., 152
Clark, L., 141, 143, 149
Clark, Nicole (single case)
and cognitive level, 109
discussion questions for, 107–8
and factors, 110–11
goals of, 102, 108, 111
implementation of tasks by, 104–7
and layers of interpretation, 111
opening activity for, 101
and organizing data, 101–11
overview about, 101–2
and patterns of decline, 31
setup of tasks by, 103–4
as single case, 31
as talking about her class, 102–3
teaching notes for, 108–11
Classroom management, 20
Cognitive demands. *See also* Cognitive
level; type or level of demand
alteration of, 15
analyzing, 8, 10, 12, 138–40
decline in, 18–22, 98–99, 110–11,
119–20, 134
defining levels of, 2, 4
definition of, 1
differentiating levels of, 5, 7–8, 10,
12, 139
importance of, 1
and theoretical considerations of
cases, 24
variation in level of, 137–40, 154–56

Cognitive levels. *See* specific case or level
Cognitive tasks. *See* Cognitive demands; Tasks
Cohen, D. K., 133
Collaboration, 71, 86, 91–92, 93–95, 100, 146, 159. *See also* Cooper, Kevin; Gorman, Fran; Hernandez, Ursula; Naruda, Trina
Conjecture, and Naruda and Hernandez cases, 74, 76–77, 78, 79, 80, 81, 83, 84, 85
Connected Mathematics curriculum, 13
Connections, conceptual, 50, 71. *See also* Procedures with connections; Procedures without connections
Cooke, G., 149–50, 152
Cooper, Kevin (dual case)
    and changing teaching, 68
    and cognitive levels, 68–69
    and deprivatization of practice, 160
    discussion questions for, 67
    and factors, 69, 70–71
    implementation of tasks by, 65–67, 69, 70
    issues for, 31
    and learning and professional practice of principals, 159
    and linking particulars with generalities, 134
    and multiplying fractions with pattern blocks, 56–71
    opening activity for, 57
    overview about, 56
    setup of tasks by, 64–65, 68
    shared meeting time of Gorman and, 56, 63, 64, 68, 159
    as talking about his class, 64
    teaching notes for, 68–71
    and theoretical considerations of cases, 24
    and type of case, 31
Correct answers, 70, 119, 120
Cortes, Diana (Hernandez assistant), 79, 80, 86
Curriculum, 121, 151, 161–62
Curriculum and Evaluation Standards for School Mathematics (NCTM), 12–13, 56, 68, 73, 82–83, 96, 108, 118, 119, 120–21, 146

Data, collection and analysis of, 101–11
Decimals, and linking fractions, decimals and percents using an area model, 37–55
Diagrams. *See* Castleman, Ron (dual case)
Dilemmas, 23, 47, 108–9
Discovery process, 74–75, 80
Discussion questions. *See* specific case
Discussions
    ending of, 35
    facilitating case, 35
    large group, 35, 142
    preparing for, 34–35
    questions for, 46–47
    reflection in case based, 25–26
    small group, 142
Doing mathematics
    and Castleman case, 47–48
    categorization of, 10
    characteristics of, 5, 10, 13n
    and Clark case, 109
    decline in, 19
    and differentiating levels of cognitive demands, 5, 7–8
    and differentiating variable high-level tasks, 156–57
    and Hernandez case, 83
    and learning and professional practice of principals, 156–57, 158
    as level of cognitive demand, 4
    and Naruda case, 84
    and patterns of task setup and implementation, 19, 20
    and professional development of teachers, 139, 141
    and Robinson case, 119
Doyle, W., 13n, 14, 19, 131, 152

Education, international comparison with U.S., 152
Edwards, Ms. (special education teacher), 73–74, 75, 76, 77, 78, 79–80, 84–85

Elmore, R. F., 160

Enactment. *See also* Implementation
  definition of, 22n

Engle, R. A., 142

English as a second language, 101, 103

Explanation, sustained press for, 49–50

Exploration, 99, 111. *See also* Unsystematic
  exploration

Ezoto, Mr. (Vietnamese teacher), 74, 75,
  76, 77, 79, 87

Factors. *See also* specific case
  and learning and professional prac-
    tice of principals, 158

Factors Associated with Maintenance
  and Decline, 135

Fencing Task, 5, 15, 17–20, 138, 154,
  156–57

Fennema, E., 139

Fey, J., 13

Fitzgerald, W., 13

Follow-up activities, and cases, 36

Fonzi, J., 134

Fox, Ms. (case), 17–18, 20

Fractions
  and linking fractions, decimals and
    percents using an area model,
    37–55
  multiplication of, 56–71

Friel, S., 13

Fuson, K. C., 139

Generalities, linking particulars with,
  134, 148–49

Ghousseini, H., 141, 142, 146

Ginsburg, A., 149–50, 152

Goals/objectives. *See also* specific case
  and cases, 34
  and creation and selection of tasks, 1–2
  for learning, 1–2
  matching tasks with, 4–5

Goldenstein, D., 23

Gonzalez, E. J., 152

Gorman, Fran (dual case)
  and changing teaching, 68

and cognitive levels, 68–69

and deprivatization of practicee, 160

discussion questions for, 67

and factors, 69–70

implementation of tasks by, 60–63, 69

issues in, 31

and learning and professional practice of principals, 159

and linking particulars with generalities, 134

and multiplying fractions with pattern blocks, 56–71

opening activity for, 57

overview about, 56

and professional development of
  teachers, 143

setup of tasks by, 59–60, 68

shared meeting time of Cooper and,
  56, 63, 64, 68, 159

as talking about her class, 58–59

and teachers as analyzers and interpreters, 143

teaching notes for, 35, 68–71

and theoretical considerations of
  cases, 24

and type of case, 31

Gosen, D., 142, 149

Graphs, and Clark case, 102–11

Grossman, P., 131

Grover, B., 5, 7, 13, 13n, 14, 15, 17, 134

Henningsen, M. A., 5, 7, 13, 13n, 14, 15,
  17, 36, 134

Hernandez, Ursula (dual case)
  and cognitive levels, 83–84
  discussion questions for, 82
  and factors, 84, 85–86
  and giving meaning to measures of
    central tendency, 72–87
  goals of, 82
  implementation of tasks by, 80–81,
    84
  and layers of interpretation, 86–87
  Naruda consultations with, 76, 78,
    79, 80

Naruda as model for, 79–80, 81, 86
opening activity for, 72
overview about, 73
reflection of, 79
setup of tasks by, 79–80, 83
as talking about her class, 79
teaching notes for, 82–87
and type of case, 31
Hiebert, J., 14, 132, 139, 152
High-level demands/tasks. *See also* specific type of task
accountability for, 99, 110, 120
characteristics of, 19
decline in, 19
differentiating variable classroom enactments of, 156–58
importance of, 162
increase in use of, 13
maintenance of, 17–18
modeling of, 50, 110–11
and type of case, 31
unintended and unanticipated outcomes of, 13
Hillen, A., 36
Hogel, M., 137
Hughes, E. K., 36, 135, 137, 142, 146, 160
Human, P., 139

Implementation of tasks, 14, 15–22, 22n, 131, 150, 152, 156–58, 160–62. *See also* specific case
Instructional leadership. *See also* Principals
role of subject matter in, 151

Jackson, B., 23
Jocelyn, L., 152
Johnson, Mr. (case), 4
Justification, sustained press for, 49–50

Kastberg, D., 152
Kaufman, J., 160
Key professional activities, relationship to tasks of, 137–49

Kim, G., 135, 162
Knowledge. *See also* Prior knowledge
procedural distinguished from conceptual, 33

Lane, S., 13n, 17, 22n, 143, 152
Lappan, G., 13, 131, 151
Leinwand, S., 149–50, 152
Lemke, M., 152
Lemonade Task, 7
Limited English Proficient (LEP) students. *See* Hernandez, Ursula; Naruda, Trina
Little, J. W., 71

McCarthey, S., 160
McDonald, M., 131
Magone, M., 143
Manipulatives, 7, 24, 38, 90, 96, 98, 141, 154–55
Martha's Carpeting Task, 7, 138, 154
Martin, M. O., 152
Mathematical Tasks Framework (MTF)
advantages of, 27–28, 33
analyzing instructional tasks as first phase of, 1–13
and analyzing the teaching of others, 147–48
and assisting the learning and professional practice of principals, 151
and cases, 24, 25, 26, 27–28
and Castleman case, 147–48
and differentiating variable high-level tasks, 158
and Hernandez Naruda cases, 86
and learning and professional practice of principals, 153, 158, 161
linking particulars with generalities through, 134
and professional development of teachers, 132, 133, 134, 135, 147–49
purpose of, 15
The Mathematics in Context Development Team, 13

Meaning. *See also* Procedures with connection; Procedures without connection
  developing a shared, 10, 12
  and Naruda case, 85
  sustained pressure for, 49–50, 71, 85
Memorization, 2, 5, 96, 131
Merseth, K. K., 133
Miller, D., 152
Mills, V., 146, 149
Modeling
  by Butler, 89
  and Castleman, 50
  and Clark, 110–11
  and Cooper, 70–71
  and Hernandez, 86
  of high-level thinking/performance, 50, 70–71, 86, 110–11
  and Naruda as model for Hernandez, 79–80, 81, 86
  and patterns of task setup and implementation, 18
  by principals, 161
Monomials, algebra tiles to multiply, 88–100
Moon, J., 142–43
Mossgrove, J., 8, 138, 154
Mullis, I.V.S., 152
Multilingual settings, challenges of teaching in, 86–87
Murray, H., 139

Naruda, Trina (dual case)
  and cognitive levels, 83–84
  discussion questions for, 82
  and factors, 84–85
  and giving meaning to measures of central tendency, 72–87
  goals of, 82
  Hernandez consultation with, 76, 78, 79, 80
  Hernandez reflection on conversation with, 79
  implementation of tasks by, 76–78, 84–85
  and layers of interpretation, 86–87

  as model for Hernandez, 79–80, 81, 86
  opening activity for, 72
  overview about, 73
  setup of tasks by, 74–76, 84
  as talking about her class, 73–74
  teaching notes for, 82–87
  and type of case, 31
National Academy of Education, 135
National Center for Education Statistics (NCES), 131, 132, 152
National Council of Teachers of Mathematics (NCTM), 1, 5, 7, 12, 27, 34, 51, 56, 68, 73, 82–83, 96, 108, 118, 119, 120–21, 140, 146
Nelson, B. S., 151
No mathematical activity, 20–22, 109
Noell, J., 149–50, 152

Observations, by principals, 152, 153–58, 161
Ohio Resource Center, 140
Olivier, A., 139

Pahike, E., 152
Paradigm cases, 23
Parents, 162
Parke, C. S., 143
Partelow, L., 152
Particulars, linking generalities with, 134, 148–49
Partners, reflection with, 26–27
Pattern blocks
  and linking particulars with generalities, 134
  multiplying fractions with, 56–71
  and professional development of teachers, 141
Patterns
  and Naruda case, 75
  and professional development of teachers, 148–49
  of task setup and implementation, 17–22
  and theoretical considerations of cases, 24

Percents, and linking fractions, decimals and percents using an area model, 37–55
Peterson, P., 160
Phillips, E., 13
Pollock, E., 149–50, 152
Polya, George, 114, 118, 139
Possible solution strategies
  and Castleman case, 51–55
  function of, 119
  and Robinson case, 119, 121–27
Practice
  analyzing and reflecting on, 146–49
  authentic, 133
  bridging professional development with improvement in, 133, 134–37, 150
  changing/transforming, 36, 68, 163
  connecting cases to, 36
  considerations of one's own, 25–27
  and core practices, 131
  deprivatization of, 160
  influence of case approach on, 24–25
  professional development as based on, 133
  reflection as influence on, 23–24
Principals
  assisting the learning and professional practice of, 151–63
  as instructional leader, 151
  modeling by, 161
  observations by, 152, 153–58, 161
  and professional development for teachers, 151, 153–60
  and resources, 152, 153, 160–62
  role of, 151–53
Prior knowledge
  building on student, 50, 70, 75, 84–85, 111
  and Butler case, 98
  and Castleman case, 50
  and Clark case, 111
  and Cooper case, 70
  and Gorman case, 70
  and Naruda case, 75, 84–85

and professional development of teachers, 141
Problem solving
  as central mathematical process, 121
  four step method of, 114, 118
  importance of, 117, 118–19
  and professional development of teachers, 142
  and Robinson case, 112–27
  role in learning of, 120–21
  skills developed by, 113
Problems, maintaining complexity of, 49
Procedures. See Procedures with connections; Procedures without connections
Procedures with connections
  and Butler case, 97
  categorization of, 10
  characteristics of, 10
  and Cooper case, 68, 69, 134
  and differentiating levels of cognitive demands, 5
  and Gorman case, 68, 134
  and learning and professional practice of principals, 154, 158
  as level of cognitive demand, 2
  and linking particulars with generalities, 134
  and patterns of task setup and implementation, 22n
  and professional development of teachers, 131, 139, 140–41
  purpose of, 68
Procedures without connections
  and Butler case, 97–98
  and Castleman case, 48
  categorization of, 10
  characteristics of, 10
  and decline in cognitive demands, 18–19
  and differentiating levels of cognitive demands, 5, 7
  and differentiating variable high-level tasks, 157
  and Gorman case, 69

Procedures without connections (*cont'd*)
  and learning and professional prac-
    tice of principals, 157
  as level of cognitive demand, 2
  and matching tasks with goals, 5
  and patterns of task setup and imple-
    mentation, 18–19
  and Robinson case, 119
Professional development
  arranging for tailored, 158–59
  bridging improvement in practice
    with, 133, 134–37, 150
  and implementation of tasks, 131
  and learning and professional prac-
    tice of principals, 151, 152
  and observations by principals, 153–58
  practice based, 133
  of principals, 158–60
  resources for, 160–63
  and scaffolding field experiences,
    134–37
  task focused, 150
  of teachers, 131–50, 151, 152, 153–60
  transformative, 132–37
Professional judgment, 142–43
Program for International Student Assessment (PISA), 150
Public presentations, and Clark case,
  103–11

QUASAR Cognitive Assessment Instrument, 17, 22n
QUASAR Project, 4, 13n, 14, 17
Questions. *See also* specific case
  and cases, 33, 35, 36

Railside High School, 17
Ramirez, A., 147
Reasoning
  by extending diagrams, 54–55
  from visual diagrams, 52–54
Reflection
  advantages to guided, 27–28
  and assisting the learning of teachers,
    146–49
  in case based discussion group, 25–26

and cases, 25–27, 36
  of Castleman, 42, 43–46, 47, 51
  of Hernandez, 79
  individual, 27
  as influence on instructional practice,
    23–24
  and Naruda and Hernandez cases, 86
  with partners, 26–27
  and patterns of task setup and imple-
    mentation, 22
  and professional development of
    teachers, 133, 135, 141–42
  of Rosa, 24
  and shared meeting time of Gorman
    and Cooper, 68
  and teacher collaboration, 86
  and theoretical considerations of
    cases, 24–25
  and videotapes, 27
Resnick, L. B., 13n
Resources, 152, 153, 160–62
Richardson, V., 28
Robinson, Jerome (single case)
  background of, 112–13
  case of, 31
  and cognitive levels, 119
  discussion questions for, 118
  and factors, 119–20
  goals of, 113, 118
  implementation by, 115–17
  and layers of interpretation, 120–21
  opening activity for, 112
  and patterns of decline, 31
  possible solution strategies for, 119,
    121–27
  setup by, 114
  as single case, 31
  and solving problems, 112–27
  as talking about his class, 113–14
  teaching notes for, 118–21
Romagnano, L. R., 19
Rosa, reflection of, 24

Scaffolded Field Experiences (SFEs),
  133, 134–37, 140, 143, 149, 154,
  160–61

Scaffolding. *See also* Scaffolded Field
    Experiences
    of student thinking, 18, 49, 85, 111, 149
School board members, 162
Sealy, J. T., 141
Sen, A., 152
Setup of tasks, 14, 15–22. *See also* specific
    case
Shared meeting time, of Gorman and
    Cooper, 56, 63, 64, 68, 159
Shulman, L. S., 23, 28, 148
Silver, E. A., 4, 13n, 17, 22n, 36, 133, 141,
    142, 143, 146, 149
Smith, M. S., 4, 8, 16, 25, 36, 133, 135,
    137, 138, 142, 146, 150, 154, 160
Solutions. *See also* Possible solution
    strategies
    and teaching notes, 33
Special education students. *See* Hernandez,
    Ursula; Naruda, Trina
Square Pattern Task, 138
Stakeholders, and importance of high
    level tasks, 162
Staples, M., 17
Steele, M. D., 142
Stein, M. K., 5, 7, 8, 13, 13n, 14, 15, 16,
    17, 25, 36, 134, 135, 138, 142, 151,
    152, 154, 160, 162
Stigler, J. W., 14, 132, 152
Strawhun, B.T.F., 142
Students
    accountability of, 70, 85–86, 110, 120
    collaboration of, 91–92, 93–95, 100
    and differentiating levels of cognitive
        demands, 8
    prior knowledge of, 50, 70, 75, 84–85,
        111
    social and emotional needs of, 101, 102

Task Analysis Guide (TAG), 5, 10, 12,
    135, 137, 139, 140, 153, 154, 161–62
Tasks. *See also* Cognitive demands;
    Implementation of tasks; Setup of
    tasks; specific type of task
    analyzing, 1–13, 138–40
    and cases, 32–33

categorization of, 10
comparing two, 138
complexity of, 14–22, 48, 149
creation of, 1–2, 12–13, 131–32
definition of, 14–15
differentiation of high- versus low-
    level, 154–56
evolution of, 14–17, 20
expectations for, 110
exploring challenging, 140–46
function/purpose of, 17, 131
identifying, 14
importance of cumulative effect of
    student experiences with, 1
key professional activities related to,
    137–49
during a lesson, 14–17
matching goals with, 4–5
patterns of setup and implementation
    of, 17–22
phases of, 142
selection of, 1–2, 12–13, 18, 131–32,
    143, 150, 152
simplification of, 99
superficial features of, 154–55, 156
transformation/shift of, 17, 70
Teachable moments, 50, 111
Teachers. *See also* Professional develop-
    ment; specific case
    accountability of, 152, 153–54
    as analyzers and interpreters, 142–43
    assisting the learning of, 131–50
    collaboration among, 159
    as doers and learners, 140–42
    as learners, 147
    as making conceptual connections,
        50
    as planners of mathematical activity,
        143–44
Teaching notes. See also specific case
    and cases, 33, 35
Teaching. *See* Practice
Television programs, survey of favorite,
    104–7
Tests, high-stake, 114, 121
Thinking, modeling high level, 50

Thinking Through a Lesson Protocol (TTLP), 135, 143, 146, 160
Thompson, C. L., 132
Thurston Middle School. *See* Robinson, Jerome
Time. *See also* Shared meeting time
appropriate amount of, 85
and Butler case, 99–100
and Castleman case, 50–51
and Hernandez case, 86
and learning and professional practice of principals, 152, 153
and Naruda case, 85
provision of enough, 50–51
and resources for ongoing teacher development, 160–61
and Robinson case, 114, 115, 116, 117, 120
Tools, 34, 135, 137, 139, 141, 147. *See also* specific tool

Trends in International Mathematics and Science Study (TIMSS), 14, 131, 132, 149–50, 152

Unsystematic exploration, 19–20, 84, 158
Videotapes, and reflection, 27
Vietnamese students. *See* Naruda, Trina
Visual diagrams
and levels of cognitive demand, 4
reasoning by extending the, 54–55
reasoning from the, 52–54

Wearne, D., 139, 152
Williams, T., 152

Zeuli, J. S., 132
Zulie, M. E., 58

ABOUT THE AUTHORS

Mary Kay Stein holds a joint appointment at the University of Pittsburgh as Professor of Learning Sciences and Policy and Senior Scientist at the Learning Research and Development Center. Her early research focused on classroom-based teaching and learning with the aim of understanding the nature of effective instructional practices in mathematics. In the past decade, Dr. Stein's research interests have expanded to include the school, district, and policy contexts of teacher learning and professional development. Most notably, she has studied the connections between district policy and classroom practice in New York City's Community School District #2, as well as districtwide instructional reforms in the San Diego city schools. Currently, she is co-PI of an IERI grant, *Scaling Up Mathematics: The Interface of Curricula with Human and Social Capital,* that is investigating how the teacher learning demands of different curricula (*Everyday Mathematics* vs. *Investigations*) influence teacher learning in large-scale reforms in two urban districts. In 2005, Dr. Stein was named Director of the Learning Policy Center at the University of Pittsburgh.

Margaret Schwan Smith is a Professor in the Department of Instruction and Learning in the School of Education and a Research Scientist at the Learning Research and Development Center, both at the University of Pittsburgh. She works with pre-service mathematics teachers at the University of Pittsburgh, with doctoral students in mathematics education who are interested in becoming teacher educators, and with practicing mathematics teachers and coaches locally and nationally. Over the past decade, she has been developing research-based materials for use in the professional development of mathematics teachers and studying what teachers learn from the professional development in which they engage. She is currently the director of the NSF-funded CORP project, which is developing materials focused on reasoning and proving for mathematics teachers' professional development. She is a member of the Board of Directors of the National Council of Teachers of Mathematics (2006–2009). In 2006, she was selected to receive the Chancellor's Distinguished Teaching Award given annually to honor outstanding faculty at the University of Pittsburgh.

Marjorie A. Henningsen is the Head of School at Wellspring Learning Community in Beirut, Lebanon, a nonsectarian, private international school she helped to found in 2007. She has a B.A. in mathematics and psychology from Benedictine College, an M.Ed. from the University of Pittsburgh in mathematics education, and an Ed.D. from the University of Pittsburgh in curriculum and instruction. She worked as a researcher, teacher developer, and author for the QUASAR and COMET projects at the University of Pittsburgh during the 1990s. In 2000, she became an assistant professor of mathematics education at the American University of Beirut (AUB) where she also served as Director of the Science and Mathematics Education Center (SMEC) until 2007. Her research interests include studying elementary mathematics classroom processes and using cases in teacher development. She still teaches part-time at AUB and remains active in designing and conducting case-based professional development for teachers and administrators in the United States, Saudi Arabia, Egypt, Qatar, and Lebanon.

Edward A. Silver is the William A. Brownell Collegiate Professor of Education and Professor of Mathematics at the University of Michigan. His scholarly interests include the study of mathematical thinking, especially mathematical problem solving and problem posing; the design and analysis of intellectually engaging and equitable mathematics instruction for students; innovative methods of assessing and reporting mathematics achievement; and effective models for enhancing the knowledge of teachers of mathematics. For much of the 1990s, Silver directed the QUASAR Project, which both stimulated and studied efforts to improve mathematics instruction in urban middle schools. From 2000 to 2004, he served as editor of the *Journal for Research in Mathematics Education*. He was the 2004 recipient of the Award for Outstanding Contributions of Educational Research to Practice from the American Educational Research Association and the 2007 recipient of the Iris Carl Memorial Leadership and Equity Award from *TODOS*.